CLASSROOMS IN THE CROSSFIRE

The Rights and Interests of Students, Parents, Teachers, Administrators, Librarians, and the Community

BY ROBERT M. O'NEIL

Over the past fifteen years America's schools have become a battlefield of controversy involving curriculum content, textbook selection, religious expression, cultural values, and personal freedom. *Classrooms in the Crossfire* is a provocative yet thoughtful and balanced discussion of the legal complexities and social implications of the clash between First Amendment freedoms and community standards for public schools.

Robert O'Neil describes the more prominent cases of recent date (Kanawha County, W. Va.; West Clark, Ind.; St. Anthony, Idaho; Suffolk County, N.Y.) as well as those less well-known but of great significance for the future of judicial intervention in school systems. These cases come from all parts of the United States, from small rural communities to large cosmopolitan areas, and suggest that no single geographic region or religious or ethnic group has a monopoly on the issue.

O'Neil looks at the controversy from the point of view of all the groups who are affected—parents whose religious and child-rearing beliefs differ from the larger community's; teachers and administrators, who must respond to the community's will as well as to legal requirements; librarians; special interest groups; ethnic minorities; private schools; and, finally, the community as a whole.

CLASSROOMS

IN THE

CROSSFIRE

THE RIGHTS AND INTERESTS

CLASSROOMS

OF STUDENTS, PARENTS,

IN THE

TEACHERS, ADMINISTRATORS,

CROSSFIRE

LIBRARIANS, AND THE COMMUNITY

Robert M. O'Neil

Indiana University Press

BLOOMINGTON

Library of Congress Cataloging in Publication Data

O'Neil, Robert M   1934–
   Classrooms in the crossfire.

   Bibliography: p.
   1. Educational law and legislation—United States.
2. Students—Legal status, laws, etc.—United States.
3. Text-books—United States—Censorship. I. Title.
KF4119.053   344.73'077   80-8153
ISBN 0-253-17933-5   1 2 3 4 5 85 84 83 82 81

For my children
Elizabeth, Peter, David, and Benjamin
with hope

CONTENTS

PREFACE

This book emerges from a long-standing concern about the condition of First Amendment freedoms in the schools and libraries of this country. Nearly ten years ago, I first became aware of the pernicious effects of censorship of school libraries, texts, and teaching. Soon thereafter the controversy over curriculum erupted in Charleston, West Virginia. I was at first amazed, then horrified, that brutal mob violence could alter the selection of teaching materials for the public school. As the months went by and the Charleston dispute remained unresolved—indeed, in many respects it remains unsettled today—I gathered material in the hope of writing an analysis of the subject. With the addition of many other incidents and the adjudication of several such disputes, the raw material for such a book has taken shape.

If this study has a bias, it is simply my own commitment to the preservation of the freedoms of the Bill of Rights in the classrooms and libraries in which the views of our next generation's citizens will be shaped. Despite the inclination of some to dispense with or relax those liberties in the interests of discipline or order, or even orthodoxy, the need for protection of free expression and thought in the schools has seldom been greater. For a variety of reasons which are explored in this book, the pressures upon the schools have become intense, and the restriction of curricular experimentation and library collection development has been a regrettable (though understandable) consequence. As a nation, we should not tolerate the current degree of restriction of free inquiry in the schoolroom; the problem is that most citizens know relatively little about the situation, the risks which it poses to a coming generation of citizens, or about the governing legal principles. A major premise of this book is that more and better information about such conditions and hazards will better maintain the freedom which is a cornerstone of our educational system.

Both inspiration and valuable material have come from many sources, but two colleagues deserve special appreciation. Mrs. Judith F. Krug, who for a decade has directed the Office of Intellectual Freedom of the American Library Association, has been a tireless worker for free expression in the schools and public libraries of this country. She not only has provided invaluable aid and encouragement to librarians under attack, but has collected and published in the *Newsletter on Intellectual Freedom* the best current compendium of cases and reports. My other special debt goes to Professor Edward B. Jenkinson of Indiana University, long-term chairman of the Censorship Committee of the National Council of Teachers of English, who has been a most vigilant protector of intellectual freedom in the public schools. If there were more Judith Krugs and Edward Jenkinsons, there would be no occasion for such a book as this.

In the preparation of this study I have been greatly aided by the diligent and perceptive work of Suzanne Matt O'Shea, of the Indiana University Law School Class of 1979, who was my research assistant for several years. I am deeply indebted to Donna Harbstreit, of the Office of the Vice President–Bloomington, Indiana University, who prepared the manuscript through several rather substantial revisions—always with good cheer and wise counsel. During that time several of my Indiana University colleagues—Ward B. Schaap, Perry Metz, and Norma Fox—bore heavier burdens than they would otherwise have carried, leaving me freer to develop this project. Finally, my wife, Karen, who has a unique appreciation of the values of freedom and knows the school setting from her own experience as a teacher, has made a profound contribution through her wise and patient counsel and by careful reading of every chapter. Hers should be the credit for the better portions, mine the onus for those that turn out less well. This book, as others, has been a joint effort in many ways.

Madison, Wisconsin
August 1980

While the bitter debate over curriculum content—and the concomitant issues of censorship and free expression—has dominated court dockets until now, new disputes have recently become subjects for litigation. O'Neil considers the arguments for those who say that individuals have a constitutional right to be educated, to attain at least a minimum level of competence, which many schools have failed to deliver; while others, the Amish, for example, or parents who disapprove of an entire philosophical approach to education, declare their children have a right *not* to be educated—at least in schools where the state has "interfered" in determining subject matter, point of view, and teacher standards.

From his extensive experience as an educator and administrator, O'Neil is well acquainted with the pressures that have forced the nation's school systems to face these passionate questions. His careful explication is essential to all citizens who share his concern for the preservation of our First Amendment freedoms.

ROBERT M. O'NEIL, President of the University of Wisconsin, is author of *Free Speech, Civil Liberties: Case Studies and the Law* and *Discriminating Against Discrimination: Preferential Admissions and the DeFunis Case.*

CLASSROOMS

IN THE

CROSSFIRE

1

THE COURTS AND
THE SCHOOL CURRICULUM

EVERY YEAR hundreds of thousands of textbooks are adopted, lesson plans are developed, new curricular units approved, and new courses initiated—all without legal challenge. But every so often something goes awry and a school board will find itself in court, having been sued for taking action which someone claims to be unlawful, or even unconstitutional. The fact that such cases are extremely rare does not, of course, deprive them of importance. Indeed, the frequency (or infrequency) of resort to the courts over curricular issues has little to do with the importance of the underlying disputes, or of the role of the courts in resolving them. The purpose of this first chapter is to review several recent legal conflicts over public school curriculum, and to gain perspective on the problem in that way.

West Clark, Indiana

Textbook adoption procedure in Indiana is fairly typical. The State Textbook Commission approves a list of books for each grade level in each subject. Local districts are then free to choose from the approved list. In 1976 the commission approved seven textbooks for high school biology, including one—*Biology: A Search for Order in Complexity*—which took an avowedly

1

creationist view of the origins of human life. Several districts decided to use this text as an alternative or supplement to a more traditional biology book. In one district, West Clark in the rural south central part of the state, a parent-teacher committee was appointed for the purpose of proposing a biology text. They recommended one of the traditional books. But the school board, under considerable pressure from citizens who held quite conservative religious views, opted for *Biology: A Search for Order*— not simply as a supplement, but (as state law allowed) as the sole text. Soon after this action a group of concerned parents went to state court, claiming that the board had acted in violation of the federal constitution. The suit alleged that to adopt such a textbook was an "establishment" of religion, which the Bill of Rights forbade. The premise was that a book which took only the biblical side of the debate over human origins, and said little or nothing about evolution, injected theology into the classroom in a way the Framers of the Constitution had meant to foreclose.

The state judge before whom the case came asked the Textbook Commission to reconsider its list, but the agency declined to do so. Then the West Clark School Board dropped out of the case, leaving the dispute between the parents and the State Commission. The judge reviewed carefully both the textbook and the teacher's manual, and found in both an improper bias in favor of the Genesis theory of the origin of life. Not only did the text devote a far larger amount of space and emphasis to the biblical view than to the scientific view; the difficulty was compounded by the teacher's manual, which propounded a demand for "correct" Christian answers to questions about the origins of life. The court concluded: "The prospect of biology teachers and students alike, forced to answer and respond to continued demand for correct fundamentalist Christian doctrine, has no place in the public schools." On this basis the judge held that the text could no longer remain even on the state-approved list, much less be adopted as the sole biology book, for a local district.

The judgment was not self-executing, however. The West Clark School Board maintained for a time that the edict did not really affect it, since it had ceased to be a party to the suit. But the State Textbook Commission soon decided not to appeal, and in time the West Clark board quietly adopted a different text— one that mentioned creationism, but stressed evolution—for the following years. Remaining copies of the controversial book were eventually sold to a private Christian academy near Indianapolis, where they could be used without fear of court intervention.

Kanawha County, West Virginia

The bitterest controversy over teaching materials was that which erupted in the fall of 1974 in and around Charleston, West Virginia. A brief chronology may aid our understanding of the struggle, which eventually reached both the streets and the courts. In the late 1960s, a dispute over the role of sex education in the schools had been the pivotal issue in a school board election. Tension surfaced again in the spring of 1974 when the school board adopted some 325 language arts textbooks on the recommendation of a teachers committee. A newly elected school board member, Mrs. Alice Moore (who had played a role in the 1969 sex education dispute), asked that final decision on the books be deferred until fall. During the summer she circulated within the community some of the more controversial texts, and community feeling became more intense as the new school year approached.

Events on the first day of classes made it clear that the issue would be deeply divisive. Many of the area's coal mines were shut down as a direct result of the ensuing conflict, for anti-textbook feeling was strongest among miners, who constituted a significant portion of the district's parents. Several days later, an uneasy administration decided to withdraw the texts from use and to appoint a committee with sizable citizen representation to review the language arts series. But the momentum of the protest was now so great that this conciliatory step brought only boos and jeers when it was announced. Soon the tension had so escalated that the superintendent decided to close the schools for the rest of the week in hopes that the weekend might bring peace.

The schools did reopen later in September, and attendance returned to about 90 percent of normal. While the textbooks were being reviewed by the citizens committee, an uneasy truce persisted. But violence erupted again in mid-October. Eighteen persons were arrested for physically blocking the path of school buses in direct violation of a court order. Vandalism directed against school buildings spread throughout the community and several structures were visibly damaged by dynamite and fire-bombs. The leaders of the protest publicly took credit for these acts of violence, and local law enforcement authorities seemed powerless to protect the schools.

The worst was yet to come. Early in November the citizens committee reported its conclusion: the language arts series was educationally sound and should be retained. Several days later the school board met and (with Mrs. Moore dissenting) approved that recommendation. The majority added, however, two important provisos: several notably controversial titles within the language arts group were to be removed from the classroom and placed in the libraries, with an alternate series to be selected later; and no student would be required to use a book that is "objectionable to that student's parents on either moral or religious grounds." This compromise was immediately hailed by the supporters of the texts, but violence flared anew. The most militant of the parents took their children out of school again, and attendance dropped. Buses were hit by gunshot blasts, and a car owned by parents who continued to send their children to school was firebombed (the driver escaped only by leaping from the car).

A week later three members of the school board and the

superintendent were served with arrest warrants charging them with contributing to the delinquency of minors by allowing the use of allegedly un-American and un-Christian textbooks. The warrants were obtained by the Upper Kanawha Valley Mayors Association, and were served during a meeting to which the school officials had been invited by a Methodist bishop who was trying to mediate the conflict.

Five days later the school board met again, and took a step which seemed to appease the protestors. Under a new set of guidelines for textbook adoption, materials in the future "must encourage loyalty to the United States," "must not contain profanity," "must recognize the sanctity of the home," "must not intrude into the privacy of the student's home by asking personal questions about the interfeelings [sic] or behavior of themselves or their parents, or encourage them to criticize their parents by direct question, statement or inference." The impact of these guidelines was accelerated by a new review process; the screening committees for each subject area would consist of three-quarters lay citizens (a certain number to be nominated by each board member), thus drastically reducing the role of teachers and other experts in the selection process. Soon the new screening groups were appointed, and the protestors now appeared to have gained control.

As the schools reopened in January, it seemed at first that the winter might be even worse than the fall. Representatives of the national Ku Klux Klan appeared in Charleston to proclaim their support for the textbook protest. But miraculously the situation soon began to improve. There were no serious acts of violence during the winter. Attendance returned almost to normal, and school board meetings settled back to their regular routine. By June, the Kanawha Valley was relatively calm.

Several steps helped to alleviate the tension. The State Commissioner of Education ruled in March that the citizen-dominated screening committees were in violation of state law because the school board had entrusted a professional task to a lay body. A new and moderate set of social studies texts was adopted during the spring, in apparent disregard of the November guidelines. An alternate to the rejected language arts series was adopted with little controversy, although the status of the original books remained in limbo. The criminal charges against the three board members and the superintendent were quietly dropped during the summer. The persons chiefly responsible for the dynamiting of the schools were indicted by a local grand jury, brought to trial and convicted, and rather severe sentences were upheld by a state appellate court. The federal judiciary also contributed to the return of calm and reason. At the height of the crisis, anti-textbook parents had brought suit in federal court, claiming that adoption of the materials to which they objected involved the "establishment" of anti-religion or non-religion, and thus violated the Constitution. The federal judge now dismissed this novel claim, holding that the use of the challenged texts was quite consistent with the national Bill of Rights. The next fall, a father who had earlier been arrested for taking his children out of school decided to send them back to class, explaining that he had abandoned the fight. "I'm fed up with keeping my kids out while everybody else's are in school," he told the press with a sense of resignation.

Several causal factors were unusual, if not unique, to Charleston. The merger into a single school district of people with such totally disparate values and views as the "creekers" (the rural residents of the county) and the city residents produced an extremely heterogenous constituency. Within the consolidated district, the rural people felt a loss of influence over the curriculum at the very time when more sophisticated (and to them more alien) teaching materials became available. Then there was the central role of the coal mines, and the strong tradition of independence among the miners, which spilled over into the streets and eventually into the schools. Tensions already present in the community—partly philosophical, partly socioeconomic and demographic—were simply exacerbated by the conflict over the teaching materials.

The stated concern about the textbooks was primarily religious. One target book, for example, referred to the parting of the Red Sea as a phenomenon "which probably happened naturally." This explanation jarred the fundamentalist beliefs of people in the hollows of Kanawha County, as did recognition of the Darwinian theory of the origin of human life and the seeming denigration of the Genesis theory of creation. A story in which animals were portrayed as invoking the aid of God was sharply attacked because the protestors believed that only man is capable of prayer. Mark Twain's humorously irreverent account of the diary of Adam also came under fire, as did several other liberal or figurative presentations of biblical material.

The opposition was not exclusively religious, however. At least three other themes were evident: politics, privacy, and race. Several books were attacked because they characterized the United States as a "representative Democracy," or because they gave an overly sympathetic view of the United Nations. The presence of antiwar poems, along with other selections that seemed to question traditional American values, made at least one anthology a target of opposition. The role of political issues in the controversy was thus clear, if secondary to the religious division. At another level, there was deep concern about material which seemed to threaten the privacy of the home and the family—a question which asked each child whether his parents rented or owned their home, and another which invited the reader to say what he or she thought the families in several pictures were doing. Concern was expressed about anything in the curriculum that involved "sensitivity training," a practice felt to be dangerously intrusive into family privacy.

Related to the privacy issue were concerns about obedience and decorum. A second grade reader contained "The Travels of a Fox," a folktale about a clever creature who outwits people but in the end is outsmarted himself; the objection was that such a story demeaned parents because the fox managed to get the better of several adults. Similarly, a third grade story drew criticism because it described a boy who cheated the grocer out of a penny; it was felt that by leaving the reader to speculate whether the boy was ever punished, the story might encourage children to steal. A story about a mischievous inner city boy who commits petty vandalism in the sight of adults who make no attempt to stop him drew protest for similar reasons.

Finally, there was the recurrent theme of race. Some of the texts contained selections from black writers such as Eldridge Cleaver and George Jackson, and drew objection because they portrayed violence, or because they seemed to excite hostility between the races, or because their "street language" was thought inappropriate for use in the schools. (Mrs. Moore stated at one board meeting, for example, that she did not object to "black literature, but to the kinds of writers represented" in the anthologies.) It was presumably for this reason that the national Ku Klux Klan thought Charleston might provide fertile ground, and thus entered the fray. A panel of inquiry sent in by the National Education Association later reported "undercurrents of racism" evidenced, for example, by a painted slogan on an outlying school building, "Get the Nigger Books out!" The black population of the county was less than 1 percent (though making up 10 percent of the people of the city of Charleston, where some evidence of racial tension existed). Such specific objections gave more than superficial support to the view that race, as well as religion, politics, and privacy, fueled the fires of protest.

Thus the combination of elements in the Charleston crisis was unusual, and the resulting conflict uniquely intense. But many of those same elements have been present in curricular disputes in other parts of the country. If violence has not erupted and schools have not been closed, that is only because accommodation has been reached short of physical force. In this respect— a matter of degree rather than of quality or kind—Charleston may have been a unique collision of values, but one that surely bears careful analysis and understanding.

One Flew Over the Cuckoo's Nest—
St. Anthony, Idaho

Late in the summer of 1977 John Fogarty, a young teacher who had recently joined the high school faculty in St. Anthony, Idaho, ordered for his fall English literature class fifteen copies of Ken Kesey's novel *One Flew Over the Cuckoo's Nest.* The order went through without difficulty, routinely signed by persons in the principal's and superintendent's offices. The books arrived on schedule, and were ready for classroom use early in the semester.

In November Fogarty told his class that *Cuckoo's Nest* would be one of seven novels to be studied in the final fall unit. He explained that some students might find language in the book objectionable, and that other books could be substituted if anyone wished. None of the students asked for an alternative assignment.

Parental reaction was, however, less enthusiastic. St. Anthony, a community of some 3,000 persons, is located on the western slope of the Continental Divide, not far from the Grand Tetons and Yellowstone Park. Most of its wage earners grow potatoes, and raise some cattle, wheat, and hay; a much smaller number work in the local lumber mill or at a nearby national forest. Eighty percent of the people of St. Anthony are Mormon, and many have rather recently moved to this area to escape more populous areas with urban problems and pressures. Thus it might have been predicted that not all the parents of Fogarty's students would welcome the assignment. One father complained to the principal that he had "got through just a few pages of the blasted thing," but found it unacceptable fare for his daughter.

Another parent read further, at least far enough to conclude that it was full of "vulgar and suggestive language" of a kind "we don't speak . . . in this family."

School officials photocopied about fourteen pages of the book and circulated the excerpts throughout the community, asking for comment. The appraisal was almost wholly negative. Apparently in response to parental pressure and community reaction, the principal demanded on December 3 that Fogarty stop using the book. He refused to do so, insisting that the novel presented a realistic view of life to which mature students should be exposed.

The controversy gradually widened. Fogarty sent packets of materials about his case to various persons and groups outside the community. The matter came to the attention of the *Idaho State Journal*, a Pocatello daily, which offered editorial support for Fogarty—calling the restriction of the book "well intentioned but badly aimed" and arguing that the book is "a genuine work of literature" which should be available to the students. The issue even reached the city desk of the *Los Angeles Times*, which dispatched a reporter to St. Anthony to cover the burgeoning dispute.

Early in February the school board took more drastic action, suspending Fogarty for the balance of the year. The basis of the action was said to be more his handling of the issue—and some veiled references to other misconduct—than the content of *Cuckoo's Nest* as such. But the context left little doubt that parental and community reaction to the novel had triggered this action.

Fogarty then sought outside legal help. The Idaho and Colorado Civil Liberties Union affiliates took up his case, and filed on his behalf a suit in the federal district court. The complaint alleged that Fogarty's constitutional right of free expression had been violated, and asked that he be reinstated with back pay and with money damages. The suit also asked that school officials be ordered not to interfere with the use of *Cuckoo's Nest* in literature classes.

One unusual feature of the Fogarty case deserves special mention. Among the persons to whom Fogarty sent packets of materials was Ken Kesey, the author of the novel. For reasons never disclosed, Kesey decided to respond to Fogarty's plea. He addressed a long open letter to the faculty, students, and administration of the school. He offered two strangely contrasting views on the whole situation. On the one hand, he took sharp issue with the administration and the board. They were, in his words, "obviously too stiff necked and thick headed to be taught any but the harshest lessons." He especially deplored the dissemination of the fourteen-page excerpts: "When you underlined those nasty words and xeroxed those pages and distributed your little package, you not only outraged the inviolability of my published work, you infringed upon my legal copyright. . . . You will hear from my lawyers."

This part of the letter greatly pleased Fogarty and his supporters. But Kesey went on in a very different vein:

> I object to *Cuckoo's Nest* being taught. What's there to teach? It's an entirely simple work, a book that any high school kid can read and comprehend without help. Let *Cuckoo's Nest* alone on the drugstore rack, and teach instead "Moby Dick" or "The Sound and the Fury" or works by Dickens or Hardy or Shakespeare, for crying out loud! I'm amazed at the number of kids who go all the way through high school and never read a classic. *Cuckoo's Nest* is no classic and needs no teaching. Kids can get it on their own whereas "Moby Dick" is long and difficult and unlikely to be read these days unless it is assigned. Don't let McMurphy crowd "Moby Dick" out of the classrooms.

Finally, Kesey had some advice for the students who were caught up in the middle of the controversy: "Don't look for what is easy. There is much wonderful in literature that is hard and obscure, and needs your efforts to learn."

There the matter rests at the moment. The community found in the Kesey letter something to please almost all attitudes and perspectives, and the case has yet to come to trial.

Chelsea, Massachusetts—"The City to a Young Girl"

It is difficult to imagine a community more different from St. Anthony, Idaho, than Chelsea, Massachusetts. An old and densely populated enclave, Chelsea is one of the grimy cities in the inner belt of Boston's neighbors, and is for all practical purposes a part of Boston. Once heavily Jewish, Chelsea has been a way station for immigrant groups moving from the core of the city to the two-family houses of Somerville, Mattapan, Watertown, and other parts of the buffer zone between middle-class Boston and its suburbs. Its schools, like its dwellings, are old and crowded.

Into the Chelsea High School Library in the summer of 1977 came an anthology of poems written by fledgling authors, entitled *Male and Female Under 18*—a collection thought by the librarian to have special appeal to her patrons. Some 40,000 copies of the anthology had been sold, and the book had been shelved in 3,500 libraries, apparently without incident. But a particular poem caught the eye of several Chelsea parents, and eventually of the school officials. "The City to a Young Girl" had been written by Jody Caravaglia, then a fifteen-year-old student at Hunter High School in New York, as she observed construction workers ogling her and other passing females. The sixteen lines of the simple verse reflected her youthful resentment at being treated as "a piece of meat." Two lines especially raised eyebrows in Chelsea: "One million horny lip-smacking men / screaming for my body."

The school committee, upon learning that such a poem could be found in their library, removed the anthology. The chairman of the school committee, former mayor Andrew Quigley, called the poem "objectionable, salacious, and obscene." He explained the committee's action: "A girl reading that without proper instruction could arrive at the opinion that every man walking down the street is considering her only as a sex object to be violated. It is not good education, and it is not something to be found in the halls of a school." Quigley also set forth in a column his critical views of the book and the librarian. The column appeared in the city's only daily paper, of which Quigley was the publisher.

There soon emerged a group called the Right to Read Committee, consisting of two teachers, several students, and the parents of one of the students, who joined with the librarian to seek a reversal of the school committee's action. Since it was apparent that requests for reconsideration would fall on deaf ears, the group filed a lawsuit in the federal district court in Boston, asking that the ban be rescinded and the book returned. The issue was not one of obscenity, since before the trial lawyers for both sides agreed that the poem was not legally obscene. Rather, as one reporter observed, "it is a clash of differing mores between youthful educators and conservative politicians."

The case came to trial in the late fall of 1977. Supporting the views of school committee chairman Quigley, another member testified that she voted to ban the poem from the library because it had "no message" and was the product of a "sick mind." While she did not consider the poem obscene in the technical sense, she thought it was no more than "just a bunch of dirty words written in order." Lawyers for the Right to Read Committee argued that such a ban violated the constitutional rights of free expression of students, teachers, and the librarian.

The judge came down solidly on the plaintiffs' side. He ruled that the action of the school committee in withdrawing the book from circulation was clearly a violation of the legal rights of the students, the parents, and the teachers. In the course of the opinion, he expressed some strong and supportive views on the freedoms of libraries, concluding: "What is at stake here is the right to read and to be exposed to controversial thought and language—a valuable right subject to first amendment protection." The school committee decided not to appeal the ruling—to which we shall turn in more detail in chapter six.

Sex Education and Birth Control in Michigan

Sex education is now required by law or by board of education policy in many states, but nowhere has the status of this subject been more checkered than in Michigan. A 1969 state law defines sex education as "preparation for personal relationships between the sexes by providing appropriate educational opportunities designed to help the individual develop understanding, acceptance, respect and trust for himself and others." More specifically, sex education involves the "responsibilities of each [sex] toward the other throughout life and the development of responsible use of human sexuality as a positive and creative force."

Sex education, thus defined, has been encouraged in Michigan public schools for many years, under a provision dealing with physical education. That law contained, however, one significant constraint: It forbade "any person to offer or give any instruction in [the] subject of birth control or offer any advice or information with respect to [that] subject." The law allowed any parent to request that his or her child be excused, without penalty, from any class in which sex hygiene was to be discussed.

In 1973 a Detroit physician named Goldfine and a school teacher named Mercer brought suit in federal court claiming that the birth control prohibition violated their rights of free expression. The teacher argued that he would risk losing his job if, for example, he were to respond to a student's question about birth control or contraception. The physician argued that he could not even accept an invitation to address any school class anywhere in the state on medical issues on which he was an expert and on which he could freely give information to patients, regardless of age, in any other setting.

The court rejected the claims of both plaintiffs. The physician, it felt, lacked a sufficient legal stake in the controversy to raise the constitutional issues; he was not personally and directly affected, since he was not a student, a teacher, or even (so far as the record appeared) a parent of a student seeking such information. The case of the teacher was more difficult, because even the state board of education agreed that he was a proper person to raise the constitutional issues. The court went on to sustain the validity of the state law, however, since it felt such a restriction on the school curriculum was a reasonable one, and fell within the authority of the legislature. A teacher, said the court, could be told in general terms what to teach and what not to teach. As far as parents were concerned, the court offered two additional comments—one, that they were under no legal compulsion to send their children to a public school, but could choose a private school with a more congenial curriculum; and second, that as citizens and voters they might press for changes in laws they felt unduly restrictive. Taking all these factors into account, the court felt the law was constitutionally valid and on that basis dismissed the suit.

The plaintiffs, having lost in the courts, did not abandon their fight. The birth control controversy was returned to the forum where the law had originated. On December 1, 1977, the Michigan legislature repealed the ban on teaching about birth control in the public schools, leaving Louisiana as the only state with such a prohibition. The new law required the creation of local advisory boards to review any programs put into effect, and forbade teaching about abortion as a method of contraception. But the major constraint which had been the subject of the unsuccessful federal suit was at length abolished through legislation.

The Michigan account does not end there, however. Shortly after the federal case was decided, a group of parents went to state court with a quite opposite claim. They argued that the existing state law was unconstitutional because it permitted sex education at all. The school board responded, and the state courts agreed, however, that a program from which any child could be excused did not raise the issues which the anti-sex-education parents sought to raise. The nonmandatory feature of the law, in the court's view, made it legally unassailable.

Siba Baum—Suffolk County, New York

Siba Baum is half Blackfoot Indian. She began her formal education in the public schools of Selden (Long Island), New York. In the fall of 1975, her mother decided to withdraw the girl from junior high school. The reason for this action was a long-standing belief on the mother's part—based on experience with two older children who had gone through the system—that the environment in the Selden schools was hostile to American Indians. This feeling came partly from the attitudes of other students, who would let out war whoops when the Baum children entered the classroom. But the final straw was a teacher's comments on a book review which Siba Baum had written about an autobiography of the Indian leader Geronimo.

In the paper, the girl explained:

> Geronimo, as other Indians, is seen as a blood-thirsty savage. But he and his people were trying to defend their lands and their way of life from invaders, who are pictured as heroes, settlers and explorers. When the Indian fought back, he was the villian. And it still goes on now.

The teacher gave the report a "B," but wrote in the margin some disparaging comments, including the remark that "the Indians got what they deserved." The same teacher admitted having said in class that some Indians were "lazy" and "preferred to stay on the reservation."

It was at this point that Mrs. Baum decided to withdraw

her daughter from school. Suffolk County officials soon brought a petition in family court charging the mother with child neglect based on her violation of the state's compulsory school laws. Mrs. Baum contested the charge, but the family court held against her. On July 4, 1978, county officials came to the Baum home to take custody of Siba. Before dawn that day, Mrs. Baum and Siba had left on a tour of Indian reservations in the west. It was the mother's claim that such visits would provide for her daughter a far better education than she had received in the Selden public schools.

The issue had by now became a cause célèbre. Civil Liberties lawyer William Kunstler, defender of the "Chicago 7" and other radical groups, came to Mrs. Baum's aid and filed an appeal. Kunstler argued that "the refusal of the school authorities even to see any element of racism in the incident, much less to take any corrective action, left a parent with very little choice." He maintained in his oral argument that "Indian children and black children are receiving an inferior education because of the failure to correct racism." It would be preferable, he suggested, to remove the child from school "and provide him with no education than for him to face racism."

The appellate court ruled against Mrs. Baum, finding her guilty of child neglect. The opinion reflected a feeling that Mrs. Baum had overreacted to a single incident, and that she was seeking publicity for herself as much as equal opportunity for her daughter. The court also considered Mrs. Baum's position unreasonable: She had insisted that she would keep her daughter out of school "no matter what happened" unless her specific demands were met. Among other things, she insisted that the school officials issue a statement that racism would no longer be tolerated. But the heart of her concern was the classroom, and she insisted that more attention be given to the problems of the American Indian in the Selden school curriculum.

The Baums were well beyond the reach of the New York

school, did in fact attempt to make the objectivity of the curriculum, rather than her responsibility to her daughter and to society, the central question in the courts. Such issues as these are, of course, plausibly open to adjudication. In contrast, courts would not be willing to allow one of the Kanawha County school firebombers or bus blockers to defend his conduct on the ground that opposition to the language arts textbooks was the motivating sentiment; in such cases the extenuating circumstances (if any) are far too remote from the offense.

Our cases illustrate a range of another sort—the diversity of the parties who raise such issues. Many of the cases involve parents, sometimes asserting a distinct parental interest in the educational process, and at other times simply asserting the interests of their children. (In practice, of course, the views of parents and children on curricular matters may be anything but concordant, but if a plaintiff claims to represent the interest of his or her child, the courts are not likely to demand proof of family consensus.)

We have also seen these issues raised by teachers in several cases and a librarian in at least one. School board members and administrators are usually defending action rather than initiating litigation, but in their responsive roles they often ask the courts to consider questions not covered in the plaintiffs' pleadings. Organizations sometimes have a substantial interest in such litigation, though they usually appear as *amici curiae* (friends of the court), or they may finance and guide litigation, as did the local civil liberties unions in the Indiana textbook and Fogarty cases. Finally, the issue may be brought to court by an interested citizen who is not an immediate participant in the educational process; but such claims, like those of Dr. Goldfine in the Michigan birth control case, are more remote and are thus more often turned aside by the courts.

Just as the cases reflect different parties, they also involve quite different elements of the curriculum. The focus of controversy may be as narrow as the 77-word poem in the Chelsea case, or it may be as broad as the allegations of racism in the Baum case or of "anti-religion" in the Kanawha County cases. Between these two extremes lie the more familiar targets—a book like the Kesey novel or the Indiana biology text; a unit in the curriculum like the Michigan sex education program or the New York social science unit, "Man: A Course of Study"; or a legislative or administrative policy (the Michigan statute proscribing classroom discussion of birth control). Such mandates may emerge, of course, at different levels; educational policy is made quite as much by local boards and even by individual principals as by state agencies or commissioners.

Finally, the reasons why curricular content or instructional materials evoke controversy are varied and complex. As we have seen in the cases discussed in this chapter, much controversy revolves about the issue of religion. Concerns are raised both by those who feel that religion has been unfairly removed from or kept out of the classroom, and by those who fear that any reference to religion in the school curriculum is dangerous and divisive. But the concerns go well beyond religion, as the cases show. Much parental and community attention has been given to the role of taboo words (sometimes improperly identified as "obscene"), and to the portrayal in textbooks of a lifestyle deeply disquieting to more traditional readers. (Sex, drugs, violence, and other themes in contemporary literature have been particular targets of recent protests, although they do not exhaust the range of concern.) Some books have been attacked because they are seen as unpatriotic—because they disparage or deprecate revered American traditions, or fail sufficiently to inculcate certain values, or seem unduly sympathetic to the United Nations or to other countries. There is also a growing concern about possible invasions of family privacy, not only from materials which seem to advance alien values, but also from instructional units which contain questions about family status and relationships, sexual attitudes and practices, and other matters which protesting parents feel should not be probed in school but should be left to the home.

This brief survey of disputes over instructional materials and curricular content leads naturally to an inquiry into causation. We need to know more about the reasons for the apparent recent growth of such conflicts. The next chapter probes some of those causes. From that probing, a better understanding of the roots of conflict over the public school curriculum should emerge. The background to which we now turn should also illuminate further the issues underlying the disputes we have observed in this initial survey.

2

THE ROOTS OF CONTROVERSY

No SINGLE CASE really explains why disputes over teaching materials find their way into the courts. Litigation about the school curriculum is not a wholly new phenomenon. As long ago as 1949, a group of Jewish parents in Brooklyn went to court claiming that the assignment of Shakespeare's *Merchant of Venice* and Dickens's *Oliver Twist* to senior literature classes violated the rights of their children to receive an education free of religious bias. The suit was a novel one, essentially without precedent. The trial judge eventually dismissed the claim, but only after satisfying himself that the presentation of both works would be objective, and that students would be warned not to infer racial or religious stereotypes from fictional characters. During the 1950s there were a few additional cases on similar issues, including one which reached the federal courts in Maryland after a Baltimore teacher was dismissed for assigning *Brave New World* to his senior literature class. But the cases were few and far between until the 1960s, and no precedent of consequence emerged. Then in the late 1960s and early '70s there occurred a veritable explosion of lawsuits over curricular matters. The task of this book is to describe the process by which a body of law concerning school curricula has developed. First, however, we should understand some of the factors that have created this new relationship between the courts and the curricula. Several forces appear to have contributed to the recent trends.

The Changing Character of Curricula and Materials

Everyone knows we have come a long way since the Mc-Guffey Readers—although one of the cases we will encounter in a later chapter shows a small-town Ohio school board demanding that the library replace several banned novels with copies of the latest edition of McGuffey. Until rather recently, the school curriculum was simple, traditional, and familiar. A survey of high schools in 1894 found that, at most, some 40 subjects were offered. By 1959, no fewer than 274 discrete subjects constituted the curricula of high schools in essentially the same communities included in the survey sixty-five years before. Many of the innovations were not likely to evoke controversy—driver education for example, or domestic science, or manual arts, all of which were added to the original "three R's" during the twentieth century in response to community pressures or perceived student needs. But other topics which have been added to meet new interests or demands are less bland—sex education, for instance, which is a relatively recent but now nearly universal curricular component, or the new mandates to teach about the Holocaust or about Black history. It is not simply that the *range* of offerings has become broader in recent years, but more that communities now demand that the schools offer instruction in the very areas that are most sensitive and most divisive. The schools are damned if they do and damned if they don't; when a community wants teaching about sex, or race relations, or consumer behavior, it can generally force the schools to comply. Yet the very response to these pressures may open a whole new range of problems which were unknown in times of simpler curricula.

There has been a significant shift, too, in the way in which controversial issues have been handled in the curriculum. In the

1920s the evolution/creation controversy was often resolved simply by forbidding the schools to teach that man descended from apes. In the 1960s and '70s, creationists have insisted that the schools teach both views, not that they eschew either. Minority parents do not ask simply that disparaging references or stereotypes be removed, but that positive steps be taken to remedy omissions of the past by adding new units or materials. The school that is compelled to enter the arena of controversy in this way incurs myriad risks and invites challenge to a degree not present in earlier times.

Meanwhile, changes in both content and format of teaching materials have compounded the risks. Professor Ken Donelson of Arizona State University, a long-time observer of children's literature, notes how recent is the emergence of a controversial or potentially censorable body of adolescent reading matter:

> Most of the books of the forties and fifties, and even the sixties remained simplistic, unrealistic, sticky and even saccharine exercises in devising puerile plots with stick figures marching inevitably and fully through them. Whatever else could be objected to such literature, they but rarely suffered any kind of criticism or attacks, even less anything bordering on censorship. The adolescent novel prior to 1965 would have prepared almost no one for the books that would follow that date.

Edwin Barber, a veteran textbook editor, wrote recently in the *New York Times* of this dramatic change in available materials:

> Until the late 1950's, schoolbooks were homogenized and largely without individual voice or point of view. Suddenly, the television generation grew up, and with the 1960's came Vietnam, the generation gap, race consciousness, women's liberation, student activism and many other issues.
>
> Homogenization was out and myths were outmoded; individualism and sensitivity to diversity were in. Textbook publishers heard complaints that their books were unreflective of the real world, and the industry hustled to catch up, "recycling" old series and creating new ones.

A partial explanation of the change in content comes from Mary
Jane Anderson, executive secretary of the American Library Association's Library Service to Children program:

> Children's authors are more accurately reflecting actual family
> life in their stories. As adults become more open with each other
> and their children about sex and love, divorce, child abuse, and
> other similar issues, authors are translating these concerns into
> subjects, settings and situations in their books.

The changing content of materials has been paralleled by a
change in format. One recent study of English curricula in the
1970s reported:

> The availability of standard literary selections in paperback edi-
> tions made them a natural resource for the academically oriented
> teacher, with a corresponding shift in emphasis from their value in
> outside reading to their use in the program for direct class study.

The number of schools offering senior electives in English or
even in comparative literature has increased markedly in recent
years, as much because of the change in format as for content
reasons. (The kind of course which John Fogarty offered in St.
Anthony, Idaho, for example, would have been virtually unknown even in city and large suburban districts a decade earlier;
not only Ken Kesey, but more substantial authors would have
been available in the library or the drugstore, but not in the
classroom.)

One would expect a close correlation between the diversity
of the materials used in the classroom and the level of controversy. Surely the cases in chapter one suggest such a correlation;
Kanawha County, for example, did not explode until the bold
new language arts series was approved in the spring of 1974.
Professor Lee Burress of the University of Wisconsin–Stevens
Point has noted a striking parallel in his studies of school censorship:

I found strong indications that the highest incidence of censorship was in the northeastern part of the United States; there was a strong suggestion that the schools with the best libraries had the most censorship pressure. The old South reported both fewer books in the libraries and fewer attempted or completed censorship acts. Thus the supposedly best educated and socioeconomically highest status communities seem to report the most censorship pressure on the schools.

Much as with the diversity of the curriculum itself, the very expansion in availability of materials may measurably have heightened the risk of controversy.

There is a third type of change in content: the recent rise in the use of innovative teaching approaches and units prepared by national or regional curriculum centers. Many of these centers were launched by appropriations under the Elementary and Secondary Education Act of 1965, and some received additional support in the 1960s from foundations concerned about the quality of the American school curriculum in the post-Sputnik era. The recurrent controversy over "Man: A Course of Study" illustrates the issue well. MACOS consists of a series of sophisticated "units" adapted to various levels of the social studies, elaborately prepared and neatly packaged by a national curriculum laboratory. The initial cost of preparation and dissemination was substantial. Since its introduction in the early 1970s, MACOS has been under attack, and has been removed by parental pressure even in such districts as Montclair, New Jersey. The basic attack has been religious in nature; parents claimed that the unit violates or disparages parental beliefs and values which have deep theological roots. While similar concerns have been raised about other materials, the novelty of the format in a unit like MACOS poses an additional risk. There is no parallel anywhere to the $2.5 million suit brought against the East Greenbush (New York) Board of Education for damages allegedly inflicted by MACOS on the plaintiffs' children. Elsewhere, there have been parental objections to the use of novel teaching formats, such as "Individually Guided Education" (which seeks to adapt instruction better to the individual learner through detailed questionnaires, parent conferences, and other instruments often seen as threatening to the privacy of family and home). The problem is not simply that the unit comes from a sophisticated national curriculum laboratory financed by the Ford Foundation or by the federal government. In some quarters such origins alone might arouse suspicion. The problem, and therefore the potential for opposition, is compounded by the fact that such materials are designed to fit into the established curriculum, rather than to exist apart from or outside it as "optional" exercises.

These several changes in the substance of education—expanded and diversified curricula, bolder texts and more paperbacks, and innovative formats—partly explain the rising level of controversy in the 1970s. They also help us understand the broadening of the focus of parental protest from sex to dirty words to politics, privacy, and religion—areas of concern which in the past were seldom mentioned in the classroom. But the change in curriculum and materials does not tell the whole story. There have also been changes in the attitudes and expectations of the principal actors in the drama, to whom we now turn.

Changing Parental Expectations and Growing Frustration

At the height of the Kanawha County controversy, a nationally syndicated column spoke of "Parents Lib" as a "new liberation movement . . . which is not yet in full swing, but is gaining steam rapidly." Across the country, said the reporter, "parents are in rebellion and demanding their rights. . . ." Another columnist explained both Kanawha County and the equally violent parental protest against school desegregation in South Boston as "symptoms of a general malaise that afflicts us all." But there does seem to be a narrower and more specific set of concerns in the textbook area, where, unlike South Boston, it is the very *content* of education which draws parental wrath.

There is nothing new about parental interest in what the schools teach and how well they teach it. The concern over quality and content of instruction has, however, been increased by several trends. One, of course, is the rapidly rising cost of the public schools (both directly through local taxes and indirectly through a rising federal contribution). Even if the value and quality of education were perceived as improving with the rise in cost, there would likely have been greater parental concerns and demands. But when increased expenditures seemed to produce lower SAT scores, greater violence, more drug-taking, and other questionable performance criteria, parental intervention was almost certain to increase.

Meanwhile, the sheer importance of the schools to society and the economy grew steadily; the number of high school graduates going to college rose from less than 25 percent in the 1930s to 50 percent in the 1970s, with the result that the performance of the schools assumed critical importance for a far larger portion of American parents.

Ironically, the mounting cost and importance of the school systems have been accomplished not only by doubts about their quality but also by a felt loss of control. Fred Hechinger, the *New York Times* senior education writer, recently reported a widespread perception that "control of schools is passing from parents and local school boards to agencies of state and federal governments and the teachers unions"—not only in the suburbs, but also in the central cities. Part of this sense of distance comes from increased centralization of funding sources, but also reflects the federal locus of pressure to desegregate, to meet uniform standards, and to achieve other goals that were once locally initiated.

There is another ironic dimension to the control issue.

While some groups that once had control—the politically influential upper socioeconomic groups—have been losing it, others who were historically excluded are fighting for a share of what is left. Kanawha County seemed to some observers more a class conflict than a collision of values—a violent attempt by the alienated people of the rural regions to gain some measure of self-determination. In this view, textbooks just happened to provide the battleground; had there been no curricular issues, then personnel, construction, or other questions would have drawn the same fire. Lee Burress observes: "It may be that an increasing number of censorship problems such as the one in Kanawha County . . . reflect the desire of lower middle class people to achieve the same degree of control of the schools that has characteristically been true of the middle class."

Such tensions are not only socioeconomic; they are also in part racial. Within the past several years there has been a new and ominous pressure from minority parents for the removal of objectionable materials. In the summer of 1976 the New Trier (Illinois) School Board agreed in response to pressure from black parents to remove *Huckleberry Finn* from all required reading lists and to relegate it to optional status. The parents claimed that the portrayal of blacks in the book, and especially that of "Nigger Jim," was demeaning. A year later, the Oakland, California, school administration removed *Daddy Was a Numbers Runner* from all junior high school libraries and restricted its availability in senior high schools, following a complaint from a middle-class black parent that the book gave too explicit a view of ghetto life. Such incidents are still rare; they were unknown even a few years ago, but may well increase along with demands from historically neglected white parent groups. The schools are caught in a crosscurrent of parental pressures of a far more complex character than those of earlier times. More controversy, and more court cases, seem an inevitable result.

While parental concern about education and the curriculum

has been rising, the alternatives available to families disenchanted by the current options have diminished. Differences and variations among public schools, which parents could once sample by moving from one suburb to another within a metropolitan area, have lessened in the last decade or so. Consolidation of once local and distinct rural school systems into huge unified regional districts has hastened the process of homogenization. There results what Professors John Coons and Stephen Sugarman characterize as a "certain sameness" in curricula as in other aspects of education:

> Among the majority of school districts there are important likenesses. Indeed, these similarities in style or curriculum are the most common complaint; schools are said to be too much the same and seek too uniform a product.
>
> Explicitly the schools emphasize technology, uncontroversial information, and skills, an approach officially deemed to be "neutral." On its surface the intended message appears to have little philosophical content; by and large the schools shun explicit treatment of controversial moral or political issues. Implicitly, however, they endorse majoritarian social and political norms. Historically and currently they have striven with enthusiasm to produce "true Americans" by conditioning the children to the mind-set accepted in the larger—or at least local—society. This "hidden curriculum" relies principally on the social ambience of the teaching personnel, who are generally middle class and trained in similar institutions.
>
> The similarities in the schools' message are matched by the standardization of the setting in which it is delivered. Indeed, the most striking regularity is that of two dozen children sequestered five hours a day in the same room in the same building from September to June.

If the "sameness" of the public school system restricts choice, there is theoretically the final alternative of private education. Half a century ago the United States Supreme Court held that states could not compel all students to attend public schools, since freedom of choice in education was a federally guaranteed right. But the practical availability of that choice for most American families is quite a different matter. Several factors sharply restrict its exercise. One limitation is of course that of cost of private schooling. Tuition even at the more modest private institutions is substantial, and comes on top of the roughly $770 which the average American family already pays each year in taxes for the support of the public school system. As Coons and Sugarman observe, "under these circumstances even wealthier people often forego the private alternative they might prefer."

Second, there is the limitation of geography. The parents who originally succeeded in having the creationist biology text adopted live in rural Indiana counties far beyond commuting distance of the private school where the book would still be used. In fact, those parent groups which protest most vigorously tend to live furthest from the metropolitan areas in which the rather small number of remaining private schools are concentrated.

Finally, the law restricts this choice in two additional ways. Under federal civil rights statutes, the Supreme Court has held that private schools may not practice racial segregation in their admissions policies, and in that sense are not truly "private." Moreover, state accreditation standards impinge upon the private schools in ways that restrict the range of options for the dissenting parent. Several conservative Christian schools in Kentucky have challenged the science requirements of that state's accreditation laws, arguing that teaching biology the way the state says it must be taught would impair the religious freedom of parents who are willing to pay the tuition.

The narrowing of private sector alternatives inevitably channels into the public schools the separatist pressures of a complex society. If white parents cannot choose totally segregated schools, if Jewish parents cannot rely on traditional yeshivas, and if fundamentalist parents in Kentucky cannot have biology taught according to the Bible, then the public schools become the battlegrounds for issues that are central to and divisive in the larger society. Yet the community has said that the issues which particularly strain an already fragile consensus—sex education, civics, contemporary literature, and the like—should be taught in the public schools. The resulting controversy should surprise no one.

Growth of Censorship: New Pressures and New Groups React to New Materials

A dangerous tension begins to emerge. If teaching materials are more varied and more challenging, and if parents expect more from the schools, we should not be surprised to see growing debate and conflict over the adoption and use of texts and curricular units. Seasoned observers of the public education scene have remarked that pressures for curricular censorship appear to have reached uncommonly intense levels. A *New York Times* headline in the spring of 1979 warned that "censorship [is] on the rise around the Nation." Fred Hechinger wrote a few weeks later: "The public schools have never enjoyed more than brief periods of cease-fire with the censors. Whenever the national mood is angry, frustrated or conservative, the blue-pencil brigade mobilizes. . . ." The occasion for Hechinger's column was the recent release of a report by the National Council of Teachers of English describing a dramatic rise in censorship during the late 1970s with evidence drawn from all parts of the country. Judith Krug, director of the Office of Intellectual Freedom of the American Library Association, has followed such matters closely for more than a decade. She reported that the school year 1977–78 saw more cases (some 300 incidents were reported to her office alone) of book removal, censorship, library restriction, and the like than had occurred in the preceding quarter century. Her gloomy appraisal is shared by other close observers, such as Professor Edward Jenkinson of Indiana University, who chairs the censorship committee of the National Council of Teachers of English and receives reports of book banning throughout the country. The lead article in the May 1980 issue of *Phi Delta*

Kappan (a national professional journal for teachers and school administrators) bore the ominous title "Preachers, Politics and Public Education: A Review of Right-Wing Pressures Against Public Schooling in America." In the informed view of such experts, something is happening which not only evokes great concern but demands an explanation.

Changes in Organization and Structure

It would be surprising if changes in the organization and structure of American public education had not in some way contributed to curricular conflicts. Several possibly relevant factors deserve comment here. In earlier times, the governing board of a school or district served a relatively small and typically homogeneous population. The march toward amalgamation of increasingly larger (and inevitably more diverse) populations into consolidated school districts brought concomitant tensions which were bound to spill over into the curriculum. Kanawha County provides an apt, if extreme, case in point. The unification into a single district of the urban population of the city of Charleston and the starkly dissimilar Appalachian "creekers" was bound to create conflict over school policies. The rural people, who would have been able to shape the curriculum in a smaller and more homogeneous district, felt powerless in the governance of the consolidated district; that sense of alienation ultimately triggered the controversy over sex education and the language arts books.

Conditions are less explosive in other parts of the country. Yet similar structural changes may have contributed to the escalation of tension we have observed. The process of adopting instructional materials illustrates a different problem. There is a paradox here: On the one hand, general curricular requirements are being set increasingly at the state level for all districts—sex education in Michigan, creationism in California, and similar mandates elsewhere. Broad policies are made either by the state legislature or by a statewide education board or commissioner. Yet the actual process of textbook adoption and approval seems to have been more and more localized. Some states still require a state agency to make basic approvals, but leave the choice among approved texts to the local districts. (In Indiana, the state agency approved seven biology texts; the decision to use *A Search for Order* was left entirely to the local board and only five districts did in fact select it before the lawsuit.) In other states, even the formality of central state approval has been eliminated; Kansas, for example, used to handle all textbook adoptions centrally in Topeka, but the 1971 legislature repealed the law and since that time local districts have handled all screening and adoption. In Alaska there exists on paper a State Schools Textbook Committee, but the legislature has declined to fund this agency in recent years, and the state education department is seeking to have repealed a meaningless and potentially confusing enabling law.

In fact, the decentralization of textbook selection has in many states proceeded even further. Despite a pervasive parental perception that key decisions about classroom materials are made in Washington or the state capital, or at least at district headquarters, in many cases the operative decisions are made at the local school level, with substantial flexibility given to the individual teacher. The increasing variety of materials has contributed in part to the individualization of the judgment. Ironically, the financial plight of many school districts in the 1970s has also played a part; as budgets get tighter, schools are more likely to use whatever materials are available—including experimental texts or units provided free by publishers. When the state or the district provides inadequate funding for teaching materials, its claim to insist on uniform reading lists loses considerable force. Thus current decentralization of textbook selection may in part be the unplanned result of conditions only remotely related to curriculum, although there has also been some conscious preference for local initiative.

Community control is by no means an exclusive demand of right-wing groups. In fact, pressures for the direct involvement of parents and citizens of the immediate area have nowhere been more vigorous than in New York City, where the Ford Foundation sponsored a notable experiment in "community control" during the 1960s. Ironically, many who favored the effort to enhance the choice of minority parents in Ocean Hill–Brownsville decry comparable pressures from the "creekers" of West Virginia. There is much justice to the critique of conservative columnist James Kilpatrick: "A considerable intellectual agility is required to maintain the proposition that community censorship of textbooks is fine for militant blacks in Manhattan but altogether abhorrent for militant whites in Appalachia." From both sides, there is little question that the attempt to regain or restore local control, within the large unified district, has intensified the risk of focussing community pressures on the curriculum that were once blurred in the larger community.

These disparate forces have converged on school curricula at an especially bad time. Schools which were already vulnerable have now been made even more dependent on dwindling local resources by tax-reduction measures such as California's Proposition 13. The current condition is well summarized by Edward Jenkinson:

> [One] reason for the rise in censorship is that the schools are a convenient target for unhappy citizens. Many people feel that they cannot fight Washington, the state capitol, or even city hall. When they become unhappy because of inflation, federal or state laws, the so-called moral decline, or anything else, they want to lash out. But they don't always know how to attack the problems that really trouble them. So they vent their spleen on the schools.

Accessibility of the Courts

Litigation over curricular choices could not have expanded

as it has if the courts had been reluctant to entertain such suits. Traditionally judges had shied away from school matters, turning away many students and teachers with claims that had at least some plausible basis in the Constitution. In the late 1960s, suddenly the doors of the courts opened, chiefly as a result of the wave of lawsuits during the Vietnam era. For the first time students squarely challenged the legal authority of school boards and administrators to enforce rules governing conduct, grooming, and dress. The opening of the courts also reflected the rising activism of teachers and their national organizations, which began to compete vigorously for membership through litigation of teachers' claims as well as in more familiar and conventional arenas. Thus the volume of suits filed against school officials rose markedly during the early 1970s, and for a set of compatible reasons. Once the doors of the courts were open to students seeking legal protection for their hair length and to teachers challenging rules of decorum and other restrictions, it was only a matter of time until the curriculum itself became the object of litigation.

While most current cases address a particular facet of the curriculum, there is no inherent reason why the focus should be so limited. There is at least one quite recent lawsuit which seeks to place the entire curriculum on trial, and asks a judge to determine its validity. Mr. and Mrs. Ronald Irwin brought suit early in 1979 against the McHenry (Illinois) School District because (they claimed) their fifth grade son Thomas had been "bored" by the standard curriculum. The boy had an IQ of 170, and his parents felt he deserved something more challenging than the standard fifth grade program. They rejected the possibility of skipping grades, suggested by the schools, because they feared acceleration would harm his social development. Private schooling was theoretically available, but the Irwins said they could not afford the substantial tuition. Moreover, they argued that the public school curriculum should offer as much stimulation to the genius as to the average pupil. When school officials refused to permit Thomas to enroll in a high school Spanish course to supplement his regular studies, the parents decided their only recourse lay in the courts. Thus they filed suit seeking $1 million in damages on the ground that the standard curriculum had "denied adequate mental stimulation" to their son and had "hindered his educational development."

It is rare indeed that the courts are used in this way to challenge the *whole* curriculum. Most cases deal with some portion of the academic program that has aroused parental or community concern, or has been the object of administrative sanction. But the Irwin case may suggest that little—if anything—about the curriculum is beyond the reach of the courts.

3

A RIGHT TO BE EDUCATED?

THERE WOULD BE little point in worrying about details if no basic right exists. The threshold legal question, then, is whether our Constitution and laws guarantee in some way the right to an education. At first the question may seem perverse, and the answer obvious. Not only is there a *right* to be educated, most people would say, there is a *duty* to be educated as a result of the compulsory education laws. But the issue is not simply whether one may (or must) sit in a classroom for six hours a day, thirty-two weeks a year for ten or twelve years. The central concern we are raising at the start of our legal analysis goes much deeper. It is an essential beginning point for any discussion of legal disputes over the content of education.

Let us begin with the case of Edward Donohue, who graduated from a high school in Suffolk County, New York, in June 1976. He tried to get a job as a carpenter but found that he lacked certain essential skills. As he was trying one day to comprehend the menu at a diner in Lindenhurst, the thought occurred to him (and to his parents) that his education had left him "unable to cope properly with the affairs of the world." Young Donohue thereupon contacted a lawyer and brought suit against the Copiague school district for $5 million damages on the basis of alleged "educational malpractice." The *Donohue*

39

case was not the first of its kind. In 1974 a California high school graduate filed a claim for damages because he claimed he could not read beyond the fifth grade level, and was thus unprepared for life. The California courts dismissed the claim on the ground that state law imposed on the schools no legal duty to provide a specific quality or level of education. The New York court followed that precedent, and held that Donohue had stated no cause of action:

> Clearly, recognition of a legal duty of care in this case would inevitably result in judicial interference. Of necessity, plaintiff would have to call upon jurors to decide which subjects should have been taught, which teaching methods were appropriate, whether certain tests should have been administered, and so on ad infinitum. Further, public education involves an inherent stress between satisfying the educational needs of the individual and the needs of the student body. It is not for the courts to determine how best to utilize scarce educational resources to achieve these sometimes conflicting objectives. Simply stated, recognition of an action of "educational malpractice" would impermissibly require the courts to oversee the administration of the public school system.

There was, however, a dissent. One appellate judge felt Donohue should at least have his day in court; "Whether the plaintiff's failure to achieve a basic level of literacy was caused by the school district's negligence, or was the product of forces outside the teaching process is a question of proof to be resolved at a trial." Moreover, an editorial in the *New York Times* warned that "the Donohue case poses knotty questions" and added that "if he loses, it will not be the kind of victory our schools or the rest of us can celebrate."

The *Donohue* case is one of several recent "educational malpractice" suits. Implicitly these cases ask whether the Constitution guarantees to citizens of school age any particular content or quality of education, or even meaningful access to education at all. While the courts in rejecting (as they have quite uniformly) the malpractice claims have not considered the constitutional dimension, we should do so here. Parents and others may well believe that education is among their fundamental rights. They may well assume that, should a dispute arise, they would be able to press in court a legal claim to an education—even (as in the case of the Donohues) a claim to an education of a certain quality. There is not much law that really answers the question directly, but this is the place to bring together what we know.

The text of the Constitution is the appropriate starting point. The word "education" nowhere appears either in the main document or in any of the amendments. The omission is not entirely the result of inadvertence; the Framers did give some thought to authorizing the creation of a federal college or university, but deleted such a specific power along with others that were better left to implication. At the time of the Constitutional Convention, there were really no public school systems as such; the modern school is a creature of the nineteenth century. As school systems did emerge, they naturally responded to local needs and operated under general state authority, with remarkably little federal control or support. Early state laws dealing with education were very general, leaving most of the details to elected local officials.

During these early times, the prospect of a constitutional claim of access to education would have seemed remote indeed. While education was of course not universally available—to women, blacks, and other minorities, for example—few of those excluded from the system would have raised any constitutional challenge. The earliest racial segregation suits were unsuccessful, even where separate schools for blacks were not (as the Supreme Court later held they must be) of quality equal to those for whites. Thus the notion of a legal right to education simply was not meaningful during this formative period.

Then in 1954 the Supreme Court offered a rather different view of the legal status of education. The precise issue presented by *Brown* v. *Board of Education* was the compatibility of racially segregated schools with the equal protection guarantees of the Fourteenth Amendment. But the segregation cases posed inescapably the question of where elementary and secondary education fit among the basic elements of a democratic society. The Court's response is highly significant:

> Today, education is perhaps the most important function of state and local governments. Compulsory school attendance laws and the great expenditures for education both demonstrate our recognition of the importance of education to our democratic society. It is required in the performance of our most basic public responsibilities, even service in the armed forces. It is the very foundation of good citizenship. Today it is a principal instrument in awakening the child to cultural values, in preparing him for later professional training, and in helping him to adjust normally to his environment. In these days, it is doubtful that any child may reasonably be expected to succeed in life if he is denied the opportunity of an education. Such an opportunity, where the state has undertaken to provide it, is a right which must be made available to all on equal terms.

Little noticed at the time, given the preoccupation with *Brown*'s central theme, was the Court's reluctance to recognize education, per se, as a fundamental right. The qualifications were deliberate and portentous: the term "opportunity" was carefully used in place of "right" at the critical points, and the guarantee of an equal education existed where "the state has undertaken to provide" some education, but on racially separate terms. Of course there was no need to say more in 1954, and one could not reasonably fault the Court for not announcing a clear "right." In retrospect, the carefully circumscribed references to "opportunity" told us more than we realized.

Soon after *Brown* the Court reviewed a case in which the putative "right" to education could have played a clearer role. Southeastern states in the late 1950s used various strategems to avoid desegregation. In Virginia some counties (with the state's blessing) closed all their public schools and channeled the released funds to the support of private "academies" which turned out to be exclusively white. A group of black parents in Prince Edward County brought suit in the federal district court claiming that such a practice violated *Brown's* guarantee of equality in public education. The issue eventually reached the Supreme Court. The majority held that Virginia had indeed denied equality to the black citizens of Prince Edward County by keeping public schools open in other areas while closing them (or allowing them to be closed) in one county. The case might have posed the question whether the state had a duty to maintain a public school system—another way of phrasing the "right to an education" claim. But the Court found it unnecessary to reach so broad an issue in the much narrower context of manifest inequality between counties of the same state. (The Court will decide broad questions only where there are no narrower grounds, and will reach a constitutional issue only when necessary.) Since the reason for the closing of the Prince Edward schools had been unmistakably racial—in fact to flout a desegregation decree— there was no need to reach the broader question whether states had any basic duty to their citizens at all in the realm of education.

A decade later the Supreme Court came much closer to the central issue. A group of parents in Texas challenged the state school finance formula by which some districts (with large and wealthy property bases) maintained high quality schools while poorer communities simply could not afford facilities or programs of comparable quality. The California Supreme Court had already held, in a similar case, that the state constitution guaranteed some measure of financial equality among school districts regardless of variations in wealth.

The resolution of the basic legal issue in the Texas case depended largely on the appropriate criterion of "equality." Many classifications which treat people or groups differently—for example, business regulations—will pass muster under a rather loose test of "rationality." On the other hand, where "fundamental" human interests are affected—freedoms of expression and religion, for example—a classification must undergo "strict scrutiny." Several years earlier the Justices struck down state laws which required newcomers to wait long periods before they were eligible for welfare; such restrictions impermissibly burdened the fundamental right of interstate travel. The question in the school finance case, then, was whether *education* would be deemed a "fundamental interest"; if so, then the widely disparate levels of financial support would probably not survive the test of "strict scrutiny."

But the Court disagreed that public education was such a basic human right. In *San Antonio School District* v. *Rodriguez*, a 5–4 majority held that education, though important, was not "fundamental" in the same sense as the liberties of the Bill of Rights. Although the parents argued that a sound education was essential to the exercise, for example, of political participation and free expression, the majority responded:

> We have never presumed to possess either the ability or the authority to guarantee to the citizenry the most *effective* speech or the most informed electoral choice. That these may be desirable goals is not to be doubted. But they are not values to be implemented by judicial intrusion into otherwise legitimate state activities.

There was another dimension to the majority decision: Although the education of the poorer children in the ghetto and barrio was inferior in some respects to that which wealthier Anglo children received in the suburbs, "we have no indication that the present . . . system fails to provide each child with an opportunity to acquire the basic minimal skills necessary. . . ."

Four members of the Court forcefully dissented. They argued that the majority had erroneously drawn the line between fundamental interests and those which deserved lesser constitutional protection. For them, education was indeed a basic right:

> Education directly affects the ability of a child to exercise his First Amendment interests both as a source and as a receiver of information and ideas. . . . Education may instill the interest and provide the tools necessary for political discourse and debate. Indeed, it has frequently been suggested that education is the dominant factor affecting political consciousness and participation.

Thus, for the dissenters (as for the California Supreme Court) the interest in access to education deserved the highest measure of constitutional protection.

There were important qualifications to the *Rodriguez* decision. All the Court held was that states were not bound by the federal constitution to treat all school districts equally. The California Supreme Court had already reached a different conclusion, relying partly on the state constitution, and reaffirmed that view after *Rodriguez*. State courts in New Jersey, New York, Colorado, and elsewhere agreed with the California justices that equal support levels were a duty of state government, though the federal constitution did not so require.

The scope of the Supreme Court holding was qualified in other ways as well. The Court noted that the parent-plaintiffs did not argue that their children had been excluded from any part of the educational system, but simply that the facilities and programs to which they had access were of poorer quality than those in other districts. Had there been either a claim of total denial or exclusion, or even a more fully developed proof of the effects of unequal support levels on educational opportunity, at least one Justice might have reached a different conclusion. Finally, the case reveals some deference to the political process by which levels of tax support for education are determined. To the extent that the majority believed or assumed that the voters of Texas had opted in favor of unequally financed schools, that judgment may have claimed a special respect from the federal courts. Thus the disinclination of the Supreme Court to hold public education a "fundamental right" may be less significant than the ungenerous language of the *Rodriguez* opinion would suggest.

Moreover, much of what the Constitution does not guarantee has now been provided by statute. Under a recent federal law—the Education for All Handicapped Children Act—school districts must identify and provide special educational opportunities for handicapped pupils. Such children must, for example, be educated with their peers "to the maximum extent possible" and must receive access to all portions of the school program normally provided for nonhandicapped children. Substantial expense may be involved in meeting these new obligations—for example, the obligation imposed by the 1980 federal court decision that New York public schools must provide sign language interpreters for deaf children in regular classrooms. For handicapped children and their parents, at least, the absence of a constitutional right to education is largely meaningless; Congress has provided substantially more than the Constitution could ever have reasonably been expected to guarantee.

Much the same is true for another group—students from non-English-speaking homes. A group of Chinese parents in San Francisco brought suit in the federal courts several years ago, claiming that their children need supplemental instruction in English to make the educational experience as meaningful to them as to their native-speaking classmates. They based this claim partly on the constitutional guarantee of equality and partly on a provision of the 1964 Civil Rights Act which bars discrimination in programs receiving federal funds. The lower court initially upheld the constitutional claim, but the Supreme Court found it unnecessary to go beyond the Civil Rights Act. Soon after rejecting the broader constitutional claim in *Rodriguez*, the Justices held that the Chinese students did have a legal right to supplemental language instruction. The opinion offered some pertinent comments about the nature and importance of education:

> Under . . . state-imposed standards there is no equality of treatment merely providing students with the same facilities, textbooks, teachers, and curriculum; for students who do not understand English are effectively foreclosed from any meaningful education.
>
> Basic English skills are at the very core of what these public schools teach. Imposition of a requirement that, before a child can effectively participate in the educational program, he must already have acquired those basic skills is to make a mockery of public education. We know that those who do not understand English are certain to find their classroom experiences wholly incomprehensible and in no way meaningful.

Other courts have applied this reasoning to require supplemental instruction for children who have grown up in Spanish-speaking homes, and who thus come to school with educational needs similar to those of the Chinese-speaking children in San Francisco. A federal judge has recently extended this theory to a group of black students in Ann Arbor, Michigan, and ordered special instruction to supplement the "Black English" which they speak in their own community.

Such protection extends, of course, only to certain subgroups within the pupil population—those who are mentally retarded, physically handicapped, or for whom English is not the native language. But these are the groups who would be most likely to assert (and to benefit from) a constitutional interest, which the Supreme Court rejected in *Rodriguez*. Thus the absence of a *constitutional* right of access to education may be far less important. Statutory protection of such special groups will increase, not diminish, if recent history is any guide. The willingness of courts to fashion new remedies even without legislative authority is also likely to increase. Even where there is no clear statutory basis, courts have recognized the educational needs of groups for whom access is impeded or restricted. As long as such solicitude exists, the ultimate question whether a *right* to education exists under the Constitution may not really be presented—at least not in a context in which its denial would seem callous.

There may be an even better answer to the question left open by the *Rodriguez* case. *Rights* may not be denied, and that is why many people believe that *only* rights are inviolable. There was a time when the courts drew a sharp distinction between certain interests that were "rights" and others that were merely "privileges." The former could not be abridged, while the latter could be given or taken away at will. But the courts in the last quarter century or so have rejected this neat dichotomy. In its place they have developed a more flexible concept of interests, or benefits—some of which may be qualified or conditioned more readily than others, but few of which can be restricted or terminated at will. The field of government employment offers an instructive example of the new approach. It has always been true that no person could insist on being hired by a government agency, nor could anyone demand that government create jobs for needy citizens. In this sense public employment is something less than a "right." And it used to follow that government jobs could be denied, or terminated, for almost any reason (or for no reason). Then gradually the courts came to recognize that working for the government was a relationship of substantial value. Various types of conditions on employment that had once been allowed were increasingly struck down—demeaning loyalty oaths, for example, and restrictions on the free public speech of government workers. What emerged was a doctrine of "unconstitutional conditions," which replaced the old right/privilege dichotomy and made certain kinds of conditions invalid even where the opportunity was not formerly a "right." Public employment might be less exalted in the order of government benefits than the vote, and might be conditioned in different ways. But no longer could a benefit or its denial be used indirectly to suppress freedom of speech, religion, or other basic liberties.

The significance of this development to public education should be clear. Even publicly supported *higher* education has been held to be a benefit of substantial value, so that a state university student may not be expelled without a hearing. Thus it is no longer useful to dismiss public education as a "privilege" in the abstract—even though no person may have a firm "right" to claim it. Surely the same should be true of elementary and secondary education, given its universality and the value of which the Supreme Court spoke in the *Brown* case.

Several decisions defining the rights of students within public education become clearer in this light. As early as 1943, the Supreme Court held that states could not compel public school pupils to salute the flag at the start of the school day—although the basis for the judgment was limits on government power imposed by the general precepts of the due process clause. The Court might have held that such actions abridged the religious liberty of the students, since their opposition to the pledge was religiously based, but took instead a broader ground which made unnecessary any inquiry into the extent of religious freedom in the public schools. This early decision is quite consistent with the later doctrine: Public education may well be something less than a "right," but its availability could not be conditioned upon an act contrary to conscience. Even at this stage in the evolution of students' legal interests, the usefulness of the right/privilege distinction was suspect. Later cases continued this trend.

The issue of high school students' legal status squarely reached the Supreme Court in 1969. The Vietnam War, and its impact on youth, made inevitable the litigation of conflicts over school authority. A student named Mary Beth Tinker was suspended from school in Des Moines, Iowa, for wearing a black armband to class in protest against the government's Vietnam policies. A school rule forbade such symbols (although it apparently permitted more traditional and less controversial insignia). Tinker and her parents brought suit against the school district,

continued access to education could not be denied without due process. In light of this judgment, the quest for a "right" becomes even less meaningful.

The *Goss* case provided more than simply a beachhead for students' procedural claims. One legal analyst has assessed its larger import in this way:

> The real significance of *Goss* is that it indicates a pronounced shift in the judiciary's proclivity to interfere in the public schools. Instead of simply setting limits on the actions of school officials, *Goss* tells administrators how they must proceed in certain situations. The Court was less willing to defer to the "expertise" of community authorities; indeed the Court expressed concern that school authorities may take "erroneous action" in discipline cases. In effect, the Court has dictated the manner in which educational authorities perform their "discretionary function" by requiring "at least an informal give-and-take between student and disciplinarian."

The Supreme Court has spoken once more, since *Goss*, on the relationship between student and school. The precise issue was again one of discipline—this time whether or not schools could use corporal punishment. A Florida law provided for the use of limited physical force against students, and the local school board had adopted additional regulations. The typical punishment consisted of one to five blows on the buttocks with a paddle. The student in the particular case claimed that the blows had been so severe as to require medical attention and keep him out of school for eleven days. But a majority of the Supreme Court in *Ingraham* v. *Wright* disagreed that such treatment constituted "cruel and unusual punishment." Although the Court had invoked the Eighth Amendment's guarantee in other settings, mainly involving prisoners, it found no basis for "wrenching the Eighth Amendment from its historical context and extending it to traditional disciplinary practices in the public schools." But the deeper meaning of *Ingraham*, as with the previous cases, lay beyond its narrow holding. Mr. Justice Powell

gave at least a hint that the Court may have withdrawn some of the sympathy for the public school pupil which *Tinker* revealed a decade earlier:

> The school child has little need for the protection of the Eighth Amendment. Though attendance may not always be voluntary, the public school remains an open institution. Except perhaps when very young, the child is not physically restrained from leaving school during school hours; and at the end of the school day the child is invariably free to return home. Even while at school, the child brings with him the support of family and friends and is rarely apart from teachers and other pupils who may witness and protest any instances of mistreatment.

While the results are not in all ways consistent, *Tinker*, *Goss*, and *Ingraham* do at least establish some important and relatively new law. Young people now have constitutional rights they did not have a bit more than a decade ago. Courts are willing to entertain claims based on these rights. It used to be that such issues got to court only when parents had claims of their own; when such claims were pressed, the court might also consider what were essentially the legal interests of the children as well. Now the courts are willing to receive and decide claims that are personal to the children—even when, as occasionally happens, those claims are actually adverse to the interests of the parents. In both situations, the courts have moved more and more deeply into the administration and policies of the public school systems of this country. Some school board members and administrators deplore the whole development, and feel their authority has been crippled by the Courts. Others—advocates of youth rights, for example—take a more benign view. It is not necessary for us to judge the new trend, but only to appreciate that legal grounds now exist for judicial entry into the content of education. How far the courts will, and should, intrude in such matters is the focus of the balance of this book.

4

THE RIGHT *NOT* TO BE
EDUCATED

IF THERE IS some legal basis for claiming access to education, one
may well ask whether there is a right *not* to be educated. The
question is sometimes posed by persons seeking an alternative
to all formal education—either by educating their children at
home, or by refusing to educate them at all. More commonly,
the issue arises when a parent finds some part of the school program abhorrent or intrusive, and wishes to have his or her child
excused. Sometimes provision is made for excusal, although
schools have become less receptive to such requests as curricula
become more uniform, consolidated schools become larger, and
concern over reported enrollments mounts. Thus the collision
between parental wishes and school policies is an increasingly
substantial one. It is the subject of this chapter.

We begin with the poignant case of Mr. and Mrs. Robert
LaMon, a Nashau, New Hampshire, couple who went to jail for
taking their fifteen-year-old daughter out of school. They had
withdrawn her from the public schools because they found offensive the required course in sex education. They believed that
such matters as sex should be discussed only in the privacy of
the home, and not in the semipublic setting of the school classroom. They next enrolled their daughter in a private school, but
soon found that choice unacceptable because of "open-ended

discussions of prostitution and pimps" in the required religion class. When the child was removed from the private school, she became a truant. The parents were cited for contempt of court because they refused to appear and explain the reasons for their daughter's absence. A state judge ordered them to jail.

The conflict between the LaMons and the New Hampshire authorities is as acute as any that occurs in our society. The basic issues need now to be explored more fully. We will consider briefly the case to be made by persons like the LaMons, and the reply which school officials would give. We will then see what the courts have done to resolve these conflicts.

First, the case for the LaMons can be stated rather simply. Schools historically derive their authority to educate from the parental relationship. Indeed, one often describes the school as acting *in loco parentis.* The United Nations Declaration of Human Rights recognizes that "parents have a prior right to choose the kind of education that shall be given to their children." One scholar observes that under early common law on this question, "the parents' authority over the education of their children was a natural right arising out of the familiar prerogatives of custody, care and nurture of offspring." A similar relationship has been recognized by many major religions; the primacy of parental judgment in matters of education has been repeatedly reaffirmed by Catholic papal encyclicals and other doctrinal statements. Until rather recently, the courts also unquestioningly recognized that parents could decide what was best for their children, in or out of school.

The philosophical basis for parental primacy is not hard to identify. If parents are legally and morally responsible for the upbringing of children, and for the values and beliefs they hold, then surely parents should have a major voice in what their children are taught (or not taught) in school. If parents cannot determine the content of their children's learning, then they lose influence over what may be the single most important shaper of values and beliefs. When parental responsibility ceases —at the age of majority or when a parent is legally deprived of custody—then control over education should also cease. But until that time comes, the argument runs, parents should be able to decide what their children should and should not learn. When the curriculum touches on such intimate matters as sex, family life, procreation, and the like, the claim for parental intervention and determination becomes even stronger.

School officials would offer several lines of response. At least one is practical: If every parent can determine what each child will study, the control of education would become chaotic. Moreover, as schools increasingly certify the content of a diploma —for college admission, employment, and the like—the need for uniformity in the curriculum becomes greater. To have the curriculum individually determined—beyond the kinds of electives that are allowed in many secondary schools—would seriously undermine the claims for acceptance and support on which the school systems of this country depend.

There are more philosophical foundations for the school's position. Public education serves as a kind of harmonizing force in a basically diverse and hetergeneous society:

> Public education is intended primarily to serve the collectivist function of promoting equality of attitude and of experience, thus advancing social uniformity and national cohesion. Both the individual and society benefit when each individual achieves the academic competence needed for political literacy and economic self-sufficiency and acquires sufficient social awareness to assure his adherence to fundamental societal norms.

Indeed, the most controversial areas of the curriculum are those closest to the basic "socialization" function of the school system: The achievement of good citizenship through education, and the preparation of students for their civic roles and responsibilities, require attention to values, principles, traditions, and beliefs in ways that may not be universally accepted. For schools to avoid controversy in such matters would imply abdication of what may be the most vital function of education.

The schools also offer a related concern: Where the *parents* may object to a particular course of instruction, the school may have a duty to enable the *child* to choose among options broader than those found within the family setting. Professor Mary-Michelle Hirschoff has argued that a value-based curriculum may be justified—against parental objection—"because of the need to protect the child's interest in being able to choose a life different from his parents upon reaching majority." If the curriculum simply perpetuates parental values and beliefs, regardless of external principles, then the schools fail to serve a basic function in a society where education has been an avenue not only for growth and development but also for change.

Two further arguments emerge on the schools' side of the debate. There is a claim of deference to the professional expertise of developers of curricula—teachers, administrators, and others who typically possess graduate professional degrees either in subject matter or in pedagogical methods. While parents may indeed know their own children best, they are seldom professionally competent in education. Thus if a parent claims that his or her child should not discuss sex in school, and a teacher or curriculum specialist defends such a unit for children in general, some deference is due the expert despite parental primacy in other areas.

Finally, something might be said about the process by which educational decisions are made in the United States. School boards are democratically elected and represent the people of their communities. While the percentage of actual participation in school board elections varies, and is often appallingly low, citizens have the chance to vote—and when they feel strongly about curricular or other school matters, they do exercise their franchise. Thus a single parental challenge to a unit or course that has been approved by an elected board (or its appointed

58 CLASSROOMS IN THE CROSSFIRE

surrogates) is antidemocratic. The clash is inevitable even where the intervention seeks to have only a single child excused, because others may seek comparable relief and may claim unequal treatment if they are not also excused. The clash is more severe, of course, where the objecting parent seeks to have the whole unit removed from the curriculum. While the majority cannot, of course, deprive even a tiny minority of its civil rights and liberties no matter how "democratic" the process of the majority, deference is surely due to the majority in balancing otherwise doubtful claims. Thus, if the majority decides that sex education should be offered in the schools, and the basis of parental objection is personal preference, the process by which curricular decisions are made is surely important.

The Courts and the Parental Plea

Several ingredients of the law become pertinent at this point. We shall review the way in which the courts have responded specifically to parental objections like those of the LaMons—including the current requirements of compulsory education. We shall also review the law on the role of values in the school curriculum, and will then consider recent changes in law governing broader parental rights and interests. Finally, we shall look specifically at the legal aspects of the sex education controversy.

Compulsory Education and Parental Protest. Not so long ago, a case like that of the LaMons probably would not even have reached the courts—either because schools simply did not venture into such troubled curricular waters, or because principals and superintendents would routinely have granted almost any parental request for excusal. In the unlikely event that a reluctant principal denied such a request, and the aid of a court was sought, judges would summarily have held in the parents' favor. From early common law roots, there had been a premise that parents control the upbringing of their children, and could thus shape the school curriculum. If the true parents did not wish the school—acting *in loco parentis*—to teach their children a given subject, the common law would respect that wish. Yet within the last half century, the courts have completely reversed that presumption, to the point where they are now willing to send the LaMons to jail for exercising the very option which the common law once guaranteed. How could such a change occur? And what is left (if anything) of the parental right to shape the curriculum?

In large measure the shift results from the evolving law of compulsory education. The role and function of American public education have changed dramatically as mandatory attendance has replaced the once optional pattern of schooling. Since 1918 all states have required school attendance by children up to a certain age, typically sixteen. Compulsory attendance laws, often challenged, have been almost universally upheld. Courts sometimes assert that the value of education is too great to allow a parent to deprive his or her child of its benefit. Compulsory attendance laws do, however, contain exceptions which have doubtless forestalled much litigation. Many states permit children to be taught at home by a private tutor or by a person (possibly a parent) who holds a teaching credential or is otherwise qualified. California law also exempts, not surprisingly, "children who are in entertainment or allied industries and who are taught by qualified persons or organizations." An exemption is sometimes provided for children who are blind, deaf, or otherwise handicapped in ways that would keep them from participating fully in a regular school classroom. But the exceptions are specific, narrowly defined, and often subject to administrative review in the case of "special qualifications."

Another type of challenge to compulsory attendance recently produced a major Supreme Court case. The Old Order Amish object on religious grounds to sending children to school after the eighth grade. They believe that formal schooling at the high school level would expose their children to alien values, would risk the censure of their church, and would jeopardize their children's chances (and their own) for salvation. Some states excuse Amish children beyond the eighth grade, but others (including Wisconsin) do not. When a group of Amish parents were convicted for violation of the Wisconsin compulsory attendance law, they appealed their religious freedom claim to the Supreme Court. In *Wisconsin* v. *Yoder*, a majority of the Justices held that Amish children could not constitutionally be required to attend school beyond the eighth grade. Although the Court reaffirmed the general validity of compulsory school laws, it created an exception for such deep and religiously based objections as those of the Amish. The Court noted some special and persuasive factors in the Amish community:

> It is one thing to say that compulsory education for a year or two beyond the eighth grade may be necessary when its purpose is the preparation of the child for life in modern society as the majority live, but is quite another if the goal of education be viewed as the preparation of the child for life in the separate agrarian community that is the keystone of the Amish faith.

Moreover, the Amish provided alternative educational experiences for their children which, observed the Court, might be more valuable than the formal instruction they would receive in the high school classroom.

The validity of compulsory attendance laws remains unimpaired; indeed, the special quality of the Amish exception reinforces their general applicability. The decision is important, but quite as much because it sustains the general rule as because it recognizes a limited exception.

The changing relationship between parents and schools has

not resulted simply from the universality of compulsory attendance laws. There have been subtler changes of two other sorts. One gradual but highly significant change has been a lessening of parental choice with regard to the curriculum. Even after attendance came to be generally required, many state laws rather liberally entertained requests for individual excusal. Even where statutes were less generous, the courts tended to accept a broad range of reasons for excusal requests, or even unexplained requests. At least through the end of the nineteenth century, courts routinely respected a parent's subjective desire to exempt a child from some part of the regular curriculum. The reasons for withdrawal could be as whimsical as the judgment of a Nebraska father in 1890 that his daughter should not study grammar because it was no longer taught as it had been when he was a youth—a judgment duly approved by the supreme court of the state. As late as 1914, the Nebraska courts still accepted highly subjective reasons for taking a child out of a music class.

Even as compulsory education requirements tightened, judicial deference to parental judgment persisted. In 1921, for example, the California Supreme Court proclaimed the right of a parent to withdraw his child from a public school dance class to which the parents were morally opposed; courts could not sanction "a power over home life that might result in denying to parents their natural as well as their constitutional right to govern or control, within the scope of their parental authority, their own progeny. . . ." Several years later the Colorado Supreme Court concurred, announcing as basic "the right of parents to select, within limits, what their children shall learn," and concluding that "parents . . . can refuse to have their children taught what they think harmful, barring what must be taught, i.e., the essentials of good citizenship."

In recent years not only have the statutory grounds for excusal narrowed, but the courts have become increasingly sparing about recognizing both value-based and pedagogically-based parental objections. At least two factors have contributed to this trend, in the judgment of Mary-Michelle Hirschoff:

> First, lack of effective exercise may have weakened the common law right of parental control over the education of one's child. Second, today's teachers may be considered to have greater expertise than parents because of the more rigorous training requirements imposed by most states.

As a result, Hirschoff notes, in most states "parents who wish to have their children excused from objectionable instruction must find protection in constitutional law."

Clearly, then, forces stronger and broader than compulsory education have recently operated on the curriculum. If the old attitude toward excusal persisted, then the mere existence of compulsory attendance laws would be largely irrelevant. If children could still be excused from particular classes for any reason, or on grounds far short of clear constitutional interests, then most of the recent controversy would simply not have occurred. Yet the school systems of today could not allow parents and students to pick and choose or to fashion their own curriculum. Thus the rise of compulsion, and the curtailment of individual choice with regard to the curriculum, are concomitant factors which contribute substantially to current tensions.

The dilemma for the parent uncomfortable about the public school curriculum may therefore be acute. If state law or local regulation provides for excusal from a particular subject, all well and good. If the parent is able to afford private education, and if there exists nearby a private school which offers a genuine alternative to the public school program, again all well and good. But many parents cannot afford private schools, and many others live beyond their range. Even where the option exists financially and geographically, it may not in fact offer the desired choice. (Recall that the LaMons found the discussion of sex in the nearby parochial school as offensive as the curriculum they had forsaken in the public school.)

There is, finally, the option of home instruction. Some states do permit children to be taught elsewhere than in a formal classroom—but circumscribe that option with careful review of the qualifications of the parent or substitute teacher, and may severely limit the option in practice even where it exists in theory. Very rarely will parents succeed in persuading a court to grant a dispensation or exemption where the statute does not. Such a victory was won in a celebrated 1980 Michigan case; devoutly religious parents convinced a state trial judge that their children received just as good an education at home as they would in the local public schools, and that to require the parents to be licensed as teachers would abridge their religious liberty. But such cases are rare indeed; both the cost and the uncertainty of success in litigation offer little solace to the would-be home instructor.

The public school therefore becomes for most families the only channel of education through the age to which compulsory attendance extends. If a course or unit is objectionable, and if excusal cannot be obtained through administrative channels, the courts are a rather remote avenue of last resort. The experience of the LaMons is, therefore, extreme only because they refused to give up in the face of governmental pressure to conform to the standard curriculum.

Values and the Schools. The courts have spoken frequently, and approvingly, of inculcation of values as a function of the public schools. One of the earliest references came in the celebrated flag salute case in 1943. The majority of the Court struck down a state law which required all children to salute the flag every morning. Such a law, said the Justices, simply exceeded the power of a state to compel behavior of its citizens. One might infer from that judgment some doubt about governmental arousal of patriotism. But the year before, the Justices had anticipated that issue and had given an answer which they now reaffirmed in the flag salute case: A state may "require teaching by instruction and study of all in our history and in the structure and organization of our government, including the guarantees of civil liberty, which tend to inspire patriotism and love of country." The flaw in the West Virginia approach was that it bypassed "the slow and easily neglected route to arouse loyalties" that other states had taken—by requiring, for example, American history or civics courses. One could mandate such *instruction* within the school curriculum; what one could not do was to coerce the *behavior* the flag salute involved.

These views about the appropriateness of values in the curriculum have been often reaffirmed. As recently as 1979, the Supreme Court declined to hold unconstitutional a New York law which required all public school teachers to be United States citizens. (The Court had earlier held that citizenship could be required only where it bore some significant relationship to the nature of the job.) The New York law disqualified aliens regardless of the country of origin, the subject they taught (for example, foreign languages), or other evidence of loyalty to the United States. In upholding this requirement, the Court recognized the special role which teachers played in imparting the values of a democratic society:

> Through both the presentation of course materials and the example he sets, the teacher has an opportunity to influence the attitudes of students toward the government and the political process, and a citizen's social responsibilities. This influence is crucial to the continued good health of a democracy. . . . Teachers, regardless of their specialty, may be called upon to teach other subjects, including those expressly dedicated to social and political subjects. Most important, a state may properly regard all teachers as having an obligation to promote civic virtues and understanding in their classes, regardless of the subject taught.

Many lower courts' decisions have been even more explicit in recognizing the role of values in the curriculum. Quite recently a Chicago teacher objected, because of her religious beliefs, to taking part in patriotic songs, exercises, and the like as part of her pedagogical duties. She was dismissed and brought suit for reinstatement, claiming that her religious liberty had been abridged. The court of appeals rejected her claim, and recognized quite explicitly the legitimacy of such value-oriented activities in the larger role of the public schools:

> Parents have a vital interest in what their children are taught. Their elected representatives on the school board have prescribed a curriculum. There is a compelling state interest in the choice and adherence to a suitable curriculum for the benefit of our young citizens and society. It cannot be left to individual teachers to teach what they please.

Thus to question the basic value-inculcation role of public education would today be quite futile. Schools have been perceived by the courts for some time as avenues through which values, principles, and traditions are properly passed from one generation to the next. Indeed, were a student subjected to a totally value-free curriculum, there might even be a claim of educational deficiency. For the moment we need not, of course, consider that side of the coin. We are concerned here only with the parent (or child) who argues that schools ought to avoid controversy by eschewing all value inculcation in instruction. There is little legal basis for such a claim.

The Shifting Law of Parental Control. A whole volume could profitably be devoted to recent changes in the law of parent-child relations. There have been crosscurrents, and the pattern remains too mixed to be very helpful. On one hand, the Supreme Court has several times struck down on due process grounds state laws requiring a minor to obtain the consent of her parents for an abortion. Judicial recognition of the minor's interests reflects in part the Court's dislike of any third-party veto over a decision to terminate pregnancy. In addition, the Court seems to doubt whether such laws really preserve the integrity of the family or reinforce parental authority where parent and child are already at odds over the abortion decision. While such interests—parental authority and family integrity—are respected by the Court and entitled to defense, they have consistently been outweighed in this context by "the right of privacy of the competent minor mature enough to have become pregnant."

Other recent cases have, however, paid greater deference to the parental position. In 1979 the Court agreed to decide whether minors committed by their parents to mental hospitals had any right to a lawyer or an adversary proceeding at which to challenge the commitment. By a 6-3 majority, the Court ruled in favor of the parental action: "The law's concept of the family . . . has recognized that natural bonds of affection lead parents to act in the best interests of their children." Thus even a summary parental commitment did not deprive children of constitutional rights, although the Court left open the possibility of some sort of legal procedure in extreme cases.

Conflicts between parent and child have been coming to the courts in other increasingly volatile forms. Many parents have sought the aid of courts to "deprogram" or regain custody of children who have been lured away from home by religious cults, notably the followers of the Reverend Sun Myung Moon. The results have varied widely—some courts being willing to appoint legal guardians for the purpose of bringing the children back into the parental fold, while others have declined to intervene. Suits brought by the religious groups against the self-help initiatives of the deprogrammers have fared unevenly; some courts have been willing to enjoin the deprogrammers if the children really wished not to be "rescued" in this way, while others felt they lacked jurisdiction over what was essentially a private or familial dispute. From the relatively early stages of this litigation emerge no clear guiding principles; the most that can be said is that courts are at least willing to consider parent-child disputes that once would have been summarily dismissed because the law arbitrarily presumed the views of parent and child to be in complete harmony. Now the courts recognize the potential adversity between generations, and will at least hear claims by child against parents and vice versa.

Perhaps the most novel manifestation of this trend is the suit recently brought by an adult son against his parents for negligent and wrongful rearing. The son had drifted from one job (and place) to another, and had been unable to find a niche in society. After exhausting more conventional remedies, he filed suit against his parents, seeking damages on the basis of a novel and bizarre cause of action. Such a claim would probably be dismissed even by a court that would consider a deprogramming suit; the prospect of setting legal standards by which the quality of parenting could be judged and for deviation from which damages could be awarded to an ungrateful child simply staggers the imagination. "Parental malpractice" or "wrongful upbringing" is not likely soon to find its way into the annals of tort law.

Sex Education: General Principles Applied

We might now return at length to the LaMons. They were sent to jail basically because they wanted their child excused from a required sex education class, a wish that school officials refused to honor. While their degree of persistence was unusual, the LaMons were by no means alone in the position they took. Sex education programs have become increasingly common, and have evoked growing controversy as they have spread. School boards have felt a growing responsibility to address problems of teen-age pregnancy, at a time when both the technology of contraception and the shrinking taboos about sex have made such programs more feasible. But many parents are made acutely uncomfortable by discussion in public school classrooms of such intimate and sensitive matters. Thus many schools have provided for the excusal of any child whose parents request it, without inquiring into the reason. Even where the regulation or state law does not so provide, school officials have quietly allowed small numbers of objectors to be withdrawn from sex education classes in order to avoid community upheaval. But there have been situations like that occasioned by the LaMons, where the subject was required by law and local school officials felt powerless (or disinclined) to grant dispensations.

The legal bases of such objections have been varied. Parents have sometimes challenged sex education requirements on religious grounds—either because they felt the course invaded their religious freedom, or because they felt that making this subject part of the curriculum served to "establish" the views of religious groups that favored compulsory sex education to the detriment of other groups. But both types of religious claims have been rejected for reasons that will be better understood after we probe the religious guarantees of the Bill of Rights in chapter five. Essentially, teaching about sex is not a direct affront to the belief or worship of one religious group, nor does it involve covert governmental support for other religions. While the study of family life in school may be more acceptable to some faiths than to others, and may pose problems for children of certain sectarian backgrounds, the courts have not found such parental objections sufficient to require exemption or excusal on religious liberty grounds.

More difficult have been challenges based on personal privacy. Although the United States Constitution nowhere specifically guarantees privacy, many cases during the last decade have implied such an interest. Most of the decisions involving abortion and contraception have been based on this newly recognized liberty. Because many state laws affecting procreation, family relationships, and the like have been invalidated on privacy grounds, the resort to this guarantee in the sex education context is hardly surprising. In a case which reached the California Supreme Court in 1975, for example, parents argued that their rights of privacy and those of their children were violated because sex education classes required revelation of innermost thoughts and sensitive family values and details. In the California case, the answer was easy: The course was not required of all students, although most in fact took it. Thus the objecting parents had simply failed to pursue the remedy open to them of asking that their children be excused. Many other state and lower federal court cases have been similarly resolved with the observation that an optional program or unit does not require children or parents to reveal any matters they wish to keep private.

The most difficult situation is that in which excusal is not available. Here the privacy claim has some substance, and cannot be avoided by suggesting that the parents may confine discussion of sex and family values to the home. If the child must participate in the course to complete the curriculum and graduate, then the issue must be squarely faced. Several courts have faced it, and have consistently balanced the conflicting interests in favor of the school—just as the New Hampshire court did in the LaMon case.

A basic pattern emerges from these cases: Clearly an unfocussed parental objection to some part of the curriculum does not suffice as it once did. The strength of the parent's feelings has no legal import; the fact that the LaMons were willing to go to jail may have strengthened their case in the press, and may have evoked some sympathy from the judge, but was legally quite irrelevant. An argument that some portion of the curriculum invades parental or family privacy is also not likely to avail greatly; courts routinely defer to the judgments of school officials in such matters. It is, therefore, only the rare claim which clearly invokes a provision of the Bill of Rights—freedom of worship, of speech, or of the press—or a claim that equal opportunity has been denied (for example, on the basis of race), to which the courts are likely to respond. The chapters which follow assess such claims and place them in the larger legal framework which this chapter provides.

5

RELIGION AND THE SCHOOLS

Mrs. Martha Howard of Owensboro, Kentucky, devoted almost a decade to the task of bringing religion more fully into the public schools of her state. Largely in response to her persistent plea, the Kentucky General Assembly in 1978 passed a law requiring that copies of the Ten Commandments be posted in every one of the state's 31,000 public school classrooms. The costs of printing, framing, and displaying the Commandments were to be met entirely by private donations. Within a short time Mrs. Howard and her friends set about to raise the necessary funds.

At precisely the same time, Kentucky state officials were trying to tighten state control over the curriculum of a group of private Christian schools. In May 1977 the State Department of Education denied accreditation to twenty church-related schools (all affiliated with fundamentalist Protestant sects). Parents who continued to send their children to these schools were threatened with criminal prosecution. State education officials insisted that such schools not only had to offer certain courses, but must also meet minimal standards for teacher certification and in the content of textbooks and instructional materials.

Both issues ended up in the Kentucky courts in a way that

71

nicely illustrates the duality of our constitutional guarantees of religious freedom. On one hand, the fundamentalist schools and parents sued the state claiming that the denial of accreditation violated their rights to free exercise of religion; to take away their ability to offer religious instruction during the week as well as on Sunday would, they said, abridge their values and beliefs. On the other hand, a group of parents who believed in the complete separation of church and state brought suit against the same education officials over the Ten Commandments issue; they argued that religion should be kept completely out of the public schools, and that placing copies of Scripture on the walls would represent a constitutionally forbidden "establishment" of religion. Both cases worked their way through the Kentucky courts under two sections of the First Amendment to the Bill of Rights.

The two cases are technically quite different, but there may be significance to their simultaneous emergence. Mrs. Howard apparently felt that religion should play a larger role in the public schools because it had become less central in contemporary life. Not only has the Supreme Court forbidden the reading of the Bible and the saying of prayers in the public schools, but courts have also restricted severely the ways in which government may aid church-related private schools. Thus the options available to the deeply devout parent have lessened in recent years, and the blame quite naturally falls on the courts. People like Mrs. Howard have been increasingly resourceful in seeking constitutionally valid areas of religious emphasis—one of which may be the posting of the Ten Commandments at private expense. To the extent that private education becomes less available to fundamentalist parents, attention will turn increasingly to the role of religion in the public schools. It is at that point that Mrs. Howard and the Christian academies become pieces of the same puzzle.

The Constitutional Setting

The federal constitution guarantees religious freedom through two interrelated clauses. One forbids "any law respecting an establishment of religion"; the other protects against any abridgement of "the free exercise of religion." Many state constitutions have similar provisions, and the federal guarantees have been held to protect against state as well as congressional action. Although religious freedom is ensured in all aspects of national life, the public schools have been the focus of much constitutional litigation in the last half century. The Supreme Court has dealt mainly with practices claimed to violate the "establishment" clause—that is, possible breaches of the historic wall of separation between church and state. Although an early case allowed the payment of public funds for transporting children to parochial schools, and the Court later upheld the lending of secular textbooks to church schools, recent decisions have progressively narrowed the permissible scope of governmental support to nonpublic schools and their students. The Supreme Court has consistently warned of the risks of involving government unduly in the affairs or policies of private schools. A host of state programs designed to relieve the mounting financial burdens of church-related schools have therefore been held unconstitutional because they reflect "excessive entanglement" between government and religion.

We are concerned here primarily with the role of religion in the *public* schools. The major court cases have been fewer, although the lines of separation have been equally distinct. In 1949 the Supreme Court held that religious teachers could not come into the public schools to offer regular instruction, but the next year the Court upheld a program of "released time" by which students were excused early to attend religious classes at their churches. The latter program, said the Court, was a convenient accommodation between the two spheres, and did not permit the intrusion of religion into the life of the school or place governmental support behind religious instruction.

The most notable decisions about religion in the public schools, of course, involved the reading of the Bible and the saying of prayers at the start of the school day. In 1962 the Court struck down a rather innocuous prayer devised by the New York Board of Regents and used to open school each morning. The next year, in two celebrated cases, the Justices held that the reading of passages from the Bible and the saying of the Lord's Prayer were equally unconstitutional because they breached that historic wall of separation between church and state. The Court rejected arguments that such exercises merely served the secular purpose of quieting active youngsters before they began their lessons, and that no public funding was being committed to religion. Nor was the Court impressed by the provision for excusing students whose parents did not wish them to take part in the ceremony; excusal might avoid an infringement of free exercise of religion, but would not blunt the claim of an illegal "establishment." The core of the decisions was that government had, by building religious exercises into the public school program, departed from the "strict neutrality" which the Constitution requires in all such matters. If that departure seemed slight, "the breach of neutrality that is today a trickling stream may all too soon become a torrent."

The prayer and Bible decisions relied solely on the establishment clause. Although in the lower courts substantial claims had been based on the free exercise clause, the Supreme Court avoided the temptation to pursue both dimensions of religious freedom. Thus the scope of free exercise interests in the public schools remained largely unsettled until the *Yoder* case, in which the Court held that children of the Old Order Amish could not be compelled to attend school beyond the eighth grade. *Yoder* does not, of course, say much about the possible free exercise claims of parents who merely object to some particular course or unit, since the Amish challenge went to the very heart of the educational process and the exemption which the Court gave them was total. But the doctrine which *Yoder* announced does at least suggest the principles which would govern a more conventional free exercise case.

Since *Yoder*, the Supreme Court has had little to say about religion in the public schools. The lower courts, both federal and state, have been left to work out the meaning of the prayer and Bible decisions for other practices. The problems have been of several distinct types, each of which deserves a separate section in this chapter. First, there have been concerns about the formal inclusion of religion or religious material in the curriculum—teaching about the Bible as literature, for example, or singing Christmas carols or hymns in music classes. Second, there has been dispute over the role of religion in the classroom apart from the instructional program—the posting of the Ten Commandments in Kentucky schools, requirements that teachers "inculcate Christian virtues" in their students, and the like. A third troubled area has been the role of religion in the *secular* curriculum—notably the treatment of evolution in the biology course. Finally, there has been a long-standing concern from certain religious groups about wholly secular curricula—not only biology, but also physical education, sex education, and other seemingly less sensitive parts of the school program. We will examine in turn each of these areas of tension.

Religion in the Curriculum

If one may not open the school day by reading passages from the Bible, may a teacher nonetheless assign the Bible to be read as literature? After the 1963 Supreme Court decisions some critics charged that a hostile Court had "taken God out of the schools" altogether. Even a cursory reading of the opinions would, however, reveal the unfairness of that claim. The majority was careful to note that "the Bible is worthy of study for its literary and historic qualities" and that a liberal education would be incomplete without some exposure to Scripture. Justice Brennan, who wrote the longest of the concurring opinions, added that "it would be impossible to teach meaningfully many subjects in the social sciences or humanities without some mention of religion."

Some states seized this invitation all too eagerly. Alabama, only months after the Supreme Court decision, decreed that devotional Bible reading be incorporated into the curriculum as a regular course of study. This policy was soon challenged, and the state courts found it to be a subterfuge forbidden by the spirit if not the letter of the Supreme Court decisions. More common was the subtler response of many states and school districts—to offer courses or units in comparative religion, including a study of the role and content of the Bible, and to increase the emphasis upon the Scriptures in courses on world literature and the like. Such programs have seldom been controversial.

For many years, the only case even close to the issue involved a challenge to an elective course at the University of Washington. A conservative religious organization brought suit against the University claiming, in part, that an English course on the Bible as literature should not be offered at a state institution, but objecting as well to a perceived lack of sympathy in the course to the fundamentalist views of the plaintiffs. The Washington state courts upheld the course after reviewing the Supreme Court precedents, and found that the challenged course did not "advance any particular religious interest or theology." Such a judgment would have been easy had not the Washington Supreme Court in 1931 held that the state constitution forbade giving public school credit for certain courses offered under church auspices. It was therefore necessary to distinguish this precedent before sustaining the university English course. But such distinctions were readily available and seemed entirely consistent with the United States Supreme Court's views in the prayer and Bible-reading cases.

Two very recent cases offer additional insight on the issues left open by the prayer and Bible decisions. Early in 1979 a federal district court in Tennessee struck down a Chattanooga public school Bible study course. Special Bible teachers were assigned to various public schools and were paid directly by a private religious group which raised funds for that purpose. The courses were elective, and students enrolled only on the written permission of parents. If grades were given in the course—a matter which varied by school—those grades were not to be entered on the student's transcript. Proponents of the program (which had been in existence since 1922) argued that the courses stressed the literary, historic, and social elements of the Bible rather than its religious content. But since the course was shaped by the outside private group—an admittedly religious organization—the court concluded that religion was excessively intruded into the curriculum in violation of the establishment clause. The court did, however, suggest that the religious emphasis might be removed and the allegedly secular purposes of the program could still save it. The Chattanooga School Board promptly accepted this invitation and assumed a greater responsibility for the program. Some six months later, the court approved the modified program, apparently persuaded that the dangerously religious elements had been sufficiently muted.

A few months earlier another federal judge had stuck down on constitutional grounds a Utah program under which public students received academic credit for Bible study courses taken under church auspices. The basis of the program was a released time arrangement—students being let out of school early once or twice a week to attend religious classes—of a kind the Supreme Court had approved many years earlier. But the special feature of the Utah program was a commitment to grant public school credit for religious study. The court felt distinguishable a program whereby, for example, public schools accept on transfer the credits already earned by students at parochial schools. The judge now found no possible secular purpose in the Utah arrangement, and feared that "the academic recognition awarded for completion of the Bible history courses by the granting of public high school credit may have an effect of advancing and sponsoring religion by indirectly encouraging students to participate in the program." Much as with the original prayer and Bible-reading programs which the Supreme Court had invalidated in the early 1960s, these practices violated the establishment clause.

The validity of secular Bible study classes remains unsettled. The Washington case dealt with an elective university course, and the courts have always been more lenient about relations between religion and government in higher education. Neither the Tennessee nor the Utah case really dealt with the kind of course the Justices had in mind when they left open the option of studying the Bible for literary or historical purposes as part of the regular English or social studies curriculum. Until some court decides the issue differently, school officials would seem reasonably safe in relying on the Washington decision even though it is not precisely on point.

Not all concern about religion in the classroom relates to the Bible. Several years ago a parent in Michigan brought suit to enjoin the study of Kurt Vonnegut's *Slaughterhouse Five* because, the plaintiff claimed, the novel "contains and makes reference to religious matters" and thus fell within the ban of the establishment clause. (This claim was not the sole basis of the suit, and may well have been an afterthought to the plaintiff's primary concern about Vonnegut's taboo language and earthy dialogue.) The trial judge actually granted an injunction against teaching the book, but the appellate court reversed and upheld the position of the school and the teacher. The higher court observed that there was no claim that studying *Slaughterhouse Five* was "derogatory to Christianity" nor was there any suggestion that the views of one sect were favored over others. The court went on to warn of the dangers of restricting the choice of literary works:

> If plaintiff's contention were correct, then public school students could no longer marvel at Sir Galahad's saintly quest for the Holy Grail, nor be introduced to the dangers of Hitler's Mein Kampf, nor read the mellifluous poetry of John Milton or John Donne. Unhappily, Robin Hood would be forced to forage without Friar Tuck and Shakespeare would have to delete Shylock from the Merchant of Venice. . . . Our Constitution does not command ignorance; on the contrary, it assures the people that the state may not relegate them to such a status and guarantees to all the precious and unfettered freedom of pursuing one's own intellectual pleasures in one's own personal way.

This judgment, sound as it is, leaves open the possibility that a different kind of assignment might be challenged on establishment clause grounds. If, for example, an English teacher were to assign only the works of Paul Blanshard, Catholic students might well have a valid claim of free exercise—if not of establishment—of religion. There is a profound difference between simply including in a general curriculum a work which takes one point of view with regard to religious matters, and stressing a particular sectarian perspective to the exclusion of others. Reviewing reading lists is an uncomfortable exercise for courts, although it may occasionally become unavoidable. Judges quite properly give broad latitude to teachers and school authorities in the selection of reading materials, and they would be loath to find a violation of the religious guarantees unless the facts went far beyond those of the Michigan case.

It is not always so obvious that a "religion" is in fact involved in challenged curricula. Take, for example, the recent controversy over the teaching of Transcendental Meditation in

New Jersey. In the early 1970s a national organization obtained federal funding to develop a TM unit for school use. Recordings of a "meaningless sound"—apparently essential to the meditation process—were made under the grant; a workbook and other materials were prepared, and the unit was reproduced for distribution. Five New Jersey high schools agreed, with the backing of the state education department, to offer the unit on an optional basis to senior students. The teachers were to be representatives of the national TM organization, specially trained for this purpose and skilled in TM. They were to be paid by sources external to the school districts.

Soon after the units were introduced, a group of parents brought suit to enjoin the TM program on constitutional grounds. There was no question about the formal involvement of public education officials, from the state commissioner on through the local high schools. The issue was whether "religion" was involved at all. Answering that question took a troubled and curious district judge through many days of testimony, hundreds of exhibits, and generated an opinion of 44 pages of fine print.

The judge came at length to the conclusion that an unlawful "establishment of religion" was involved. Clearly the TM unit was not Christian, nor was it even sectarian in the usual sense. Yet the Science of Creative Intelligence—the parent philosophy—had many qualities of a religion, and a formal organization analogous to those of more familiar sects. Adherents held its tenets in much the same perspective as did believers in the Judeo-Christian scriptures and the seminal works of other faiths. The ceremony which the TM unit introduced into the public schools also had a quasi-religious character, replete with chanting and other devotional exercises. Had the origin and content of the program been familiarly sectarian, little doubt would have remained about the outcome of the case. Since the Science of Creative Intelligence elevated a particular philosophy to the level and function of theology, the public schools which offered the unit had crossed the forbidden line which separates church and state. The secular goals of the unit—to reduce tension, to increase sociability, and to improve the general learning environment—were no more exculpatory than the fact that devotional reading of the Bible helped to calm children at the start of the school day. The district court concluded:

> Owing to the religious nature of the concept of the field of pure intelligence, it is apparent that the government agencies have sought to effect a secular goal by the propagation of a religious concept. . . . These means of effecting ostensibly secular ends are prohibited by the establishment clause. . . . The promulgation of a pure, perfect, infinite and unmanifest field of life clearly has the primary effect of advancing religion and religious concepts.

The court of appeals affirmed this decision some months later, relying heavily on the district judge's analysis. One appellate judge concurred specially, and wrote at some length in view of the novelty of the case. He wished specifically to leave open the possibility of religious programs in the public schools which might have—as the TM unit clearly did not—a secular function:

> Religious observation and instruction in public schools may be sustainable if ideas are taught in an objective fashion, or if the overall impact of the religious observance is *de minimis*. Neither was true here. . . . Although federal courts should be reluctant to interfere in the judgments of what subject matter should be taught in the schools, our constitutional duty to guard against state efforts to promote religion may not be set aside out of deference to the policy choices of other officials.

The New Jersey TM decision is surely novel, and may seem trivial. Yet it probably anticipates other challenges to the introduction into the public schools of nontraditional and eclectic philosophies that resemble only remotely the familiar sectarian theologies. Followers of the Maharishi Mahesh Yogi are not alone in seeing the schools as fertile fields for proselytizing. Other cults that have recently gained adherents, especially among the young and impressionable of high school age, may well follow suit. Though the massacre at Jonestown may well chill recruitment for a time, the underlying quest for identity will surely find other outlets. Thus the legal principles established in the TM decision, written upon a *tabula rasa*, may be valuable to future litigation over comparable curricular issues.

Religion in the Classroom

The role of religion in the public schools is by no means limited to regular courses and assigned materials. As the Kentucky Ten Commandments law suggests, other avenues have been sought for the infusion of religion and religious material into the school setting. A frequent area of controversy has been the offer of the Gideon Society to distribute free Bibles to students at certain schools. Since the Supreme Court's 1963 decisions, lower courts have generally refused to allow school officials to accept such an offer, even if no public funding were involved and sponsors of other religious materials would be equally welcome. A recent federal court of appeals decision identified several reasons to refuse even free Bibles. The Gideons, noted the court, had made several requests to appear, and apparently would try to disseminate other materials if the Bible distribution went smoothly. Thus, in time, "the board might find itself effectively defining religion or censoring the content of religious materials." To the extent that an offer to one group would invite requests from others, "the public school system could become the focal point for the competition of all religious beliefs." Ironically, the court of appeals concluded, "the more fairly and objectively the guidelines are enforced, the more the school board will become immersed in serious religious questions." The only safe policy was to prevent the school board from starting down the road at all, and that is just what this court and several others have done.

In the same case, the court of appeals considered a Florida law that sought to infuse religion into the schools in a quite different way. The legislature had required that public school officials "inculcate by precept and example . . . the practice of every Christian virtue. . . ." Teachers, specifically, must "embrace every opportunity" to transmit those "virtues," although no standards or sanctions were contained in the law. When this requirement was challenged because of its clearly sectarian reference, the court of appeals first held it unconstitutional. Had the legislature told teachers they must inculcate "Jewish virtue" or "Moslem virtue," observed the court, there would be little doubt about the invalidity of such a law. The wider acceptance of Christianity did not change the situation; indeed, if anything, stressing the majority faith only underscored the plight of members of other faiths and of nonbelievers. Later the court of appeals reconsidered the case and—deadlocked by a tie vote—upheld the statute without an opinion on its merits. Apparently some of the judges doubted whether any relief was needed in the absence of any showing that teachers were in jeopardy for failing to "inculcate Christian virtue" in the classroom. Should enforcement be threatened, a court would undoubtedly follow the lead of the first opinion and would find the law to violate both the establishment and the free exercise clauses.

If the legislature may not *compel* teachers to breach religious neutrality, it should be clear that school officials may not even *allow* them to do so. Consider the intriguing case of Joan LaRocca, a tenured art teacher in Rye, New York. Her dismissal was upheld by the state courts because she had sought to proselytize students for an obscure religious sect. The evidence showed that Mrs. LaRocca had urged her students, during school hours, to attend meetings of the Julius Movement, at which a special version of the Bible would be studied and other sectarian materials would be distributed. Mrs. LaRocca had also used her school office for a prayer session during the school day, and had apparently encouraged several students to misrepresent to their parents the degree of their involvement with her sect. The New York appellate courts had little difficulty in finding the requisite "cause" for the termination of an otherwise satisfactory teacher; such a severe breach of neutrality in matters of religion could not be condoned. While cases of open proselytizing are rare, the occasional aberration makes the point that the individual teacher, as well as the state legislature or the school board, must not breach the wall of separation.

The role of religious music in the public school has been an increasingly active area of concern. When the school board of Sioux Falls, South Dakota, ruled in the fall of 1978 that religious songs could be included in school programs, a group of parents brought suit with the help of the American Civil Liberties Union. Their claim was that singing, for example, "Silent Night" in holiday choral programs violated the establishment clause because of explicit references to Christianity. Community feeling ran high; many parents and citizens appeared before a public hearing to urge the school board to "keep Christ in Christmas."

Several weeks after the holiday season, the federal court decided in favor of the school board. The rule which allowed the performance of carols "recognizes that much of our artistic tradition has a religious origin." The opinion continued:

> Religious texts are frequently used in Christmas music. Much of this art, while religious in origin, has acquired a significance which is no longer confined to the religious sphere of life. It has become integrated into our national culture and heritage. To allow students *only* to study and *not* to perform such works when they have developed an independent secular and artistic significance would give students a truncated view of our culture.

Opinion on this judgment ran the gamut. The Catholic bishop called the decision "wonderful" and observed "we're all part of a Christmas tradition." The lawyer who had filed the suit on behalf of the objecting parents suggested, half facetiously, that "someone should set the Bible to music" since the court had, in his view, allowed the singing of verses that could not be recited in class. An appeal by the parents was unsuccessful. The appellate court, with one judge dissenting, agreed with the trial judge that the purpose of the exercises was primarily secular, and that allowing the carols did not abridge religious liberties or unduly entangle the school district in religious matters.

Meanwhile, the Classroom Teachers Association in Tulsa, Oklahoma, debated a recommendation that teachers avoid religious themes in holiday programs. The emergence of these issues in the school setting is, of course, simply a microcosm of a broader concern about religious displays (such as the nativity scene on the courthouse or city hall lawn) which has been a focus of separationist concern for some time. There is remarkably little law governing these issues.

Nowhere has the religious music issue been more controversial than in California. The State Board of Education adopted in the spring of 1978 new criteria for the evaluation of instructional materials in music. The specific focus was materials which contained "any discussion, depiction or other aspect of religion" and which were, for that reason, subject to additional scrutiny. Among the new policies were, for example, these requirements: that songs with sectarian religious content would be included in basic materials "only as required to achieve a specified educational purpose"; that teacher and student materials should not "suggest activities for students that could be considered adorational or devotional in nature and that may require students to participate in any religious observance"; and that where sectarian materials were included they should be treated with emphasis on their secular contributions to music style, music history, and "to the recognition of music as an element of cultural diversity."

Persons on both sides of the California controversy invoked the applicable state statute—a masterpiece of accommodation—which mandates neutrality in these terms:

> An explanation or description of a religious belief or practice shall be presented in a manner which neither encourages nor discourages belief in the matter, nor indoctrinates the student in any particular religious belief.

The dilemma of religious neutrality in California is especially acute, and not only for political reasons. The "separation" provisions of the state constitution are stricter than those of the federal Bill of Rights, and the California courts have imposed a rigid line between church and government. The state supreme court once held that public funds could not be used to restore the San Diego mission—despite its obvious historic value—so long as formal control remained in the Catholic archdiocese and its religious leader. Perhaps the most extreme manifestation of the California policy was an appellate court decision in the early 1960s forbidding the City of Pasadena to spend municipal funds on a promotional film of the Rose Bowl Parade because some of the floats were sponsored by church groups. Thus the approach of the California State Board of Education to the religious music issue is at least consistent with general state policy on religious matters. The public response was predictably intense, and the last word has probably not yet been heard. For the moment, California has taken a harder line on the introduction of religious music into the classroom and the assembly hall than have most other states, although comparable pressures are evident in other parts of the country.

This discussion of the role of religion in the public school brings us finally back to the Kentucky law requiring the display of the Ten Commandments in every classroom. Soon after the law was enacted, the education department asked the Attorney General for an opinion on its constitutionality. The state's chief legal officer was uncomfortable with the request, and apparently unfamiliar with such weighty constitutional problems. Without ruling directly on the merits, he implied his view that the law would be valid if carried out with private funds. The Attorney General relied on cases which had allowed, for example, engraving the Ten Commandments on statues on courthouse lawns, or their display on the walls of certain public buildings.

The Ten Commandments case does pose a more difficult issue. The display of these biblical precepts on the classroom wall is certainly less coercive to the nonbeliever, or to the non-Judeo-Christian, than the daily devotional Bible readings and Lord's Prayer. The requirement of the Kentucky law that private funds meet all the costs of the program is designed to blunt any claim of public subsidy. On the other hand, the Ten Commandments clearly reflect Judeo-Christian beliefs, and in that sense are undeniably religious in nature. Those who belong to no faith, or to a faith that does not honor the Bible, cannot insist that comparable precepts be placed in every Kentucky classroom. It is precisely because of the risk of such counterclaims that the Supreme Court has insisted on such strict separation. Moreover, the origin and purpose of the state law are unmistakably religious, and such roots are sometimes persuasive in determining constitutional issues. Thus, while the Ten Commandments case is surely closer to the line than many others we have reviewed, it should be governed by the same constitutional principles.

In the spring of 1979, the trial court ruled in favor of the school authorities, holding that the governmental role in the hanging of the Ten Commandments was minimal and for that reason did not violate the establishment clause. The concededly religious origins of the biblical precepts did not, in the court's view, "forever divorce their use for a secular purpose." A year later the Kentucky Supreme Court affirmed the trial court judgment by an equal division—an unusual circumstance which leaves the decision of the lower court intact but produces no opinion from the higher court. Justices on both sides of the state supreme court expressed individual views, but there was no majority or minority opinion. About the same time, a federal judge struck down a rather similar North Dakota law requiring that each school district in the state post a copy of the Ten Commandments in a prominent place in every classroom. The federal court found the purpose of the law to be clearly religious; this conclusion might be reconciled with the Kentucky case because North Dakota had apparently envisioned the use of public funds in the posting, while Kentucky had insisted that the display be privately funded.

On November 17, 1980, the United States Supreme Court summarily reversed the Kentucky courts' decision. By a 5–4 vote, the Court held that the Kentucky posting law was unconstitutional:

> The pre-eminent purpose for posting the Ten Commandments on schoolroom walls is plainly religious in nature. The Ten Commandments is undeniably a sacred text in the Jewish and Christian faiths, and no legislative recitation of a supposed secular purpose can blind us to that fact. . . .
>
> This is not a case in which the Ten Commandments are integrated into the school curriculum, where the Bible may constitutionally be used in an appropriate study of history, civilization, ethics, comparative religion or the like. . . . Posting of religious texts on the wall serves no such educational function. If the posted copies of the Ten Commandments are to have any effect at all, it will be to induce the school children to read, meditate upon, perhaps to venerate and obey, the Commandments. However desirable this might be as a matter of private devotion, it is not a permissible state objective under the Establishment Clause.

Religious Influences on the Secular Curriculum

There is a much subtler but possibly more difficult impact of religion on the public school curriculum. As we noted in the first chapter, the debate over the study of evolution occurs within the wholly secular biology course. Yet one cannot shape the content of introductory biology without making choices that have profound religious import—whether to stress evolution, to stress creation, to present some balance between the two views, or to leave a major gap in the students' understanding by avoiding this sensitive area entirely. Each of these options has been followed at one time or another, and no one has been wholly satisfactory. Several have been the subject of major court cases, which provide the backdrop for this section.

In the 1920s a number of states, mainly in the South, adopted laws which forbade the teaching of evolution. One such law led to the celebrated *Scopes* case in Tennessee, a case which brought fame to Clarence Darrow, humiliation to William Jennings Bryan, and martyrdom to John Scopes, but left the legality of such prohibitions unsettled. Most such laws remained on the books, in fact, until the issue finally reached the United States Supreme Court in 1968.

The Arkansas statute which settled the issue made it a crime for any teacher in a public school (or state college or university) to teach or to use a textbook which teaches "that mankind ascended or descended from a lower order of animals." The state courts upheld the law, but the teachers who were subject to its criminal sanctions appealed further on constitutional grounds. A clear majority of the Justices in *Epperson* v. *Arkansas* held the law to be in violation of the establishment clause, because its origin and inspiration were so plainly religious and because there was no possible secular justification for banning the teaching of Darwinian theory. The sole aim of the law, held the Court, was "to blot out a particular theory because of its supposed conflict with the Biblical account, literally read."

This decision finally put to rest all state laws which forbade the teaching of evolution as such. The states did not abandon the cause, however. Shortly after the Supreme Court decision, Tennessee modified its old "Scopes" law to require that any biology book which did discuss evolution must state "that it is a theory as to the origin and creation of man and his world and is not represented to be a scientific fact." Such a text must also give "commensurate attention" and "equal emphasis" to "the origins and creation of man and his world as the same is recorded in other theories including, but not limited to, the Genesis account in the Bible." This law did not in terms forbid the teaching of evolution, but instead demanded a disclaimer of its scientific validity and equal time for the Genesis theory of creation. (A final clause of the law decreed that the Holy Bible was not to be considered a "textbook" and the Bible therefore did not have to give equal time or offer any disclaimer.)

The state and federal courts in Tennessee simultaneously heard constitutional challenges to this revised law, and found that it fell squarely under the Supreme Court decision in the *Epperson* case. The law revealed a clear preference for a Judeo-Christian view which was sectarian as well as religious. The fact that evolution was not forbidden, but simply disparaged, did not avoid the force of the establishment clause. Moreover, the Tennessee law invited the very risk which the courts had cautioned against in other contexts—involving school authorities in making inevitably theological choices among various curricular options.

There has been considerable ebb and flow in the creationist movement. An April 1980 *New York Times* survey carried the headline "Darwin's Foes Lobbying for Equal Time in Schools." The essence of the report was that "in a sophisticated nationwide campaign, public schools in virtually every state are being asked to revise biology curriculums so that the biblical account of creation can be included as an explanation for the origin of life." Special note was taken of efforts in the most conservative regions, although the survey recognized that "the teaching of creation has been revived far beyond the Bible Belt areas of the South and Middle West." The California experience is especially instructive. In May 1969 the state board of education ventured that "if the origins of man were taught from the point of view of *both* evolutionists and creationists, the purpose of education would be satisfied." While this statement by itself required no change in curriculum or materials, it gave a portent of future developments during a period when the composition of the state board gradually changed to reflect more closely the philosophy of Governor Ronald Reagan.

The next year the state department of education issued a new "Science Framework," which had been long in preparation. Toward the back of the pamphlet appeared a seemingly innocuous analysis of the precept that "interdependence and interaction with the environment are universal relationships." The key paragraph quickly drew national attention:

> [A]ll scientific evidence to date concerning the origin of life implies at least a dualism or the necessity to use several theories to fully explain relationships between the data points. . . . While the Bible and other philosophic treatises mention creation, science has independently postulated various theories of creation. Therefore, creation in scientific terms is not a religious or philosophic belief. Also note that creation and evolutionary theories are not necessarily mutually exclusive.

Again, this statement did not mandate the revision of texts or curricula, but did move California another step closer to imposing some form of dual instruction. In 1972 the state board tentatively adopted several texts which included creationism, but scheduled for later that year a public hearing at which opposing points of view could be presented. Many groups appeared, among them representatives of the American Academy for the Advancement of Science and the National Academy of Sciences, both of which adopted resolutions condemning the emerging policy of the California board. The AAAS statement urged "that reference to the theory of creation, which is neither scientifically grounded nor capable of performing the roles required of scientific theories, not be required in textbooks and other classroom materials intended for use in the classroom."

After hearing these and other views, board members voted for a motion to require equal treatment of the two theories in science texts. But the motion lacked the support required by the board's own rules and thus failed. In its place the board resolved that evolution should be presented as a "theory" rather than as "scientific dogmatism." Two months later the board suddenly shifted the focus of creationism away from science, and declared unanimously that "the philosophy of origin" should be dealt with in *social science* textbooks. Although this action left unclear just how the theme was to be addressed in social studies materials, it did reflect a compromise reasonably satisfactory to both sides, and thus averted a possibly bitter showdown on the science curriculum issue. Meanwhile, however, the board also approved the preliminary results of editing which had been done by various committees in response to the 1970 science framework; the only major change was the deletion from a fifth grade text of a statement that most Christians espoused the Genesis view of life's origin before the publication of Darwin's theories (but by implication had espoused evolution thereafter).

The issue remained largely unsettled until several clarifying events occurred. In April 1975 the California Attorney General responded to inquiries from legislators about the legal aspects of the creationism debate. The Attorney General's opinion did not cover all the issues, but did make clear that the state board of education and local school boards (a) could lawfully use public funds to buy materials which presented only the evolutionary theory; and (b) were not legally or constitutionally required to adopt textbooks which contained both evolutionism and creationism.

Later that year a new social science framework appeared. In the section dealing with "views of human origin" appeared the simple statement that several "representative views of origin are studied in the social sciences because they make significant contributions to human systems of beliefs and values." The framework warned that "the teacher must be respectful of the commitments of students" and that the relevant analytic skills "should be taught only to the degree to which students are mature enough to handle them."

Perhaps more helpful is later language in the draft of a new *science* framework, submitted in 1977 to replace the troublesome 1970 framework. Under the same heading (dealing with "interdependence and interaction with the environment") this brief statement appears:

> Scientists also have developed, from experiments and observations, hypotheses concerning the development of life from the non-living matter of the prebiological Earth. This research and its hypotheses are usually referred to as "chemical evolution." Philosophic and religious considerations pertaining to the origins, meaning, and values of life are not within the realm of science because they cannot be analyzed or measured by the present methods of science.

There the California controversy might seem to have come to rest. But the creationist position is not likely to disappear so gracefully. Indeed, at the start of the 1978 session of the legislature, a resolution was introduced asking the state board of education to recommend to all state-supported educational institutions (presumably including colleges and universities) "that a balanced treatment of evolution and special creation be encouraged" in all courses and teaching materials, "such treatment to be limited to the scientific, rather than religious, aspects of the two concepts." The 1978 session closed with no action on this resolution. California lawmakers were by that time far more concerned with being able to support public schools at all in the wake of Proposition 13 than with what should be taught in them.

The invalidation of the Tennessee law did not foreclose the

one option suggested during the California evolution/creation controversy—requiring that *both* evolution and creation be taught in the biology course, without disparagement of either or reference to the biblical origin of creation. There are no court decisions on the legality of this pure "equal time" approach. On one hand, such a requirement would be less offensive than either the Arkansas flat ban or the Tennessee disclaimer. In most areas of the law, a requirement that two conflicting points of view both be taught—socialism and free enterprise, to take a common example—would be permissible. The problem here is the special role of religion. Thus, it seems likely that courts would find even the "equal time" policy in violation of the establishment clause, since the only possible reason for requiring *any* time for creationism would be religious value and belief. Only a very clear secular purpose would avoid that conclusion—for example, strong scientific evidence to support the account of life's origin found in the Book of Genesis. Should such a case reach the courts, such evidence might be submitted and would complicate the picture. But to the extent that the reason for any study of creationism remains religious, as it quite clearly has been in the past, a finding of unconstitutionality would be hard to avoid.

The ban on teaching of evolution may, of course, be enforced in subtler ways than through state legislation. In the early 1970s a student teacher in Gastonia, North Carolina, was summoned to the principal's office. She was charged with having answered student questions about the origins of life in a way that implied an approval of Darwinism. She was reported to have impugned the accuracy of the Genesis theory. When the teacher admitted she had made such statements, she was discharged. She brought suit for reinstatement in the federal district court, claiming that her dismissal violated the establishment clause as well as her freedom of speech. The court agreed, and held that muzzling an individual teacher's discussion of evolution was as clearly unconstitutional as was the Arkansas statutory prohibition. Here an individual principal had done precisely what the Supreme Court had said the state legislature could not do.

This discussion might imply that the establishment clause is the only source of protection. Clearly a teacher's freedom of expression is also in issue (this will be fully treated in the next chapter). Several of the cases we reviewed here did raise free speech or academic freedom claims as well as those of freedom of religion, but the courts have often preferred to decide these cases under the establishment clause. Had the religious freedom claim been unavailable, for any reason, there is a clear suggestion in the *Epperson* case that the teacher's freedom of expression offered an alternative and constitutionally adequate basis for the same result.

Meanwhile, there is a separate source of concern—the effect such restrictions may have on the student's ability to learn. A parent in Mississippi brought suit in federal court claiming that her state's anti-evolution law disadvantaged her daughter in the competition for college admission. Since the student had not done well on standardized tests, an incomplete science education would, the mother argued, further impede her academic progress and impair her prospects for success in later life. The claim was ingenious, the issue intriguing, and the case well made. But the court did what courts should do in constitutional cases, and decided on the issue on the narrowest available ground. Since the Mississippi statute was clearly in violation of the establishment clause as applied in *Epperson*, no more need be said. The "learning rights" issue thus remains for a later case.

Obviously the Scopes-type prohibition is the simplest way of ensuring that students will learn only the Genesis view. The equal-time approach is a subtler avenue to the same goal. Still less direct is the approach which triggered the West Clark, Indiana, textbook suit. If a school district voluntarily adopts a text which in fact presents *only* the Genesis theory, the same educational result will presumably follow. Students in that district, at least in their biology course, will learn only the biblical view of life's origin.

The question whether adopting a particular textbook violates the establishment clause is harder than the legality of the Scopes-type ban on teaching evolution. Yet the local judge in the West Clark case followed a comparable route in deciding the issue raised by parents who objected to the use of *Biology: A Search for Order.* The preface of the book was unequivocal: "The most reasonable explanation for the actual facts of biology as they are known scientifically is that of Biblical creationism." The text stated flatly that "the world was brought into existence out of nothing but the power of the creator." In the teacher's guide which accompanied the text, certain natural phenomena were explained in religious terms—a discovery, for example, attributed to the "direction of God's providence." After a careful review of the whole book, the judge concluded that its classroom use would violate the establishment clause; the adoption of such a text would foster a particular religious perspective quite as much as would a ban on teaching Darwinism.

The West Clark case left open a host of intriguing issues: What if such a book is simply available for collateral reading, or is simply made available in the library and is suggested by a teacher for students who wish more information about creationism? What if the content of the book simply balances the two theories, and does not (as *Search for Order* clearly did) take sides? And what is the scope of a judicial ban on the use of a designated book? Seemingly, school boards may not forbid the use of certain books because of objectionable content (see chapter six), though courts may (perhaps *must*) do so. Each of these cases is quite different from the one actually presented. At least the mere buying of the book for the school library would be unobjectionable. But even the supplemental classroom use of the same book poses a different issue; it is one thing for students to augment their individual study of evolution with creationist materials, but quite another for them to be *required* to do so.

The textbook which presents both sides is also a quite different issue—harder than the West Clark case, and different from the simplistic Tennessee "equal time" law. One may grant that the creationist position probably would not have found its way into the book at all but for religious pressure. But so long as a religious basis is not given in the text itself, and so long as Darwinism is not disparaged by the comparison, the mere adoption of a book which offers both views would not necessarily violate the establishment clause. Indeed, for reasons we will see shortly, such an accommodation might even help to avoid other constitutional difficulties. Surely it has political appeal in parts of the country where fundamentalist belief is pervasive and where the public schools are under pressure to respond to that belief. Constitutional principles may not of course bend to popular pressure, nor may they be shaped or modified at the polls. But the relationship of the community to the public schools, and the intensity of belief about the origins of human life, cannot be ignored.

Religious Concern about Secular Curricula

To this point we have been concerned about the inclusion of material which either reflects religious belief or discusses theology. A quite different set of issues is raised when a deeply religious parent, like those in Kanawha County, objects to the *exclusion* of religious material from the curriculum. West Virginia parents, required to send their children to the public schools, claimed that the textbooks and other instructional materials then in use and others proposed to be adopted were offensive because of their excessively secular content. This contention has constitutional dimensions, and did in fact lead to a lawsuit in the federal district court. The parent-plaintiffs argued that the secular curriculum violated their religious liberties in two ways: first, that teaching materials which avoid any reference to religion effectively "establish" non-religion, or "Secular Humanism"; second, that depriving public school students of biblical teaching abridges the free exercise of their religion. The issue clearly has two sides, and the dilemma of the school officials is a poignant one: The adoption of texts favored by religious groups may violate the Constitution in one direction, while the omission of religious material may generate constitutional challenges on the other side.

We might analyze the legal issues through the Kanawha County suit. The complaint alleged that devout parents were compelled to send children to the public schools where they had to read "articles and stories promoting and encouraging a disbelief in a Supreme Being . . . and [which] encourage them to violate the Ten Commandments as given by the Almighty to Moses. . . ." Particular texts and other materials were alleged to "violate their freedom of religious practice and belief, and . . . contain matters anti-religious and denouncing the practice of their faith."

The claim that secular materials represent an establishment of non-religion or anti-religion is an intriguing one. The historic purpose of the establishment clause was to prevent government support of recognized religious sects. The framers of the Bill of Rights would not have expected that complete avoidance of biblical references would someday be said to violate the First Amendment. Through the years, however, the definition of "religion" has steadily broadened, as we saw in the New Jersey Transcendental Meditation case. In the 1960s, the Supreme Court was called upon to decide the claims of persons seeking conscientious objector status through philosophical commitment quite unlike traditional sectarian worship or belief. The Court in 1970 held that purely ethical and moral grounds for pacifism would meet the condition for exemption, even though the objector did not hold a traditional deistic belief. Such convictions might, in the Court's view, occupy "a place parallel to that filled by God in traditionally religious persons." Earlier, the Court held that a person might not be denied a notary public's commission because he refused to swear a belief in God; the free exercise of religion protected nonbelief as well as familiar theology. Against this background, there is some basis for the claim that a wholly secular curriculum "establishes" a non-religion.

The courts have not, however, been very sympathetic to the establishment claim in this context. Two cases have considered it—the Kanawha County suit, and a rather similar case filed earlier in the federal courts in Houston. In the Texas case the plaintiffs argued that the public schools gave forbidden support to a "religion of secularism," and thus violated the establishment clause. The court found the connection, if any, between the secular curriculum and "religion" so tenuous as to fall outside the constitutional ban. School officials had not discouraged free discussion of the origins of human life, and such discussion might well include the teaching of Genesis. The Texas judge was also troubled by the matter of remedies: For a court to forbid the teaching of evolution, or require the teaching of creationism, would be the very thing the Supreme Court held in *Epperson* the Arkansas legislature could not do. If teachers were told that discussion of evolution was taboo, the specter of broader intervention would loom; "avoidance of any reference to the subject of human origins is, indeed, a decidedly totalitarian approach to the problem. . . ." The court of appeals affirmed the dismissal of the suit with the brief comment that "federal courts cannot by judicial decree do that which the Supreme Court has declared the legislature powerless to do, i.e., prevent teaching the theory of evolution in the public schools for religious reasons."

The district court in the West Virginia case gave even shorter shrift to the establishment claim: "A complete loosening of imagination is necessary to find that placing the books and materials in the schools constitutes an establishment of religion contrary to the rights contained in the Constitution." The court of appeals affirmed without even a reported opinion, and there have been no later cases.

While the conclusion reached by all four federal courts seems clearly correct, the establishment clause argument is at least ingenious and deserves a respectful rebuttal. To begin, the courts are right that the avoidance of religion in the curriculum does not constitute the *establishment* of a forbidden philosophy. One can imagine a militantly anti-religious (or actually sacrilegious) curriculum, but such was not the case either in Houston or in Charleston. The courts were also rightly concerned about the alternatives; to order that teachers avoid any reference to evolution would not only run afoul of *Epperson* but would threaten free expression in a most basic way. Thus as far as the establishment clause issue ran, judgments in favor of the school districts seem sound.

Both cases presented an alternative ground for relief: the claim that the secular curriculum abridged the free exercise of the plaintiffs' religion. This claim is quite different from that of the Wisconsin Amish in the *Yoder* case. The fundamentalist parents in Texas and West Virginia did not object to the public school per se, nor did they seek excusal from major parts of the curriculum. What they did oppose, on religious grounds, was the particular approach taken in certain courses, notably biology but also parts of the social studies. Their claim has several components: a fear that a "godless" school may undermine religious teaching from the home and the church; an apprehension of open conflict between what is taught in school about the origin of life and what is presented at home as the literal word of God; and a concern that children under peer (and teacher) pressure could espouse beliefs contrary to those instilled by parents and religious leaders. Such grounds of concern are substantial. Certain faiths require their adherents to be "separate" from teaching and practices which conflict with the tenets of their theology. Thus the risk exists in the secular school setting not only of a clash of values but of deeply unsettling doubts in the child's mind.

Despite the sincerity with which these beliefs are held and presented, however, the element of coercion necessary to an abridgment of religious liberty is absent. The alternative of private education exists, at least for those who can afford it. Where that option does not exist, the public schools often provide for the excusal of the child whose parents on religious grounds object to a particular part of the curriculum. (In the Houston case, for example, children could be excused from certain courses, and the school board argued that this proviso was broad enough to include even discussion of evolution in biology. The court agreed and thus found the possibility of coercion considerably mitigated.) Excusal is not without its costs, to be sure; the child who leaves the classroom may be stigmatized, valuable instruction may in fact be lost, and the excusal procedure may itself require the declaration of a belief which the parents wish not to reveal in such a form. But the courts have been disinclined to find here the coercion essential to a free exercise claim.

The two federal district courts which have considered the argument have rejected it on this basis. Both opinions disposed of the free exercise issue rather summarily, and the appellate courts affirmed without additional discussion. In the West Virginia case, the court observed curtly that the First Amendment "does not guarantee that nothing about religion will be taught in the schools, nor that nothing offensive to any religion will be taught in the schools," and concluded that none of the school board's curricular policies "constitutes an inhibition on or prohibition of the free exercise of religion." The Texas court said even less about the free exercise issue, having given most of its attention to the establishment clause issue along lines we have already considered. Perhaps most surprising is that neither court felt it necessary even to distinguish *Yoder*—though surely the struggle of the Wisconsin Amish bore at least superficial resemblance to the pleas of the Houston and Charleston fundamentalists.

The Texas case raised one additional issue not present in the Kanawha County suit. The plaintiffs had argued that even if the court were unwilling to enjoin the "secular" curriculum, or to forbid the teaching of evolution, it might be willing to mandate "equal time" for all plausible theories of the origin of life. The court was not impressed:

> If the beliefs of fundamentalists were the sole alternative to the Darwinian theory, such a remedy might at least be feasible. But virtually every religion known to man holds its own peculiar view of human origins. Within the scientific community itself, there is much debate over the details of the theory of evolution. This Court is hardly qualified to select from among the available theories those which merit attention in a public school biology class. Nor have plaintiffs suggested to the Court what standards might be applied in making such a selection.

The court of appeals, in one sentence of its brief affirmance, agreed on a slightly different ground: "To require the teaching of every theory of human origin . . . would be an unwarranted intrusion into the authority of public school systems to control the academic curriculum."

This judgment about the particular proposal should not totally foreclose efforts at accommodation. Even granting that a mandate to teach every known theory of the origins of life would create chaos, more plausible solutions remain to be considered. One possible option would be an open excusal plan, which would not require (as did the Houston policy) a declaration of religious opposition as the basis for the dispensation. Such a procedure would probably open the door far beyond its rationale, and for that reason would probably be unworkable. Another option—parallel science instruction for fundamentalist students—would meet the free exercise test but would raise serious problems under the establishment clause because it would use public funds to further the views of particular religious groups. Special classes would, moreover, almost certainly create serious inequities (in terms of class size, subject matter, and the like), and might therefore violate other constitutional provisions.

For the school district that genuinely wishes to find an avenue of accommodation without breaching either of the religion clauses of the Bill of Rights, some guidance may emerge from the policy statement adopted in January 1978 by the Iowa Department of Public Instruction:

The science curriculum should emphasize the theory of evolution as well supported scientific theory—not a fact—that is taught as such by certified science teachers. Students should be advised that it is their responsibility, as informed citizens, to have creationism explained to them by theological experts. They must then decide for themselves the merits of each discipline and its relevance to their lives.

6

DIRTY WORDS AND SUSPECT
BOOKS IN THE CLASSROOM

THE DISMISSAL OF English teacher John Fogarty, in St. Anthony, Idaho, was hardly a unique event. Every year dozens, perhaps hundreds, of textbooks are censored. Occasionally the censors actually burn copies of the objectionable work, as occurred recently in Warsaw, Indiana, and Drake, North Dakota. Often censorship takes a subtler form—quiet withdrawal of a book from the school library, a memorandum from the principal or superintendent warning teachers not to assign the work, or even invisible self-censorship by a teacher or librarian who decides to avoid controversy by simply not using a targeted book. But the acts of censorship which reach the courts are most often those like the dismissal of Fogarty, in which a teacher or librarian is subject to some sanction by school authorities and is not only willing to resist, but financially able to seek legal redress. Only on these rare occasions do issues of censorship ever get to court. For this reason there are relatively few decided cases defining the rights of teachers and librarians who face reprisal for using or assigning controversial literary works.

Let us take the case of John Fogarty as a starting point for an analysis of the legal issues. The position of a school board which discharges a teacher for flouting the principal's order not to use a particular book can be rather simply stated. First, it is clear under state law that local school officials and boards determine the curriculum and assign certain students to teachers (indeed, they are required to see that all students complete a stated number of hours of instruction in many prescribed areas; failure to do so would subject officials to legal liability). Should a teacher be hired to teach English and insist instead on teaching algebra or history, there would be little question about the propriety of a nonrenewal of the contract. Likewise, the English teacher who insisted on exploring great works of literature with students who badly needed remedial instruction in grammar, spelling, and punctuation would receive little sympathy from the most ardent civil libertarian. The case of John Fogarty—the teacher who exercises his own judgment in selecting a controversial work for an assigned course—seems to present a special facet of this general principle. (One parent in St. Anthony compared his own needs to those of the schools: "If I hired an agricultural expert with a degree to help on the farm, and I wanted him to plant potatoes and he said no, I'd tell him to hit the road. It's as simple as that.")

Second, school authorities reasonably expect a high standard of professional behavior from teachers, who serve in the classroom as authority figures. Deviation from duty—especially to a degree that invites public controversy—serves in the eyes of the administration to undermine the central role of the school system. Extreme departures may also violate the usually unwritten but widely accepted code of professional responsibility by which teaching has become a learned profession in American society. If respect for teachers is undermined in an individual case, respect for public education may be jeopardized.

Third, there is a continuing (and increasingly vital) need of the schools for wide community support. Most revenues for public education come from local taxes; if parents and other citizens lose confidence in the schools, tax levies may fail and the fiscal base of the educational system may be threatened. Surely, therefore, if the vast majority of citizens in a town like St. Anthony do not want *One Flew Over the Cuckoo's Nest* to be taught in the high school, the principal and the superintendent are likely to heed that sentiment. Ironically, the administration may even argue that restricting John Fogarty's freedom on this occasion will in the long run protect other teachers; such repressive measures may thus be justified in part by a desire to help those whom these measures hurt.

Fourth, school officials would point out, even the Supreme Court has said that children may be kept from reading books that are generally available to adults. Over a decade ago, during its most liberal period, the Court held that states might apply special standards to defining obscenity for young readers, and could restrict the sale and distribution to minors of works that adults have a constitutional right to read. Surely, the St. Anthony board would argue, a school may follow what law enforcement officials can do in imposing higher literary standards for minors.

Finally, school officials would argue that a basic purpose of public elementary and secondary education is subverted by a John Fogarty. From their inception, our school systems have had as one recognized goal the "indoctrination" of the youth of the nation. The preservation and perpetuation of basic values and traditions rank high among the assigned functions of the schools. To the extent that particular instruction—or even the assignment of particular materials—departs sharply from those values, a basic purpose of public education is undermined. Since it is the task of school officials to protect those values, some control over the curriculum necessarily follows. Where John Fogarty's literary tastes and interests (and even those of some students) conflict with basic values of American society, it becomes the duty of the board and the superintendent to preserve the latter even at the expense of the former.

The teacher's reply is premised on three quite different claims: first, that persons who work for the government (including public school teachers) may not be discharged for the exercise of speech which the Constitution protects; second, that teachers often assert the constitutional rights and liberties of others, most notably their students, and should thus have a "derivative" right along with the primary one; third, and most important, that teachers enjoy a special measure of legal protection—sometimes called academic freedom—above and beyond the freedom enjoyed by other public employees. Each of these claims must now be analyzed.

The Teacher as Government Employee

Teachers share with other persons who work for the government certain protections not available in the private sector. A teacher in a private school, for example, has no *constitutional* right to comment publicly on the policies of the school administration. A decade ago, however, the United States Supreme Court held that an Illinois public school teacher named Pickering could not be fired for writing an open letter critical of the conduct of school finances. Even though there were some errors in the statement, the Court held that the teacher could be discharged only if he had shown reckless disregard of the truth or had acted with malice. The *Pickering* decision has been extended to hundreds of other public employment settings, and has been a cornerstone of protection for the free speech of persons who work for the government. The underlying principle is simple enough, though it has taken decades to develop: While no person has a right to obtain or to keep a government job, the Constitution does not allow the government to condition its hiring upon the willingness of persons to give up the right of citizenship they would otherwise enjoy. Since the right to criticize government is basic among those liberties, persons who work for the government must be as free to speak publicly (even about the policies of their employer) as is anyone else.

A pair of cases in the early 1970s extended the protection of government employees into the public school classroom. Two teachers in New York State were dismissed, one for refusing to lead her students in the daily pledge to the flag, the other for wearing in class a black armband to protest the Vietnam War. Both teachers took their cases to the federal courts, and both won reinstatement. The court both times found the conduct well within the protection of a public employee's right to protest government policy; in the black armband case the court applied to teachers essentially the same standard as the Supreme Court applied to student protest in the *Tinker* case.

The public employment cases do, however, contain important limitations. In the *Pickering* decision, the Supreme Court warned that some kinds of critical speech might be punished if they disrupted the effective working of the agency. Other kinds of speech might exceed the bounds of the constitutional privilege through sheer irresponsibility or because of their *ad personam* nature. Taking "company time" or defaulting on assigned duties could also result in a sanction even if the content of the speech were otherwise protected. While these qualifications may not seem troublesome for the school teacher, one post-*Pickering* decision is highly pertinent. A civilian instructor had been hired by the federal government to teach Vietnamese military personnel. During one of his class sessions he departed from the assigned topic—military weapons—to express some personal views about the role of the United States in the Indochina war. For this deviation he was dismissed, and his dismissal was upheld by the federal courts. Such a departure from the assigned material, said the court, was not only a breach of duty, but threatened to disrupt sensitive relations with the foreign personnel who were in this case the students. Thus the value of *Pickering* and the other public employment cases for the teacher in Fogarty's position is qualified.

The Teacher as Representative of Students' Rights

It is sometimes suggested that a public school teacher should be allowed curricular discretion in order to protect the freedom of students to learn. Professor Sheldon Nahmod has thoughtfully stated the case for this sort of "derivative" teacher's freedom in the classroom:

> An unbalanced presentation on a controversial subject . . . may be harmful to the education of students. It deprives them of the opportunity to consider as many relevant facts and opinions as possible. Moreover, a classroom is one of the few places where controversial subjects can be discussed in a supervised and reasonably thorough manner. In making an unbalanced presentation, a teacher impedes the development of critical and other faculties; the point of view espoused and perhaps received so uncritically may in fact be erroneous and ultimately harmful to the students. Although this may also occur in the context of a balanced presentation, students at least will have had the opportunity to decide otherwise.

One recent case illustrates the way in which a teacher's rights may be reinforced by the interests of students. An Oregon political science teacher arranged to invite four speakers into his senior high school classroom. Three of the speakers—a Democrat, a Republican, and a John Birch Society member—appeared without incident. An invitation was extended to a Communist, and was approved by both the principal and the school board. Community pressure soon developed, however, and the board not only cancelled the invitation but imposed a broad ban on all "political speakers" anywhere in the school system. The teacher and a group of his students went to federal court to challenge the ban, asking that the Communist be allowed to speak and complete the series. The federal district court held the school policy unconstitutional—in part because it violated general First Amendment principles developed in college speaker ban cases, but also because it prevented the students from receiving information to which they had a constitutional right. The ban was declared a violation of the First Amendment rights both of the teachers and of the students.

The nature of this case suggests the rarity with which the "derivative rights" argument will in fact be available to the teacher. Only where the wishes of the students are clearly parallel is there the necessary certainty about the factual basis for the claim. Much more often, the views of students either will be unknown to the court, or will actually be opposed to those of the teacher. Where student interests are not directly reflected in the case, it is likely that either the parents or the school board (acting *in loco parentis*) will assert contrary views. Take the *Fogarty* case as an example: It was apparent from newspaper reports that many students either enjoyed *One Flew Over the Cuckoo's Nest* or at least did not find it offensive. Such views could possibly be introduced in evidence—although they would conflict with claims of the school administration, presumably reinforced by parental testimony, that students of impressionable ages should not be exposed to such material. Where a teacher argues that students want to read the book but the principal and the parents insist that they should not (at least not in class), the court is likely to defer to the latter set of "derivative rights" rather than to the former. Thus, save in the unusual situation of the Oregon Communist speaker case, where the students and their parents are actually parties to the case in support of the teacher's position, the teacher is not likely to find much comfort in this second argument.

Academic Freedom for the Teacher

If the general rights of public employees do not fully protect the beleaguered teacher, he must then seek special protection. College and university professors have long enjoyed such a special status under the doctrine of academic freedom. The contours of the doctrine have been well stated by the American Association of University Professors, in a 1940 statement which now has the imprimatur of the courts as well as of major colleges and universities and professional and learned societies:

> Institutions of higher education are conducted for the common good and not to further the interest of either the individual teacher or the institution as a whole. The common good depends upon the free search for truth and its free exposition.
> Academic freedom is essential to these purposes and applies to both teaching and research. Freedom in research is fundamental to the advancement of truth. Academic freedom in its teaching aspect is fundamental for the protection of the rights of the teacher in teaching and of the student to freedom in learning.

The uncertainty is the extent to which academic freedom is available to elementary and secondary teachers—and that is the really central issue in Fogarty's case. Had the same dispute arisen at the University of Idaho, no action would have been taken; had reprisal been even threatened, any court would have held that a university professor enjoys a constitutional right to assign to his classes any material that is not obscene or otherwise unlawful. (Even where material could be banned at newsstands or drugstores, its dissemination and study in a university classroom or laboratory may well be protected—but that is a question beyond our present scope.)

The *Fogarty* case is difficult because of a subtle tension between the high school setting and the nature of the course. The students, on the one hand, would be in college the following year, and the course in which the assignment was made had many qualities of a college level course. Elective study of literature in a college preparatory track closely resembles a college course—and, in fact, may be more demanding or sophisticated in content and depth than many literature courses offered to college freshmen. On the other hand, the expectations of the public school system, from kindergarten through senior high school, are profoundly different from those of the college or university. Public schools serve a set of specified purposes, on the basis of which they are supported by local taxes. The employment of teachers, and their relationship to the administration, differ markedly from the model of higher education. Even the teacher of senior literature courses typically comes through a quite different preparatory route and has different duties and responsibilities from those of the college professor—for example, the teacher may be expected to watch the lunchroom one day a week but is not expected to do advanced research. Thus, despite the similarities in *content* between Fogarty's course and an introductory literature course at the University of Idaho, there are significant differences in *context*. The tension between these two forces makes exceedingly difficult any simple answer to the question whether a high school teacher enjoys academic freedom on the college model.

Some concise answers have been offered. They have at least the virtue of simplicity, and perhaps that of consistency as well. For example, Professor Stephen Goldstein, a sensitive scholar both of free expression and of teachers' rights, argues that academic freedom really does not belong in the elementary or secondary classroom. Certain aspects of the elementary and secondary school—the "teacher's position as an authority figure," the importance of "inculcation of values" as a school function, the relative immaturity of the students, and the rather structured nature of the curriculum—militate against the downward extension of concepts developed at the collegiate level. On this basis, Goldstein would apparently give academic freedom to an instructor in secretarial skills or remedial English at a junior college, but would deny it to the high school teacher of a senior elective course in comparative literature, government, or religion. To

Goldstein the structure and organization are basic; the need to sustain the authority of the school officials (and ultimately that of the community which supports the school system) is paramount. Since the tension between the two forces must be resolved in some way, Goldstein argues for a formula which applies across all levels of elementary and secondary education. Some support for his view comes from the relatively small number of cases addressing the issue. In order to assess the soundness of this position, we must now turn to the courts.

It is always wise to begin with the relevant decisions of the United States Supreme Court. Those decisions are of limited value here because the Justices have never considered a curricular issue under the free speech clause of the First Amendment, from which the academic freedom claim derives. The Court has, however, shown its concern for and commitment to the principle of academic freedom in other settings. In a series of decisions going back to the 1950s, the Court struck down loyalty oaths on First Amendment grounds. In several of these cases, most of which involved college or public school teachers, the Court recognized that members of the academic profession made a special claim for freedom of thought and inquiry. The clearest such statement came in the 1967 case striking down a New York loyalty law:

> Our Nation is deeply committed to safeguarding academic freedom, which is of transcendent value to all of us and not merely to the teachers concerned. That freedom is therefore a special concern of the First Amendment, which does not tolerate laws that cast a pall of orthodoxy over the classroom. . . . The classroom is peculiarly the "marketplace of ideas." The Nation's future depends upon leaders trained through wide exposure to that robust exchange of ideas which discovers truth "out of a multitude of tongues, [rather] than through any kind of authoritative selection."

While most of the loyalty oath cases involved college professors rather than school teachers, their principles clearly apply beyond the immediate setting. It is true that these decisions really defined rights and liberties of all public employees; since oaths have been generally invalidated, no special dispensation for the teaching profession has been sought or granted. Thus the most that can be said with confidence is that such statements about academic freedom are helpful, though seldom essential to the decision.

Other cases may be even more helpful to the development of a claim of academic freedom. The origins of the Supreme Court's concern with the public school curriculum go back to the 1920s. Nebraska, like many other states, enacted shortly after World War I a law which forbade the use of German in any classroom in the state. When a German-speaking teacher in a Lutheran school appealed his conviction to the Supreme Court, a majority of the Justices held the Nebraska law unconstitutional. The Court recognized the legitimacy of the state's desire to promote assimilation among its people by requiring a common language. But the Court felt that the means Nebraska had used violated the teacher's "right thus to teach and the right of parents to engage him so to instruct their children"—a right protected by the due process clause of the Fourteenth Amendment. (Although there was evidence that such laws were aimed at the German-born population and might have been struck down on that basis, the Supreme Court instead adopted a broader ground of decision.) Two questions remain: To what extent did this decision—*Meyer* v. *Nebraska*—apply to public schools, and what elements of the curriculum did it protect?

The first question has been partially answered in the intervening years. Although the facts and much of the reasoning of the *Meyer* case would limit its effect to private schools, the Supreme Court has read it more broadly. In two cases in the late 1960s, both involving public schools, the Justices simply assumed that *Meyer* applied quite as much to public as to private schools. The Court characterized the Nebraska statute as an "arbitrary restriction upon the freedom of teachers to teach and of students to learn" and as a "restriction upon the liberty of teacher and pupil." The other question—to what parts of the curriculum does *Meyer* apply?—remains unsettled. The Supreme Court recognized in 1923 "the power of the State . . . to make reasonable regulations for all schools, including a requirement that they shall give instruction in English. . . ." The Court also disclaimed any disparagement of "the State's power to prescribe a curriculum for institutions which it supports." Later cases have reaffirmed this general language.

The possible relevance of *Meyer* to the curriculum, and to the teacher's claim of academic freedom, was measurably enhanced by the *Epperson* case. As we noted in the previous chapter, the Supreme Court there struck down state laws banning the teaching of evolution, although on a religious freedom ground and with no explicit mention of academic freedom or teachers' liberty of expression. In *Epperson* the Supreme Court underscored what was said in *Meyer* about the "State's undoubted right to prescribe the curriculum for its public schools. . . ." The problem here was that Arkansas had sought to prohibit, "on pain of criminal penalty, the teaching of a scientific theory or doctrine where that prohibition is based upon reasons that violate the First Amendment." These elements were important to the decision: the law contained criminal sanctions, it completely excluded from the schools a whole body of scientific thought, and the basis for the exclusion was a particular religious point of view.

Some additional guidance comes from the concurring opinion of Mr. Justice Black. He would have struck down the law because of the vagueness of its key provisions. He also offered a critical distinction:

> It is plain that a state law prohibiting all teaching of human development or biology is constitutionally quite different from a law that compels a teacher to teach as true only one theory of a

given doctrine. It would be difficult to make a First Amendment case out of a state law eliminating the subject of higher mathematics, or astronomy, or biology from its curriculum.

Mr. Justice Stewart, who wrote another concurring opinion, reinforced Justice Black's distinction:

> The States are most assuredly free "to choose their own curriculums for their own schools." A State is entirely free, for example, to decide that the only foreign language to be taught in its public school system shall be Spanish. But would a State be free to punish a teacher for letting his students know that there are other languages in the world? I think not.
>
> It is one thing for a State to determine that "the subject of higher mathematics, or astronomy, or biology" shall or shall not be included in its public school curriculum. It is quite another thing for a State to make it a criminal offense for a public school teacher so much as to mention the very existence of an entire system of respected human thought.

It is not quite clear what troubled Justice Stewart. Perhaps, as Goldstein suggests, he was more concerned about a state's attempt to forbid a teacher from even mentioning Darwinism in class than about totally banning a particular subject from the curriculum. Justice Stewart would, on one hand, grant that a state could decide not to offer biology in its public schools. On the other hand, he would uphold the lower federal court that reinstated the North Carolina teacher for giving Darwinian answers to student questions about evolution. It is less clear whether Justice Stewart would allow school officials, for example, to require some materials—and forbid others—on the basis of their treatment of the evolution controversy.

The cases which have addressed the curriculum provide limited guidance, but only that. The other possible source of the Supreme Court's views on the academic freedom issue is the case of *Tinker* v. *Des Moines School District*, which involved student rather than teacher rights. Several students had worn black armbands to class, in clear violation of a school rule, to express their opposition to the Vietnam War. They were suspended, and brought their claims into the federal courts. The Supreme Court eventually held that, in the absence of any actual or seriously threatened disruption, the students could not be disciplined for peaceful protest of this sort. Although the case was concerned chiefly with the rights of students vis-à-vis the authority of the public schools, the majority opinion contained a vitally important statement about the protection of the Constitution for the freedom of inquiry even at the secondary level:

> In our system, state-operated schools may not be enclaves of totalitarianism. School officials do not possess absolute authority over their students. Students in school as well as out of school are "persons" under our Constitution. They are possessed of fundamental rights which the State must respect, just as they themselves must respect their obligations to the State. In our system, students may not be regarded as closed-circuit recipients of only that which the State chooses to communicate. They may not be confined to the expression of those sentiments that are officially approved. In the absence of a specific showing of constitutionally valid reasons to regulate their speech, students are entitled to freedom of expression of their views.

Thus, the Court in *Tinker* suggested that activity protected by the First Amendment—such as the wearing of the antiwar protest symbols—may be prohibited only where there is a clear threat of disruption. As we noted earlier, one federal court of appeals applied that reasoning precisely to the teacher wearing in class a *Tinker*-like black armband. There is reason to believe that the Supreme Court would also apply the *Tinker* reasoning to a curricular case like *Fogarty*, although the absence of cases in point makes any such judgment speculative.

In fact, the Supreme Court decisions do no more than refine the issues. Professor Thomas Emerson, in his lengthy treatise on First Amendment law, offers two observations about the limited value of the cases bearing on academic freedom:

The first is that the Supreme Court has touched upon only a small fraction of the total area of academic freedom. . . . None of [the relevant cases] considers the rights of individual faculty members [or teachers] vis-à-vis the administration of their own institutions or vis-à-vis their colleagues. . . . The second conclusion is that the Supreme Court has never undertaken to establish academic freedom as an independent constitutional right. . . . All that the Court has done is to say that academic freedom considerations are relevant in the application of standard doctrine; it has not held that they possess any constitutional dimension of their own.

Since the Supreme Court has not spoken, we must look for closer precedent in the lower courts. Important, though not dispositive, are a pair of cases in the early 1970s which dealt with teacher conduct and expression. In one case the teacher was discharged for refusing to lead the morning salute to the flag; in the other, it was the peaceful display of a black armband in class that brought the sanction. Both cases involved mature high school classes, and there was no evidence of disruption or any other harmful effect. Thus the appellate court (both cases went through the same federal circuit) ordered the reinstatement of both teachers on First Amendment grounds. Given the circumstances, these were really general public employment cases that happened to involve teachers, and did not attempt to define the scope of allowable expression in the classroom. We must therefore turn to a group of cases which did more precisely address the content of the curriculum through teachers' claims of redress.

The first modern reported case had a prophetic quality. A high school teacher in Baltimore had assigned *Brave New World* to her senior English class. When parental complaint about the content of the book brought the matter to the principal's attention, the teacher was asked to cancel the assignment. She refused to do so, and found at the end of the spring that her contract for the following year was not renewed. She went to court, claiming that her constitutional liberties had been violated. The court found in favor of the school board, with some suggestion that

First Amendment activity was not centrally involved. The court of appeals, however, affirmed the decision solely on the ground that a probationary teacher simply had no "right" to continuing employment, and thus declined to reach the merits of the case. Thus the first opportunity to establish relevant precedent aborted on procedural grounds.

The next reported cases came in the late 1960s. Two judgments of the federal court of appeals for the first circuit have important factual similarities and should be considered together. The first involved a teacher named Keefe in Ipswich, Massachusetts, who gave his senior English class copies of an article in the current issue of the *Atlantic Monthly*. Written by the noted psychiatrist Robert Jay Lifton, the article discussed the mounting wave of student protest in the larger context of radicalism and revolt. Lifton used at one point the word "motherfucker" for illustrative purposes, and during discussion of the essay in class Keefe drew attention to that word. He also told the class that any student who found the assignment distasteful could choose an alternative. Apparently in response to parental protest, Keefe was summoned before the school committee and asked to defend his use of the word. He was also asked whether he would agree never to use that word again in class, but he declined to make such a commitment. He was then suspended, and his discharge was in prospect at the time he sought the aid of the federal courts.

Although the district court held for the school committee, the court of appeals reversed. The way in which the higher court posed the question anticipated its answer:

> The central issue of the case is whether a teacher may, for demonstrated educational purposes, quote a "dirty" word currently used in order to give special offense, or whether the shock is too great for high school seniors to stand. If the answer were that the students must be protected from such exposure, we would fear for their future. We do not question the good faith of the de-

fendants in believing that some parents have been offended. With the greatest of respect to such parents, their sensibilities are not the full measure of what is proper education.

The court then referred to the *Brave New World* case, which it found procedurally inapposite. Keefe's case was stronger for several reasons: The cited word was in fact available in at least five books in the school library; "it is hard to think that any student could walk into the library and receive a book, but that his teacher could not subject the content to serious discussion in class." While acknowledging the need for restraint in the classroom, "we find it difficult not to think that its application to the present case demeans any proper concept of education. The general chilling effect of permitting such rigorous censorship is even more serious."

It may be premature to ask whether the *Keefe* case really applied academic freedom to the high school classroom. There is partial support, however, for a positive answer: When the school committee argued that Keefe could be fully vindicated by seeking money damages, and that judges need therefore not intervene to protect his interests at an earlier stage, the court responded cryptically, "Academic freedom is not preserved by compulsory retirement, even at full pay." Yet other portions of the opinion stop short of a clear commitment to academic freedom for secondary teachers. And since the issue was resolved in the teacher's favor, the rationale may seem less important than the result.

The very next year, the same legal issue returned to bedevil the court of appeals in a factually different posture. Another Massachusetts high school English teacher had been dismissed for using a taboo word in class, and he too sought the aid of the federal courts. The circumstances were slightly different: The discussion revolved about a Jesse Stuart novel of life in rural Kentucky. The issue was the role of taboos in the school context, triggered by the discussion of sex-segregated seating in a rural one-room schoolhouse. The teacher, Roger Mailloux, suggested to the class that many taboos persist. He illustrated the point by writing on the board first the word "goo," which the students agreed was meaningless, and then the word "fuck," which the students recognized as meaningful but impolite. After one student offered a definition of the word, the discussion turned to other matters. Mailloux was, however, summoned to the principal's office and proceedings were set in motion which led to his dismissal. It was this personnel action which brought the dispute into the federal courts.

The district judge first thought the case was controlled by *Keefe*, and on that basis summarily ordered the teacher reinstated. The court of appeals sent the case back for a full hearing, warning that *Keefe* should not be read "to do away with what, to use an old-fashioned term, are considered the proprieties, or to give carte blanche in the name of academic freedom to conduct which can reasonably be deemed both offensive and unnecessary to the accomplishment of educational objectives."

Despite the caution, the district judge found again for Mailloux. Central to his thinking was evidence on several points: that the teaching method involved was relevant to the subject and to the students; that the approach was deemed by experts (for example, education professors from Harvard) to serve a serious educational purpose; that the teacher had acted in good faith; and that the general policies of the school district had not adequately warned him that such conduct would jeopardize his job. The case for at least a qualified academic freedom was persuasive in the senior high school literature class:

> The Constitution recognizes that freedom in order to foster open minds, creative imaginations, and adventurous spirits. Our national belief is that the heterodox as well as the orthodox are a source of individual and of social growth. We do not confine academic freedom to conventional teachers or to those who can get a majority vote from their colleagues. Our faith is that the teacher's free-

dom to choose among options for which there is any substantial support will increase his intellectual vitality and his moral strength. The teacher whose responsibility has been nourished by independence, enterprise, and free choice becomes for his student a better model of the democratic citizen. His examples of applying and adapting the values of the old order to the demands and opportunities of a constantly changing world are among the most important lessons he gives to youth.

On the other hand, the district judge was troubled by the context within which the case arose, and the uncertain relevance of the collegiate model:

> The secondary school more clearly than the college or university acts in loco parentis with respect to minors. It is closely governed by a school board selected by a local community. The faculty does not have the independent traditions, the broad discretion as to teaching methods, nor usually the intellectual qualifications, of university professors. Among secondary school teachers there are often many persons with little experience. Some teachers and most students have limited intellectual and emotional maturity. Most parents, students, school boards, and members of the community usually expect the secondary school to concentrate on transmitting basic information, teaching "the best that is known and thought in the world," training by established techniques, and, to some extent at least, indoctrinating in the mores of the surrounding society. While secondary schools are not rigid disciplinary institutions, neither are they open forums in which mature adults, already habituated to social restraints, exchange ideas on a level of parity.

These two conflicting themes had now to be resolved, and the district court relied heavily on the procedural fairness issue in doing so. The court of appeals affirmed a judgment in the teacher's favor, but solely on the procedural ground, agreeing that the school system's regulations failed to give proper warning. The appellate court restated its concern about the possible overreading of *Keefe*, warned that each case must be decided on its own facts, and confessed that "we are not of one mind as to whether [Mailloux's] conduct fell within the protection of the First Amendment." It was only the fair notice issue that resolved the case, leaving the substantive question open.

A 1974 case illustrates a similar ambivalence in another federal court of appeals. Three Illinois teachers were discharged for distributing to their classes a poem about the Woodstock rock festival. The poem contained some taboo words, and could be read as condoning or even encouraging drug use and sexual freedom. School officials focussed on such phrases as "A place to take acid," "grass smoked together," "bodies naked into the water, touching each other," and "we're a big fucking wave," among others. Copies of the brochure containing the poem were distributed in one teacher's eighth grade classes, and were displayed on the bulletin board in the classroom of another. When several students took the brochure home, parents complained, and the superintendent initiated the dismissal of the teachers. They promptly took to the federal court a claim of violation of constitutional rights.

The district judge ruled in favor of the school board, and a panel of the court of appeals (three judges out of eight) affirmed that decision. When the full court of appeals considered the case several months later, the eight judges were equally divided. Such a division has the effect of sustaining the lower court judgment, but without an opinion on either side. Thus the only opinions are those of the two judges in the majority and the one in dissent on the original hearing.

Despite some testimony that the brochure as a whole was "an admirable teaching tool," the facts of this case made it substantially different from the earlier cases in several respects. For one, the students were much younger—eighth-graders rather than seniors (in *Keefe*) or juniors (in *Mailloux*). Another obvious difference was the relationship between the suspect material and the teacher's regular assignments. One of the three plaintiffs was a French teacher, and little connection between the Woodstock festival and French could be claimed. Of the other two, one had just completed a study of the history of rock music and the other was exploring in class the construction of musical instruments; the relationship of the Woodstock brochure to these themes is a bit closer, but still tenuous. A third difference has to do with the nature and weight of the exculpatory evidence; in the earlier cases, teacher-plaintiffs brought forth substantial testimony either on the value of the material itself or on the validity of the teaching technique which provoked the controversy. Finally, there was in the Illinois case a lurking issue of illegality—the "admitted invitation," in the court's phrase, to the use of drugs in violation of state law. Without suggesting that any of the teachers could be criminally charged for circulating the brochure, the presence of the drug laws undoubtedly undermined the claim of academic freedom.

The case is still not an easy one, however. Four of the eight judges of the full court would have found in the teachers' favor, though we know the reasoning of only one (the dissenter on the original panel). An excerpt from that dissenting opinion may suggest the strength of the countervailing argument:

> Particularly where the school board has not formulated standards to guide him, academic freedom affords a teacher a certain latitude in judging whether material is relevant to his instruction. . . . These instructors did not exceed the bounds which germaneness places on protected classroom speech. . . . More importantly, however, the appropriateness of a particular classroom discussion cannot be gauged solely by its logical nexus to the subject matter of instruction. A teacher may be more successful with his students if he is able to relate to them in philosophy of life, and conversely, students may profit by learning something of a teacher's views on general subjects. Academic freedom entails the exchange of ideas which promote education in its broadest sense. [The dissenting judge then discussed the "fair notice" issue and argued that here, as in *Mailloux*, the teachers had not been adequately warned that such conduct could cost them their jobs.]

A later and consistent footnote to the Illinois case comes

from another federal appellate court. A fifth grade teacher in North Carolina had been demoted (to the position of tutor) because she had read to two of her classes a note found circulating among her students. The note contained several taboo words, which she stressed, but she apparently warned against their use in other inter-student communications. A parent complained of the incident, and the teacher was demoted after a hearing. Although the applicable school board rule forbade conduct no more precisely defined than "neglect of duty," the court of appeals felt the teacher had adequate warning that such language might jeopardize her position. The tender age of the students undoubtedly contributed to the result. There was also something in the way the offending language was used; a concurring judge remarked that the teacher "gave [the note] stature by reading it to the class and later rehearsing it before another class, each time accenting the vulgarities."

If John Fogarty (or his attorney) read these cases, he would surely share our confusion. Using "motherfucker" in a class discussion may be protected if the source is respectable and if the word is found in books already in the school library. On the other hand, writing the work "fuck" on the blackboard may not be protected, although the teacher may still win reinstatement on procedural grounds. And distributing a poem with drug and sex references and other taboos may or may not be protected, depending on which panel of the court of appeals happens to hear the case. Of course the law is not wholly without guidance; certain desiderata do begin to emerge—for example, the age and sophistication of the students; the relationship of the suspect language to the teacher's assigned tasks; the availability of those same words in the school library; and the "educational value" of the discussion or material (an issue on which the courts are apparently willing to receive expert testimony from professors of education).

It is also true that none of these decisions deals precisely with the issue in Fogarty's case—that is, the selection and assignment of literary works. Several other cases do come closer to that issue, and help to round out the discussion. We have already noted the inconclusive judgment in the *Brave New World* case, which might have given some early guidance. The next such case involved a Montgomery, Alabama, teacher named Parducci, who was dismissed for assigning Kurt Vonnegut's short story *Welcome to the Monkey House* to her eleventh grade English class. The principal and the associate superintendent called the teacher to account for the use of what they described as "literary garbage" which, in their view, promoted "the killing off of elderly people and free sex." The teacher brought suit in the federal court, asking both for reinstatement and for money damages.

The case happened to come before Judge Frank Johnson, President Carter's original nominee for FBI Director and the author of a number of major civil rights and civil liberties decisions. "That teachers are entitled to first amendment freedoms" he began, "is an issue no longer in dispute." While the legal status of academic freedom remained uncertain, "the Supreme Court has on numerous occasions emphasized that the right to teach, to inquire, to evaluate and to study is fundamental to a democratic society." The *Tinker* case, then recently decided, had obvious relevance to the classroom environment, and Judge Johnson quoted extensively from the majority opinion. Applying *Tinker* to curricular issues, a court must first decide whether the material in question "was inappropriate" reading for high school juniors. Despite the presence of taboo words and "vulgar terms," the assignment of the story could not be thought inappropriate when judged in a larger literary context:

> The slang words are contained in two short rhymes which are less ribald than those found in many of Shakespeare's plays. The reference in the story to an act of sexual intercourse is no more descriptive than the rape scene in Pope's "Rape of the Lock." As for the theme of the story, the Court notes that the anthology in which

the story was published was reviewed by several of the popular national weekly magazines, none of which found the subject matter of any of the stories to be offensive. It appears to the Court, moreover, that the author, rather than advocating the "killing off of old people," satirizes the practice to symbolize the increasing depersonalization of man in society.

The validity of the assignment on the basis of its content was reinforced by its effect within the classroom. The Supreme Court had indicated in *Tinker* that evidence of actual disruption of school activities would be necessary to restrict otherwise protected expression. In *Parducci*, the closest to "disruption" was the request of three students to be excused from the assignment; "there was no evidence that any of [the teacher's] other 87 students were planning to disrupt the normal routine of the school." Thus to the extent *Tinker* applied to the individual classroom case, there was simply not that threat of interference with the educational process or classroom decorum which would warrant restricting First Amendment freedoms.

There is some question how well the *Tinker* analysis fits this kind of case. To the extent that *Tinker* does provide the proper standard, there are obvious difficulties in measuring "disruption" by the number of students who ask to be excused from a particular assignment, or by the difficulty of offering them educationally sound alternatives. Commentators have criticized Judge Johnson's reliance on the *Tinker* standard for resolving curricular disputes —though accepting its relevance, for example, to the teacher's wearing in class of a black armband. But this concern need not detain us here. The *Tinker* side of the *Parducci* decision has not stood the test of time. The other branch of the opinion, that dealing with the "appropriateness" of the material to the students and to the course, is more durable and more useful; it roughly parallels the emphasis in the "taboo word" cases upon the "relevance" of the material to the teacher's assigned task or subject.

Several other cases decided during the 1970s add little. A federal district court in Iowa held, not surprisingly, that a drama teacher could not be discharged for allowing students to recite the words "damn" and "son of a bitch" in rehearsal of a play—although she had made them substitute "son of a biscuit" in the public performance. A federal judge in Texas ordered the reinstatement of a high school civics teacher who had been discharged for using somewhat controversial but professionally acceptable material dealing with race relations and antiwar protest, remarking that "a responsible teacher must have freedom to use the tools of his profession as he sees fit." One recent case reached a contrary result, upholding the dismissal of a Florida teacher whose discussion of prostitution and other "illegitimate" topics seemed to the court beyond the scope of constitutional protection of classroom freedom. The opinions in none of these cases added measurably to the understanding of the legal issues, and for that reason a brief summary here should suffice.

Through the course of these decisions, two elements have gone almost unnoticed. Little attention has been given to the educational purposes of the course and of the broader curriculum, or to the issue of governance—the level at which or authority by which vital decisions are made in the public school system. It remained for a 1978 case to draw first critical attention to those issues.

The case involved a school district in a Denver suburb. Early in 1976 the school board issued a directive that ten titles—works of "beat" poets like Allen Ginsberg and Lawrence Ferlinghetti, and novels dealing with the supernatural—could no longer be used in junior and senior courses in contemporary literature. At the same time the board approved 1,275 other titles. The next day a further directive explained that the ten proscribed works "will not be purchased, nor used for class assignment, nor will an individual be given credit for reading any of the books." It appeared that even reading aloud or causing to be read aloud any of the ten books, or discussing any of them in class, would violate the board's order. None of the works on the proscribed list was legally obscene.

A group of teachers brought suit in the federal district court, claiming that the board's order abridged their free expression and their academic freedom. The court was troubled by this argument at the outset: "the logical extension of plaintiffs' contention is that they can teach without accountability to their employer." On the other hand, the court was also troubled by the board's claim of unfettered authority to direct the teachers' activities: "The logical extension of [this contention] is that they have the power to cause teachers to teach from a prepared script." Nor did the court find the earlier teacher cases especially helpful; *Keefe* and *Parducci* had but "limited value" here for two reasons: "First, the existence of the constitutional right of academic freedom in the high school context is not self-evident." Second, "the courts must not assume the role of arbiters of the appropriateness of material for use in a classroom"—and that was about as far as the earlier cases had gone. A more basic issue of governance—the extent to which the Constitution imposes limits on the locus of curricular decisions—posed the central task of the court in such a case. Having defined the issue in this way, the court recognized that curriculum and instruction in the *elementary* schools should be shaped by persons directly responsible to the community. At the *secondary* level, however, the court was troubled by the implications of full community control of curricular content:

That view is the essence of tyranny, because it imposes a collectivist control on the individual's thoughts and actions. The tyranny of the majority is as contrary to the fundamental principles of the Constitution as the authoritarianism of an autocracy. Consider the possibility that the plurality in a given community may decidedly differ from the national majoritarian principles. What would be the reaction to a school board's decision to teach nothing but Maoism in the public schools? Can there be any teacher dissent to that societal value if it is representative of the plurality of the voting electorate in a given school district?

Apart from the level of instruction, the nature of the course was relevant to the degree of school board control. While many subjects, even at the high school level, properly fell within the "implantation or indoctrination stage," others were by their nature less readily subject to administrative domination. The fact that the board itself had declared the senior literature course an elective argued strongly for constitutional protection. Finally, and most significantly, the court distinguished those tasks and responsibilities of a teacher which were regulable on the "employer-employee model": taking attendance, getting students to assembly, coming promptly to class, and performing myriad other extracurricular and co-curricular tasks. There was, however, a core of *intellectual* activity which could be restricted only to the extent it was "inconsistent with or counterproductive to the objective of producing effective citizens" or to the extent it breached the bounds of "professional responsibility." (Here the judge cited as an example a recent unreported case in which he had upheld the discharge of a teacher who "turned an innovative graffiti exercise into a verbal attack upon the junior high school principal.")

The activity involved in the present case was precisely the kind which the Constitution protects: "The selection of the subject books as material for these elective courses in these grades is clearly within the protected area recognized as academic freedom." The board's decree was the "kind of broad prior restraint which is particularly offensive to First Amendment freedoms." On this basis, one would naturally suppose that the teachers won their case—and so they would have, but for one final ironic twist on the basis of which the court ruled against them. During collective bargaining the previous year, there had been discussion of a possible "academic freedom" provision in the contract between the board and the union, under which the Teachers Advisory Council would have final authority on the selection of instructional material. That draft provision was eventually replaced by the declaration that "the final responsibility in the determination of [issues of academic freedom] rests with the Board." Under this clause, the court now held that the teachers had bargained away their First Amendment rights, including an otherwise clear primacy in the selection of materials for the literature course. Since the teachers had voted for an exclusive bargaining agent, and were thus bound by the contract, "they may not now seek to avoid it by calling upon a constitutional freedom to act independently and individually."

On the final point, the Colorado case seems quite at variance with Supreme Court precedent. Many years ago the Court held that white workers and unions they controlled could not bargain away the interests of black members of the employment unit. More recently, the same principle has been applied to First Amendment rights as well, the Court holding that a dissident teacher could not be prevented from speaking out at a school board meeting on an issue which was then under discussion at the bargaining table. Thus the final point of the case is probably erroneous as well as ironic. The major premise of the decision is, however, its analysis of the restriction imposed on the text selection process, and the striking conclusion that *some* secondary teachers enjoy academic freedom with regard to *some* judgments in *some* courses.

The court was careful to qualify the holding in several respects, not only in the grade level and the type of course to which it applied, but also in the activity which was in dispute. Had the same teachers failed to maintain discipline or refused to take attendance—or perhaps even allowed their students to read fewer than a prescribed number of novels—the case would almost surely have fallen on the other side of the line. Change any of the critical factors, this court warned, and the outcome would no longer be certain; that, surely, is the meaning of the reference to a teacher's use of graffiti to lampoon the junior high principal in front of his students.

The court of appeals reversed on both issues. After holding —quite properly in light of labor law precedents—that union members could not bargain away their First Amendment rights, the court turned to the substantive issue which the district judge had resolved in the teachers' favor. The central issue was which of two groups—the school board or the teachers—had ultimate authority to choose textbooks. Since the board could decide whether or not to offer the course, and could select a major text-book, then why (the court asked) "may it not go further and exclude certain books from being assigned for instruction in the course?" The board had in fact approved a very long list of per-missible texts, and had proscribed only the ten titles which lead to the suit. Moreover, the board's rule did not forbid mention of the ten books in class, nor their citation as examples of con-temporary literature, but only their formal assignment. Under these conditions the appellate court concluded that such a ban lay within the powers of the school board and did not abridge the First Amendment freedoms of the teachers.

The *Cary* (Colorado) case represents a significant refinement of earlier precedents. In place of the monotonous focus on "rele-vance" and "disruption," other criteria now entered the picture. Two absolutely central issues have begun to receive proper atten-tion—one relating to the governance of education and the alloca-tion of decisional authority or responsibility, the other focussing on purpose or nature of the educational experience.

The question of who may decide what issues is surely cen-tral to such cases, and should have received attention in the courts much earlier, as Goldstein and others have argued. Per-haps the issue has been blurred because the earlier cases involved a single (admittedly familiar) model: the community protests the use of certain material, the board or administration orders it removed from the curriculum, and a teacher protests. In such a case it may be unnecessary to separate the governance issue—who may decide—from the substantive issue of what is being decided. But consider one other case which involves a quite different model. In the spring of 1972 a teacher in northern Ohio bought for and gave to her ninth grade English students new paperback copies of Edgar Lee Masters's *Spoon River Anthology*. The students soon discovered that two pairs of facing pages had been neatly removed from the anthologies. When they asked the teacher for an explanation, she told them that she had decided that certain poems were "inappropriate" and that their language might be offensive to some. (She made no attempt to tamper with copies which some students had bought on their own.)

Several students, with the aid of the Ohio Civil Liberties Union, brought suit against the district and the principal for having approved the deletion. The federal judge was perplexed by this novel issue, and cast about for helpful analogies. There was, he recognized, no issue of obscenity, since the reason given for deleting the questionable pages was the general subject matter rather than the impact of particular words. None of the familiar precedents seemed to fit. *Tinker* was inapposite because the students in this case "were not refused permission to express an opinion. . . ." The teacher cases (*Keefe, Parducci,* and *Mailloux*) were also distinguishable because there "the stifled party is a teacher," and here the teacher was doing the stifling to the displeasure of the students: "What a teacher chooses to teach is not equivalent to what a student decides to learn." Finally, the court rejected a claim which would have given the students their strongest support—the right to receive information, which at the time of the decision (1974) was far less well developed than it has now become. Since there was no constitutional basis on which to challenge the teacher's action, the students were left with only a tort claim—unconsented destruction of their property (since the books had been bought with money they gave to the teacher). The case was then dismissed because the federal courts lack jurisdiction over such nonconstitutional issues.

The *Spoon River* case squarely raises the governance issue. Suppose, for example, the teacher had been discharged (under pressure from a group of liberal parents) for engaging in an act of censorship, and brought suit for reinstatement. A court would then face the issue that has been conveniently avoided in the earlier cases—whether the critical question is *who does the act* complained of (teacher, administration, or board), or whether instead the critical issue is the act itself (excising non-obscene material from an anthology). If, for example, a court felt that a teacher could not be dismissed for *refusing* to remove the suspect pages, because that would constitute censorship of the *Keefe-Parducci* sort, it might also hold that the teacher could no more readily deprive the students of access to those pages on her own initiative. Conversely, the court might well say that the teacher may "edit" the book even though the principal may not force her to do so. Such a decision would say, in effect, that a decision to delete the pages is within the scope of the teacher's academic freedom, even though it denies students access to constitutionally protected material and even though the board could not have forced the teacher to delete that material.

The difference between the two foci—who decides and what is decided—emerges from this *Spoon River* variation. If removing these pages is something that *no one* may do, then the teacher would fare no better than the board. Indeed, if one believes (as Goldstein appears to) that curricular judgments are essentially administrative, then the teacher might fare even less well than the board. If, on the other hand, one differentiates according to the locus of the decision—as the federal judge in the *Cary* case did—the outcome may well depend on the identity of the actor as well as the action taken. One might conclude that the board may not remove the pages—nor may it compel a teacher to do so—but that a teacher may do so on her own. (In the actual *Spoon River* case, of course, the board and the administration approved what the teacher did, so this issue did not arise. But in the event of disagreement over such "editing" of materials, a court would have to decide whether such action is within the teacher's academic freedom, or whether it is permissible neither to teacher nor to administration. The source or level of the action—the lurking governance issue—becomes central under such circumstances.)

Apart from the focus on governance, *Cary* also brought to the fore the issue of educational mission or purpose. Earlier cases, notably *Parducci*, did consider such matters as the "appropriateness" of challenged material in the school setting, or the relationship of classroom discussion and its content to the works in the school library. But *Cary* posed a more basic inquiry: the nature of the course or part of the curriculum in which the controversy arose. To the *Cary* court a persuasive datum in the teachers' favor was the board's own listing of the course as a senior elective—thus implying its own view that orthodoxy should be minimized and freedom of choice should be encouraged. For the board to restrict the teacher's freedom of choice after encouraging student freedom of choice would be as inconsistent as forbidding a teacher to discuss in class words found widely in books available at the school library. If the school board decided no longer to offer an advanced elective course in contemporary literature, that would be a different matter; but so long as the course was available to college-bound seniors who opted for an enriching experience, restrictions of the kind imposed in the *Cary* case were simply unsuited to the educational goals declared by the very authority which imposed the restrictions. Freedom of choice could be curtailed, to be sure, by simply discontinuing the course (and precisely that step has in fact been taken by other communities seeking to stifle controversy in the classroom). But so long as the elective curriculum remains intact, its effectiveness cannot be undermined by winnowing out particular titles.

Such a conclusion is comforting, and helps to accommodate the conflicting pressures with which we began. Academic freedom in the high school classroom clearly is not absolute. Its scope, in fact, is to some degree subject to the judgment of the school board and the administration. It is the elected and appointed officials who shape the curriculum and decide in broad terms what shall be taught. If a district chooses to offer only basic required subjects, teachers in that district will enjoy precious little freedom of expression—save in those areas where the speech of any public employee may not be curtailed. If, on the other hand, school authorities (presumably in response to parental as well as student pressure) decide to enrich the curriculum and to offer advanced courses in literature, drama, government, or economics, they must accept the consequences. A principal effect is that teachers hired to offer these courses enjoy a degree of academic freedom that is properly denied to their colleagues who teach manual arts, typing, and basic grammar. Thus the school board can vary to some extent the scope of academic freedom available within the system—not by silencing a particular teacher because it dislikes the words he writes on the blackboard or the novels he selects, but rather by reshaping the curriculum. If school officials, for whatever reason, will not tolerate the liberties essential to an open curriculum, the remedy available to them is a comprehensive rather than a selective one.

Let us by way of conclusion return to the case of Mr. Fogarty. The argument for his reinstatement seems a compelling one. The level of the course and of the students in it, and the policy of the school board itself with regard to the course, suggest a broad measure of discretion in the selection of texts. Putting aside the question whether a legally obscene work could be assigned, or one that invited students to violence, the choice of *Cuckoo's Nest* seems eminently supportable.

7

LIBRARIES, LIBRARIANS, AND CENSORSHIP

THE REMOVAL OF "objectionable" books from school libraries is probably at least as common as the restriction of classroom materials. The sequence of events in the Chelsea, Massachusetts, poetry anthology case is fairly common: A parent happens to read a passage in a book which a student brings home from the school library, and finds the language or the ideas offensive. The parent protests to the principal, who then directs the librarian to remove the book or place it on a "restricted" shelf. Usually the process ends there. The Chelsea case is one of very few ever to reach the courts.

Several factors make library censorship more elusive than the suppression of classroom discussion. Initially, the constitutional issue is not easy to frame. The First Amendment says that government may make no law abridging freedom of speech or of the press. There are profound differences between the familiar forms of censorship with which the framers of the Bill of Rights were concerned and the removal of a single volume from a large library collection. In fact, books are taken out of circulation frequently and for myriad reasons—because they are obsolete, or the bindings are frayed or the pages torn, or student interests or teacher assignments change, or space is more urgently needed for other materials. Most decisions to withdraw books from libraries do no violence to the First Amendment, a fact which makes more difficult the framing of the constitutional issue in cases of genuine censorship.

Moreover, the particular book might well never have been on the shelf in the first place. If the space or budget were smaller, or if a publisher's notice had not caught the librarian's eye, or if a teacher had not suggested the particular work, the acquisition might never had been made and the problem would never have existed. If one is to say that the removal of an objectionable work is unlawful, does this mean that the failure to acquire the same work would also be suspect? Are libraries constitutionally compelled to acquire all books the removal of which would be unlawful? Surely the argument cannot be pressed this far; the framing of the legal issue is for this reason doubly complicated.

Second, there are many different ways in which access to a suspect volume may be limited. The librarian may set aside a special shelf to which student access is restricted. Parental consent or approval may be required for the circulation of certain works. Access may be confined to students in a particular course where the work will be analyzed in class and not read casually. A school board member may simply check out all copies of the work and refuse to return them, making sure that no funds are committed to replacement. Some such restrictions on access are clearly more offensive than others, yet all such actions limit the ability of students to obtain a particular volume. The variety of sanctions does, however, complicate the analysis.

Third, there is a threshold question of *whose* constitutional rights are implicated. Presumably in such a case the aggrieved party is either the student or the librarian. If we focus on the student for a moment, the difficulty is clear: Either the student has the approval of a parent, or does not. If the parent does approve, then presumably the book could be bought from a bookstore or borrowed from the public library. If the parent disapproves, does the school librarian have any business defying parental wishes by making the book available—especially if the principal (who acts *in loco parentis* for such purposes) also disapproves?

The other set of constitutional interests would be those of the librarian. Surely the librarian's *own* access to the work is not restricted by a ban on its circulation. One could argue that the librarian has a duty to make available to patrons any materials that are not unlawful—but that argument might suggest that all such works must be acquired as well as circulated once they are in the collection. Another possible basis of the librarian's rights would be that the process of acquisition, cataloguing, and circulation represents an exercise of First Amendment rights—much like the teacher's selection of and assignment of texts, a function which courts held protected in several cases we considered in the previous chapter. Either theory would represent a novel addition to First Amendment law, but both deserve careful consideration.

These analytical problems would not, by themselves, explain the scarcity of cases defining the rights of libraries and librarians. Several practical elements also account for the infrequency with which librarians (or patrons) litigate their grievances. Librarians as a profession are in the worst possible position to assert their rights through the courts. On one hand, they lack the major economic stake that has triggered most of the major test cases in the First Amendment area; unlike movie producers and distributors, newspaper and magazine publishers, theatrical impresarios, book publishers, and others who have financed the litigation of free speech and free press claims, librarians simply cannot afford test cases as part of a commerical operation. Nor are the libraries in which they work likely to support such suits, as newspaper owners will often do for reporters threatened with subpoenas; in fact, the library board may well be the censor. On the other hand, librarians are unable to claim the benefits of the various legal service programs that have mounted many test cases on behalf of the legal rights of oppressed groups. Though generally underpaid, librarians are not indigent and thus are not eligible for such programs. Even the national civil liberties groups that have pushed for expansion of constitutional rights have been relatively slow to notice the librarian's plight. Thus the librarian is too poor to support his or her own test case, but usually not poor enough to have the costs borne by others.

In fact, the traditionally passive nature of the library profession may in part have kept its members from seeking legal support. Unlike school teachers and other groups that have been effectively organized for the mutual defense of economic and legal interests, librarians have historically been reluctant to press for redress of grievances. When the American Library Association in 1973 filed its first *amicus curiae* brief in the Supreme Court, seeking a rehearing of an obscenity decision, the *New York Times* observed editorially:

> Professional librarians as a group are hardly known as flaming radicals. As civil servants they find themselves in the delicate position of being the guardians of much that is necessarily controversial, while their place on the totem pole of authority gives them very little power to defend their professional opinions and their personal security.

The editorial closed by observing that the Library Association's plea for a rehearing "represents an expert judgment based on experience at the firing line." This foray into the legal area marked a new departure for the organized library profession, and one that has begun to reshape not only the profession's image but its legal status as well.

The inclination of librarians to capitulate rather than litigate may reveal a reluctance of another sort. One suspects that librarians are uneasy about being exposed to public scrutiny as a test case plaintiff must be. Since most controversial works are somehow suspect in the public mind—whatever their literary merits—advocacy of their free circulation may entail certain risks. No one likes to be identified in the press as a purveyor of smut, although if he makes his living by publishing salacious magazines or selling "confidential" paperbacks, the risk is at least a calculated one. But for the librarian such a public posture is uncomfortable at best, and at worst may risk grave jeopardy to reputation and to employment prospects in conservative communities.

Thus the combination of legal uncertainties and practical difficulties may largely explain why relatively few acts of library censorship ever reach the courts, and why no well-developed body of "library law" yet exists. There are, to be sure, cases involving libraries and librarians—for example, the 1965 Supreme Court decision about a racial sit-in at a Louisiana public library, or the several federal appellate decisions involving personnel claims of dismissed librarians. But none of these cases addresses at all the issue with which we are concerned: the constitutional aspects of removal of books from a library collection. In fact, until 1972, there were no decisions whatever on that issue. There are now eight, and they form the corpus of "library law" as we know it today.

The first of the cases arose in a Queens, New York, school district about 1970. Public attention had focussed on Piri Thomas's *Down These Mean Streets*, a graphic account of contemporary life in Spanish Harlem. The school board ordered that the book be limited to parents of children in the school and denied to students themselves. A group of parents and teachers brought a suit in the federal court, asking that the volume be returned to general circulation. The district court dismissed the case, finding no constitutional violation, and the court of appeals affirmed.

The appellate court gave rather short shrift to the constitutional issues. This paragraph contains the essense of the decision:

The administration of any library, whether it be a university or particularly a public junior high school, involves a constant process of selection and winnowing based not only on educational needs but financial and architectural realities. To suggest that the shelving or unshelving of a book presents a constitutional issue, particularly where there is no showing of a curtailment of freedom of speech or thought, is a proposition we cannot accept.

Several factors apparently helped the court to reach this conclusion: No teacher or librarian had been dismissed or even punished; no restriction had been placed on discussion of the book in class; the book was generally available in the community, being currently sold in paperback in many book stores; and the decision had been made after public debate by a school board which apparently reflected the strong desires of the community which supported the school system.

A key to this decision has been offered by Professor Loftus Becker of the University of Connecticut:

[The court] noted that somebody, sometime, had to make decisions about what books should be retained in public school libraries. It said that there would be nothing improper about a decision, for instance, to remove from the school library all books arguing that the earth was flat. Therefore, the court reasoned, there was nothing improper in removing this particular book about life in Spanish Harlem. In other words, having decided that the school board could properly remove *some* books, the court concluded that the school board could properly remove *any* books.

Before we turn to the next case, we might probe further a central premise of the Queens case: that the general availability of the book in the community undermines the plaintiffs' constitutional claim of access. The argument certainly has a superficial appeal; if the basis for a First Amendment claim is the right to read, presumably students are not denied that right because they must ask their parents to buy the book or check it out of the public library. There are, however, at least two answers. First, the school library is the most appropriate channel for students in the school. Some students may be unable to afford to buy the book, even if it is generally available in paperback. Surely they cannot afford to buy *all* the books they might like to check out from the school library, and a decision that one book can be removed means that others may also be restricted. The public library, even if it has the book right at hand, is surely a less convenient source for the student who first inquires at school. Thus the theoretical existence of alternatives does not always offer as broad a practical range of choice.

There is a better and more basic answer. A denial of constitutional right cannot be excused because alternative channels are available—any more than some public schools in a community may remain segregated simply because other schools are integrated. Several years ago the Supreme Court faced a similar question in the dispute over denial of the use of a city auditorium for performance of *Hair*, the rock musical. The city pointed out that several private theaters would be happy to accommodate *Hair*, and for that reason argued that no constitutional objection could be made to the city's prohibition. The Supreme Court found the availability of private alternatives to be legally irrelevant: " '[O]ne is not to have the exercise of his liberty of expression in appropriate places abridged on the plea that it may be exercised in some other place.' " If this reasoning applies to rock musicals, then it should apply at least equally to library books.

This point can be made in a slightly different way: If the school board has violated the First Amendment rights of students, librarians, or teachers, that violation will not be excused because the rights are not totally suppressed. Thus if the removal of *Down These Mean Streets* from the library of one school is unconstitutional, it matters not that the same book is available in other libraries in the community of the school system.

The next case arose several years later in a rather similar

way. During the summer of 1972 the school board of Strongsville, Ohio, resolved to remove and destroy existing copies (and
to buy no further copies) of two novels, Joseph Heller's *Catch
22* and Kurt Vonnegut's *Cat's Cradle*. The reasons for the action
were reflected in the minutes of a school board meeting at which
several members stated forcefully their displeasure with the language and content of both works. In place of the banned books,
the libraries were directed to buy copies of a biography of Her-
bert Hoover and the reminiscences of General Douglas Mac-
Arthur. The board also urged that the ancient McGuffey Readers
be revived as supplemental texts, "since they seem to offer so
many advantages in vocabulary, content and sentence structure
to the drivel being pushed today."

Soon after the school board's action, five students brought
suit seeking the return of the banned books. The district court
dismissed the complaint on the basis of the Queens decision.
The court of appeals to which the case then came acknowledged
that general authority to select books for school libraries and
classrooms resided with the school board. The court also recognized that a school library must engage in the sort of "winnowing" to which the earlier case referred: "Of course a copy of a
book may wear out. Some books may become obsolete. Shelf
space alone may require some selection of books to be retained
and books to be disposed of." But the burden was on the school
board to show a legally defensible and constitutionally valid
reason for withdrawing a book. In this case there was no such
reason, the record showing only the clear distaste of the Strongsville board members for Heller's and Vonnegut's language and
views of life.

The court's conclusion followed directly: While the state
and the school district were under no legal duty to provide a
library, much less to acquire a particular novel, "once having
created such a privilege for the benefit of its students . . . neither
body could place conditions on the use of the library which were

related solely to the social or political tastes of school board members." Removal of books on such grounds was, in this court's view, analogous to other kinds of censorship which the Supreme Court had forbidden in more familiar contexts.

Two additional points reinforced the decision. The court of appeals in the Strongsville case gave central emphasis to the educational function of the school library:

> A public school library is also a valuable adjunct to classroom discussion. If one of the English teachers considered Joseph Heller's *Catch 22* to be one of the more important modern American novels (as, indeed, at least one did), we assume that no one would dispute that the First Amendment's protection of academic freedom would protect both his right to say so in class and his students' right to hear him and find and read the book. Obviously, the students' success in this last endeavor would be greatly hindered by the fact that the book sought had been removed from the school library. The removal of books from a school library is a much more serious burden on freedom of classroom discussion than the [prohibition on the wearing of black armbands found unconstitutional in the *Tinker* case].

The Strongsville court also rejected the "alternatives" argument which the Queens court had implicitly accepted: "Restraint on expression may not generally be justified by the fact that there may be other times, places, or circumstances available for such expression." Thus the ready accessibility of both novels in public libraries and book stores had no legal bearing on the constitutional claim of the Strongsville high school students.

It is not easy to reconcile these two federal court of appeals judgments. One marginally persuasive distinction might be offered: Even though the circumstances revealed content-based objections in both cases, the court in the Queens case did not wish to explore the matter of motive. Whatever may have been said at the crucial school board meeting, the court would *presume* a content-neutral basis for the action—treating the new copy of *Down These Mean Streets* essentially like the tattered

Grimm's Fairy Tales which is consigned to the recycling center. The Strongsville court's handling of the motive issue was, of course, radically different: *Only* where a school board could demonstrate a legally valid reason would censorship *not* be found. Thus even a decision to discard a little-used book in good condition or a popular but well-worn work could be the subject of legal challenge; if the librarian had failed to record noncontent considerations, the action might be legally vulnerable. As a practical matter, such actions would be unlikely ever to get to court, since parents and students seldom feel aggrieved by the normal winnowing process. Moreover, despite the implication that any but the most innocuous book removal would be constitutionally suspect, the Strongsville court probably meant to limit its holding to a case in which there was substantial evidence of content censorship.

One other factor may help to explain, if not reconcile, the contrasting result in these two cases. In the several years between the two decisions, the Supreme Court gave explicit recognition to an emerging doctrine: the First Amendment right to receive information. By the early 1970s there were suggestions of a nascent claim of access—a postal regulation case, several decisions recognizing the interests of listeners and viewers in the broadcasting area, some lower court cases involving college and university speaker bans, and mounting judicial scrutiny of censorship of prisoners' mail. Just about the time the Queens case was decided, the Supreme Court acknowledged the importance of "a First Amendment right to receive information and ideas" and observed that "freedom of speech necessarily protects the right to receive." The development of the reader's or listener's rights reached full flower in several cases in the mid 1970s dealing with the constitutional status of commercial advertising. Several decades earlier the Court had, without explanation, held that advertising was beyond the protection of the First Amendment. Now that view was questioned and finally repudiated. But the Court seemed reluctant to elevate the advertiser to the full constitutional status of the noncommercial speaker, author, or publisher, and thus used as a "bridge" the rights of would-be readers and listeners. By the time of the Strongsville case, therefore, a new constitutional basis for the student's claim existed, and could be invoked with a conviction that would have been unwarranted four years earlier.

Against this rather mixed background, we move to the third and most recent of the cases. As we observed in chapter one, the Chelsea case had origins quite similar to those of the other two: A student checked the anthology out of the library; a parent was disturbed by a particular poem, and complained to school authorities. The issue quickly became a cause célèbre because the school board chairman was also the publisher of the local newspaper and used that medium to share his literary views with the community. A federal court suit was filed by a consortium of concerned persons—three students and their parents, the librarian who had been ordered to remove the book, two English teachers, and the Massachusetts Library Association. Shortly after the suit was brought, the court ordered the school board to take no action against the librarian or the teachers, and to return the book, without deletions, for the use of any student presenting a written permission slip from a parent or guardian.

After extensive testimony, the district judge rendered a decision in the summer of 1978. This time there was little doubt about the reasons for the removal. The school board chairman had used the pages of his own newspaper to make clear that the content of the poem was the sole basis for the removal decision. (Indeed, after the suit was filed, the editorial pages of the newspaper inveighed against the prospect of judicial intervention, and warned that the federal court "cannot be allowed to intimidate the Committee from doing what has to be done to root out all the 'filthy' literature that is being circulated in the High

School under the guise of 'education.' ") Any suggestion of a neutral basis for the ban would be implausible; not only was there no claim that so recent and timely a work was obsolete but the small space it took on the shelf could hardly have been needed for other materials. Thus the record left no doubt that the sole reason for the removal of the book was the subjective judgment of the school board that its "theme and language [were] offensive."

This was a judgment which the school committee could not make. Only a substantial and legitimate governmental interest would allow school authorities to abridge First Amendment freedoms—whether the issue was symbolic speech by students, classroom discussion by teachers, or removal of books by librarians. "The Committee," observed the court,

> claims an absolute right to remove [the offending poem] from the shelves of the school library. It has no such right, and compelling policy considerations argue against any public authority having such an unreviewable power of censorship. There is more at issue here than the poem "City." If this work may be removed by a committee hostile to its language and theme, then the precedent is set for removal of any other work. The prospect of sanitizing the school library of views divergent from their own is alarming, whether they do it book by book or one page at a time.

Finally, the district judge spoke eloquently of the role of the library in the total educational process:

> The library is a "mighty resource in the marketplace of ideas." . . . There a student can literally explore the unknown, and discover areas of interest and thought not covered by the prescribed curriculum. The student who discovers the magic of the library is on the way to a life-long experience of self-education and enrichment. That student learns that a library is a place to test or expand upon ideas presented to him, in or out of the classroom.
> The most effective antidote to the poison of mindless orthodoxy is ready access to a broad sweep of ideas and philosophies.

There is no danger in such exposure. . . .

What is at stake here is the right to read and be exposed to controversial thoughts and language—a valuable right subject to First Amendment protection.

The Chelsea holding received strong support from another federal district court about a year later. The Nashua (New Hampshire) School Board had ordered certain copies of *Ms.* magazine removed from the senior high school library. There was no doubt from the public discussions that some board members did not like the contents of the magazine (for example, articles about lesbianism and witchcraft) and had forced their views on the librarian. A group of parents, students, and a teacher went to court to challenge the removal. After hearing extensive testimony, the federal court held the removal unlawful. The objections of the board members seemed to the court to have much more to do with the "political" content of *Ms.* magazine than with anything "sexual." Moreover, the magazines were clearly not "obscene" in the legal sense of that term. Because of the clearly content-based removal, only the restoration of the issues in question would suffice. But the court later amended its decree to assure the school board that they need not subscribe to *Ms.* in perpetuity, but need only replace the copies that had been removed and complete the current subscription.

Just as the law seemed to be moving toward a clear consensus for freedom of access, another federal judge struck a dissonant note. The school board of Island Trees, New York, had ordered that eleven books be removed from the high school library. A coalition not unlike that in Chelsea and Nashua brought the issue before the federal court, claiming a denial of constitutionally protected liberties of expression. In August 1979, almost four years after the removal order, the court ruled in the school board's favor. Since the case arose in New York, the judge felt constrained by the Queens decision, which was still binding in his circuit even though it had been sharply questioned in two other federal regions. But the Island Trees court did not rely exclusively on the earlier precedent. Even if it were free to follow Strongsville or Chelsea, it would have declined to do so—mainly because it felt that decisions about the acquisition or removal of library materials inevitably reflect the content of those materials and could not always be subject to judicial review. If (as the other judges had recently held) "a federal court must guard a book against *removal* because of its content, then how could the same court avoid passing upon a school board's content-based refusal of a student's request to *acquire* a particular book when the funds were available?" In response, the district court now suggested that the judiciary "simply is not competent to decide what books are to be in a school's library" and that "the proper agency is the school board. . . ." Thus the Island Trees court found no constitutional basis for intervention, even though (unlike Queens) objectionable but not legally obscene content had clearly prompted the removal order.

There has been one other recent reversal. A district judge in Vermont (which is in the same federal circuit as New York, and is also governed by the Queens decision) upheld the action of a school board in the small town of Vergennes, which had removed several titles from the high school library and forbade the librarian to buy additional works of fiction without approval of the administration and the board. This action was challenged by a group of parents, students, and a librarian. The judge rejected the students' claims—which represented the major thrust of the suit—because he felt bound by the Queens decision, even though he acknowledged that other courts had taken a more benign view of library freedoms in the intervening years. The judge's lack of enthusiasm for the constitutional issue emerged at several points in the opinion. "Students remain free," he observed, "to purchase the books in question from private bookstores, to read them in other libraries, to carry them to school

and to discuss them freely during the school day." Thus, he concluded, First Amendment rights had not been abridged—despite
the Supreme Court's consistent protection of the plaintiff's chos-
en time and place for asserting freedoms of expression.

In the fall of 1980 the federal appellate court spoke with a
rather mixed voice. A divided panel reversed the Island Trees
decision, and directed the trial court to probe the factual allegations more fully. A sufficient claim of infringement of First
Amendment freedoms had been made, said the majority, to require further inquiry at the district court level. The complaint
of the Island Trees students and parents revealed "an unusual
and irregular intervention in the school libraries' operations by
persons not routinely concerned with their contents." The concurring judge recognized unequivocally that "the use of governmental power to condemn a book touches the central nervous
system of the First Amendment." This disposition does not settle
the case, but leaves important issues open for further exploration
on remand. Meanwhile, the appellate court on the same day
affirmed rather summarily the contrasting decision in the Vermont case, finding there a less compelling claim of First Amendment infringement.

Through the Strongsville, Chelsea, and Nashua decisions
runs the constitutional claim of access—the patron's right to receive information from the library. In Strongsville, there was no
occasion to consider the possible interest of librarians because
the plaintiffs were all students. In Chelsea, a librarian was among
the plaintiffs, but the court found the students' interests sufficient to settle the case. It is not hard to imagine, however, a case
in which there are no student plaintiffs—or where, for some
technical reason (such as the postponement of decision until
after the students' graduation) a court would need to consider
the librarian's claims. The constitutional basis of those claims
should now be considered, even though the courts have not yet
reached this issue.

The interest of the patron is relatively familiar in First Amendment terms. Many constitutional cases have considered claims of access to information, and the lawfulness of government policies which deny or restrict such access. But the claim of the librarian is quite different, and calls for a new approach. Some of the differences are fairly obvious.

The whole thrust of the First Amendment has been to get government out of the business of judging the content of protected expression. Clearly the First Amendment forbids public officers and bodies from imposing personal and subjective literary standards upon the content of libraries or classrooms. Yet the whole process of buying and shelving books for libraries involves precisely such a process; *Male and Female* would not have been in the Chelsea high school library at all if the librarian had not found it worthy of a place on the shelves. A paradox thus emerges: If the courts are to recognize a constitutional interest in the librarian, apart from the interests of patrons, they must explain why one person's content judgments about books are to be protected from another person's interference.

In part because of the difficulty of deciding that question in the librarian's favor, we should look further. One basis for the librarian's claim comes from the rights of persons who seek access to materials which the librarian has been ordered to restrict or withhold. A persuasive case can be made that the librarian serves as a facilitator for the free expression of others—the channel by which an author (or publisher) reaches a vast body of readers who cannot buy the book. If librarians are not free to make untrammeled judgments about the acquisition and circulation of controversial materials, then the First Amendment freedoms *both* of authors and of readers may suffer. This point contributed measurably to the conclusion in the Strongsville case—that a reader cannot read and a teacher cannot teach if the material is not freely available in the library.

The argument needs to be developed a bit more fully. First,

it seems clear that a librarian cannot be required to violate the constitutional rights of readers by withholding materials to which the First Amendment ensures them access. The California Supreme Court has held that a social worker may not be compelled to violate the privacy rights of his clients by conducting unannounced predawn raids. In other settings it seems clear that the public employee may not be forced to choose between losing his job and violating the rights of others. The same principle should apply no less to the librarian faced with a threat or demand to abridge a patron's right to read. Quite apart from the broad constitutional principle, there is a practical risk of civil liability for depriving the patron of his rights. Surely, then, the desire to respect the First Amendment interests of persons whom he serves should protect the librarian against reprisal. If the right to read enjoys the constitutional status we have suggested it should, the librarian is surely a most appropriate (if indirect) beneficiary.

This constitutional claim is, however, a derivative one. The question remains whether the librarian enjoys personal First Amendment rights. Although no court has so held, it would be surprising if the sensitive intellectual work of the librarian could not claim constitutional protection. Yet here again we must reason by analogy.

The most obvious and apposite analogy is to academic freedom. A substantial body of case law now protects freedom of expression and association of professors and researchers. Clearly this freedom encompasses more than simply classroom instruction. Also included are political activity and association off campus, participation in labor organizations, writing letters to the local press, and of course academic relationships with students and colleagues. Over the last twenty years or so, the courts have struck down a broad range of invasions of academic freedom that chill free thought and inquiry even though they do not directly stifle discussion in the classroom.

The relevance of libraries and librarians to academic freedom should be obvious. Professors cannot pursue controversial issues or invite student research on the frontiers of human knowledge unless the university library is free to order and circulate all relevant materials. Indeed, a free and unfettered university library may well be the cornerstone of academic freedom. Thus the college or university librarian is engaged in a pursuit which seems no less deserving of direct First Amendment protection, within the academic community, than is the teaching and research of the professor.

The relevance of academic freedom to the public school or community library is less obvious. Yet the public library shares with the university a responsibility for the gathering and transmission of knowledge from one generation to another. Effective participation in the political process requires ready access to the shelves of the library. Censorship of the acquisition and circulation of controversial materials by the public library cannot help but constrict the total intellectual and political environment of the community. If librarians are not free to gather and disseminate a broad range of materials, then the civic life of the community and the vigor of political debate are bound to suffer. Thus the function of the public library, and the need for constitutional protection of that function, relate closely to the mission of the college or university from which academic freedom springs.

There is still missing a step, needed to bring the librarian's professional activity under the purview of the First Amendment. What is lacking is a new concept of free expression which would encompass the librarian's intellectual and creative processes. Such a concept should not be difficult to fashion. In fact, some of the librarian's functions are "speech" in the narrowest and most traditional sense. Yet it would hardly do to stop there— that is, to tell the librarian that he may order any book he wishes (because that involves "speech" in the technical sense), but that he may not catalog, shelve, or circulate the work since these functions are not traditionally within the First Amendment. Rather than parsing the librarian's work in this arcane fashion, we need a broader concept which will include all the elements vital to the exercise of a librarian's professional judgment and responsibility.

Such an extension of the traditional concept of free expression hardly seems radical or novel. The Supreme Court has already recognized the concept of "symbolic speech"—notably in the case of a student wearing a black armband in protest against the Vietnam War. A lawyer's freedom of expression necessarily involves the solicitation of clients. An architect's "speech" must include drawing blueprints and the designing of buildings, as well as verbal descriptions of these works. For the sculptor and painter, the only meaningful concept of expression includes the tangible artistic work which results from the creative process, even though the only traditional "speech" involved may be the title or the catalog. Most recently the Supreme Court has brought within the protection of the First Amendment the performance of a rock musical.

In this setting the professional activity of the librarian seems to merit comparable constitutional protection. When the librarian speaks or writes words of his own the First Amendment unmistakably applies, but simply does not go far enough. Most of what the librarian does is to review, select, and disseminate the words of others. Yet the preparation of acquisition lists and the cataloging, shelving, and circulating of books all require a measure of judgment and intellectual evaluation comparable to that required of other protected professions. Moreover, the courts have never had difficulty bringing under the First Amendment the bookseller, the newsdealer, or the movie exhibitor, all of whom disseminate the words and works of others rather than their own. Surely the librarian, who performs a similar function in a noncommercial context, should not enjoy a lower level of constitutional protection.

The recognition of a distinct librarian's freedom takes us back to the perplexing question we posed early in this chapter: If the removal of a book poses constitutional problems, to what extent might the *failure to acquire a controversial* work also be a subject of legal challenge? Let us consider this issue through several situations of increasing difficulty. The starting point is the case in which the school board orders a librarian not to buy a designated work because they find its content "offensive." Such a case seems legally indistinguishable from the removal case; in fact, the Strongsville case involved both a retrospective and a prospective ban, and the court saw no need to differentiate. The censorship is quite as complete and no less pernicious in the one case as in the other—even though there seems something more offensive about forcing a book to be taken off the shelves than about preventing it from ever getting there. If school boards could simply tell librarians not to acquire suspect works, and in that way avoid the Constitution, the First Amendment safeguards developed in Strongsville and Chelsea would be of very limited value. Moreover, the temptation to "pre-screen" all possible controversial works would be a likely by-product of drawing such a distinction.

At the other end of the scale, it is clear that no school board is required to buy every book, or even all books, that may be of interest to students and teachers. Where the budget or the physical space permit the acquisition of only a small fraction of available and meritorious works, the courts have made clear that no constitutional issue arises. Even where the school board determines acquisition policy with more particularity than simply setting the overall budget—for example, urging greater emphasis on some areas and less emphasis on others—no constitutional issue would seem to exist. Should the policy be highly selective—

for example, banning the acquisition of all works of a specific author, or all works dealing with certain topics (for example, evolution, race relations, etc.)—then a constitutional claim could be based on the Strongsville and Chelsea decisions. But the typical policy of a school board, setting broad guidelines within which the acquisition process operates on a limited budget, is not likely to violate the First Amendment.

The more difficult decisions are those made by the individual librarian or the professional library staff. There may be many grounds for a negative acquisition decision, some of which surely create no constitutional problem. Such criteria as cost, potential student and teacher interest, available space, duplication of existing collections, probable longevity, and the like, are well within the scope of a librarian's discretion. Not only is consideration of such factors legally permissible; it is in fact a major basis of the claim for First Amendment protection for professional librarianship. Some discretion must be exercised, and the relevant criteria are those in which librarians are most expert.

Slightly more difficult is the case in which a librarian declines to acquire a book on essentially legal grounds. If, for example, the content could be thought obscene, or might incite readers to violence, the librarian would presumably be allowed to apply such content standards even in the absence of a binding court decision. Surely, given the risks of making an erroneous judgment, the librarian should be allowed to err on the side of caution. (There are risks in carrying this theory too far; the line between the librarian's judgment and that of the principal or school board may not always be clear. Where in fact the librarian is doing the administrator's bidding with regard to a possibly obscene book, the claim of professional responsibility and judgment of course becomes attenuated.)

As a variant, consider the librarian who seeks to avoid a controversy of a different sort—declining, for instance, to buy for the library *Biology: A Search for Order* after the courts have held its classroom use to violate the establishment clause. One may argue that such books belong in the library, even though their use in the classroom is forbidden—indeed, that the school may best respond to the wishes of deeply religious parents by making sure such works *are* accessible in the library despite their unavailability as instructional materials. Yet the librarian might well err on the side of caution in feeling that the buying of creationist materials would violate the spirit, if not the letter, of the establishment clause.

We come now to the most difficult case of all: Suppose, to be precise, that the school librarian in Chelsea had first read the contents of *Male and Female*, including the poem which triggered the controversy, and had then decided that the book was not appropriate for the age level or sophistication of her students. Suppose, further, that a student came seeking the book and was told that the library had made a decision on content grounds not to acquire it. Should the student and parents bring suit to challenge that judgment, the librarian would of course be a defendant rather than (as in the actual case) a plaintiff. No longer would the dispute be between the librarian and her employer, but rather between the librarian and her patrons. The resolution of this dispute would be far more difficult than any we have yet encountered.

The case bears a superficial resemblance to the *Spoon River Anthology* case. The precise counterpart would be a librarian's refusal to circulate a volume already on the shelf (or a decision to let it circulate only after blocking out or deleting certain selections). Where the librarian has exercised a responsible judgment not to buy a particular non-obscene work, the courts should not interfere. A range of professional discretion should be recognized within which librarians may decide to acquire or not to acquire, even at the risk of depriving their patrons of material that is constitutionally protected, educationally valid, and of current interest. Likewise, it should be permissible for librarians to designate certain works for limited or restricted circulation—requiring parental approval, imposing age limits, or confining access to students in a particular course. Again, the locus of the judgment is critical: For the school board or the principal to make such decisions would preempt the librarian's professional judgment (and thus abridge First Amendment freedoms) in much the same way classroom censorship preempts the teacher's liberty. For the librarian to make such decisions may indeed diminish access of patrons to constitutionally protected material, but deference by the courts to such judgments seems preferable to judicial review of every decision whether or not to buy a book.

There is a final situation—the only one in which judicial intervention might be appropriate. Suppose a librarian in a predominantly Catholic community buys only the works of Paul Blanshard and refuses to acquire any books by Catholic authors. Or suppose a library which serves a black neighborhood consistently favors the white side of race relations in its acquisition policies. Or suppose the professional staff of a library in a fundamentalist community provides only the Darwinian side of the controversy over the origins of life. One may feel that the political process ought to resolve such problems, since the electorate does after all provide the bulk of support for the public library. But the political remedy may not always be effective—if, for example, a branch library serves a Catholic enclave within a predominantly Protestant community, or a black neighborhood in a predominantly white city.

Recognition of judicial relief in situations amenable to the political process is not unknown; in the early 1960s, for example, the Supreme Court opened the way for judge-ordered reapportionment of state legislatures—a matter from which the courts had previously abstained under the "political question" doctrine. Moreover, the willingness of courts to vindicate the interests of racial minorities where the political process has proved elusive or unresponsive may suggest that intervention here would be warranted in extreme cases.

There are very substantial risks in asking a court to monitor the acquisition policies of a public library—and for that reason, if for no other, judicial relief should be most sparingly contemplated. But the possibility of court intervention should remain for the extraordinary case in which the patrons' First Amendment interests are clearly at variance with those of the librarian and would suffer irreparably from judicial abstention. One fervently hopes that such a case will never arise.

8

BEYOND THE FIRST AMENDMENT

MOST CURRICULAR POLICIES—including some that are highly controversial—threaten neither free speech nor religious liberty.
State education laws contain countless provisions committing the
school curriculum to the preservation of old values or the disparagement of new ones. Requirements that "free enterprise"
be stressed or that "the evils of Communism" be exposed in the
social studies curriculum are common. Many states require inculcation of precepts as vague as "patriotism," typically leaving the
implementation to curriculum planners. Such mandates as these
may well be objectionable to substantial numbers of parents and
teachers, but redress must be found through the political process
and not in the courts. Only the most exceptional of curricular
disputes can be the subject of adjudication. The central issue
of this chapter is when and on what grounds courts may inquire
into curricular policies that do not abridge First Amendment
freedoms.

The reluctance of courts to go beyond protection of the
liberties of speech and religion is deeply rooted. For more than
a half century, the Supreme Court has insisted that the role of
the judiciary in curricular matters should be an extremely limited one. One source of that limitation is the respect due to other
branches of government more expert in such matters as the
superintendence of public education:

Judicial intervention in the operation of the public school system of the Nation raises problems requiring care and restraint. . . . By and large, public education in our Nation is committed to the control of state and local authorities. Courts do not and cannot intervene in the resolution of conflicts which arise in the daily operation of school systems and which do not directly and sharply implicate the basic constitutional values.

Such a caution merely poses the question, but does not answer it. The issue to be explored here is when issues other than heavy-handed censorship or denial of religious liberty may "directly and sharply implicate the basic constitutional values."

It might be useful to start by reviewing several specific limits on the role of the courts. One restraint is *procedural*: A court can decide only those issues which come before it in the proper fashion; unlike other branches of government, courts cannot reach out and gather in those questions which may seem to need adjudication or resolution. The ways in which a curricular dispute may reach a judge are by now fairly familiar: a suit to enjoin the use of a particular text; a suit to compel the teaching of a subject or point of view not found in the current curriculum; review of a teacher dismissal or suspension; a dispute over the removal of a book from the school library; a request for the excusal of a child from some part of the curriculum; or a criminal prosecution for taking or keeping a child out of school altogether. Beyond these channels, there may be attempts to inject curricular issues into other types of proceedings—for example, the prosecution of the Charleston, West Virginia, school bombers, who claimed they should be allowed to defend with their beliefs about what was taught inside the buildings they attacked. But the courts have properly drawn the line here, and have said that destruction of property (or injury to person) will not be excused because of the catalytic beliefs or motives.

A second source of limitation is *jurisdictional*. The federal courts, at least, have power to decide only certain kinds of issues

—mainly those which arise under an act of Congress or which involve a claimed denial of constitutional rights and liberties. Thus many curricular disputes within the public schools are beyond the reach of the federal courts simply because no constitutional issue is at stake. Federal judges will often make clear in dismissing a suit of this sort that their refusal to adjudicate reflects only the absence of such an issue, and does not imply approval of the challenged practice.

A third limitation might be termed *remedial*. If a court is to decide that a wrong has occurred, the judge must be able and ready to correct that wrong. The court is called upon in most cases to fashion—and to administer—a specific remedy. It is one thing to require that a wrongfully discharged teacher be reinstated, or that a book illegally removed be restored to the library shelves. It is, however, quite another matter for a court to demand that more X, or less Y, be taught in the public schools because the judge has found the curriculum to be biased or distorted. Even if the standards for such a remedy were clear, as they seldom are, the prospect of satisfying all parent, teacher, and community groups by a single decree would be remote indeed. Thus a court which undertook to police the curriculum would thereby assume a continuing and inescapable task of monitoring. Quite apart from the heavy workload which most courts face these days, such a role would be most uncomfortable and unfamiliar to the typical trial judge. Thus remedial limitations reinforce other judicial constraints.

A fourth factor is the range of *alternatives to judicial intervention*. Of course a judge must look to the allegations and the evidence in determining what judicial response is appropriate. Yet it is not improper for a court to take account of the other options open to one or both parties. There are in fact a number of alternatives to judicial intervention in curricular disputes. In the rare case, as actually happened in Charleston, parents may actually take to the streets, and may substitute bombs or rifles for the usual weapons of persuasion. More likely, persons who fail in court will turn to the political process, hoping that like-minded citizens and parents may help them elect a school board which will make the desired changes in the curriculum. If the political process fails, and if informal accommodation (for example, excusal or transfer) cannot be achieved, then the parents may opt entirely out of the public school system. Sometimes private schools are available—costly in almost all cases, and geographically remote in many. Where there are no private schools, parents may set up their own schools, or obtain state certification to teach their children at home. Where that choice is not available (often because of high licensing standards), the parents may simply take the child out of school, provide home instruction, and risk prosecution for truancy. This final option does have potential for bringing the issue back to the courts in a more compelling form; the judge who declined to entertain a suit to enjoin a textbook or to excuse a child from class has no choice when the issue comes up on appeal from a truancy conviction. By that time the curricular dispute is no longer the central issue of the case. But the court may reasonably consider the range of alternatives; the question "What happens if I dismiss the case?" is not an irrelevant or improper one for a judge presented with a novel plea.

Yet the central issue remains, for the full range of potential legal challenge to the curriculum has not been exhausted by the First Amendment cases. The area of sex education may illustrate the relationship beween the familiar and the unfamiliar claims. To the extent that challenges to such programs have been based on religious freedom grounds, courts have at least been willing to entertain them. But there is evidence that theology is no longer the principal basis of most sex education challenges. Rather, the impelling force is a parental belief that such deeply personal matters should first be discussed at home and probably do not belong at all in so "public" a setting as the school classroom.

The real basis or reason for objecting, in short, is one of privacy and the parental role in shaping values and morals, rather than freedom of worship. The courts are in the uncomfortable position of having to decide the case on the asserted ground, even though the *real* reason may be quite different.

The sex education controversy provides a bridge between the familiar and readily cognizable constitutional claim (freedom of religion) and the less familiar parental interest in protecting the integrity of family values against external threats. Courts can deal easily with claims that books or teaching materials abridge freedom of religion; the problem is that few sex education units are really vulnerable to such a claim. The basic interest in privacy or parental guidance of values and morals is substantial, but founders when it must find a familiar constitutional peg on which to hang. Thus many curricular disputes which involve parental or student interests other than free speech or religious liberty have fared poorly in the courts—or have never even got there because of the well-founded belief of attorneys that litigation would be pointless. In this chapter, we shall examine a broad range of these "unfamiliar" claims that lie beyond the bounds of the First Amendment.

Race

Two real cases will pose the first such issue. One is a case we considered in the first chapter—that of the Blackfoot Indian girl in Suffolk County, New York, whose mother withdrew her from school in protest against allegedly insensitive classroom views of Native American history and life. The New York appellate court upheld a judgment against the mother, partly because it felt she had used the daughter as "a pawn" in "seeking martyrdom" for herself. The court also observed that whatever may have happened in the classroom did not show a pattern of racial discrimination throughout the school district—suggesting that nothing less than pervasive bias would have warranted intervention.

The other case shares with the first only its subject matter, the role of race in the curriculum. Several years ago a group of black parents and students and public and private school teachers brought suit against the Mississippi State Textbook Purchasing Board and the History Textbook Rating Committee. Their claim was that these agencies consistently adopted only history texts which "espouse notions of 'white supremacy' and/or which minimize the role of blacks in the history of Mississippi." Although the state board could adopt as many as five history books, they approved only the traditional text, which, in the judgment of one critic, "delicately bypasses the darker avenues of the state's racial past." In addition to challenging the sole selection of that book, the suit also cited the board's refusal even to consider a competing work which presents a more balanced view of Mississippi history. The alternative text, *Mississippi: Conflict and Change*, was the joint effort of a group of scholars concerned about the traditional approach. It had won critical acclaim from educators, in part because (as *Newsweek* magazine recently noted) it "rejects old-fashioned images of blood-thirsty redskins, bucolic ante-bellum society and corrupt Reconstruction government." This text offered an accurate account of the role of the government of Mississippi in the civil rights struggles of the 1960s. The state, in defending its right to select textbooks— even those which may be faulted for their portrayal of race relations—argued that "the case seeks to involve Federal courts in the textbook selection process of the States," a prerogative which Mississippi, at least, felt well worth defending against such a challenge.

These two cases inject a wholly new element into the dispute: the relationship between racial equality and the curriculum. Of course the courts have not been the only forum for this tension. Several years ago there emerged a group of librarians

and others concerned about the treatment of minorities in children's literature, under the name of Council on Interracial Books
for Children, Inc. The Council published in 1976 a report,
Human—and Anti-Human—Values in Children's Books, which
charged there was pervasive bias in current materials, offered a
"rating instrument" for applying racially balanced criteria, and
suggested that steps (not clearly defined) be taken to improve
the treatment of minorities in children's literature. Many librarians were deeply disturbed by this publication. The lead editorial in the *Library Journal* for November 1976, under the cap-
tion "The Would-Be Censors of the Left," warned that groups
like CIBC "have not only adopted the book removal tactics of
the nay-sayers, they press on to insist that their ends can only be
achieved through children's books written and evaluated according to their so-called guidelines. . . . All it takes is enough common sense among librarians to see that censorship looks, sounds
and smells the same whether its [sic] coming from the Left or
the Right." Quite apart from the work of CIBC, we have already
taken note of the black parents on the Chicago North Shore who
succeeded in having *Huckleberry Finn* removed from the required reading list.

The racial bias issue is bound to reach the courts. Indeed,
in at least one guise it is already there.

Let us begin our analysis with the case of the Long Island
Blackfoot Indian family. We should assume the absence of any
ulterior motives on the mother's part, and a classroom environment that is demonstrably demeaning to the Indian child. Presumably a parent would first be required to exhaust all administrative remedies, including a petition for a change of teacher
or classroom, or even of school. If the district failed to honor
such a request, or if a transfer failed to improve conditions, then
the mother charged with truancy for removing the child from
school would surely have a plausible claim. It would be bizarre
for a court in an individual case to require proof of racial bias

in all parts of the system. If only because the number of Native Americans in that part of New York State is small, the extent of overall discrimination is likely to be slight. Moreover, what is in issue is not the duty of the district to desegregate its schools, but the claim of a single isolated family to a reasonably congenial learning environment.

It would be easy enough for the court to dismiss the criminal charge on the ground that sufficient provocation existed for the mother's decision to withdraw her daughter. Such a judgment would resolve the particular *case*, but not the *issue.* Indeed, the mother had said she would not return her daughter to school unless certain demands were met, among them her insistence that the school district "place the problem of the American Indian in its curriculum." Such a demand called, of course, for affirmative measures well beyond the initial plea that teachers not refer to Indians as "lazy" or "savage." The appellate court may have been influenced in part by a feeling that simply dismissing the criminal charge would leave unresolved a set of curricular issues beyond its jurisdiction in a truancy proceeding. Even if the issue of the classroom environment had been properly before the court, any judge would be loath to decide how much treatment of American Indian concerns was needed. Such remedial and procedural cautions do not necessarily argue for a different result in the criminal case, but they do suggest how limited would be the effect of a finding of nontruancy.

Let us now turn to the Mississippi history case, which presents a comparably difficult issue. Here too we must assume (as the complaint alleged) that black parents, students, teachers, and administrators have come to the federal court only as a forum of last resort. So long as the allegedly "racist" book is the only one on the approved list, and so long as the course in Mississippi history is required, in private as well as in public schools, black children will perforce learn only that version of their own history and culture which that book contains. Of course their parents can furnish supplemental reading at home, but that option gives small protection against the effect of a demeaning or severely biased account in the schools. Thus there is at least warrant for a court to inquire into the allegations that a racist and required textbook denies equality to Mississippi blacks.

On the other hand, judicial intervention would pose obvious difficulties. It is one thing for a court to compel the textbook adoption agencies to consider the competing volume, as the Mississippi complaint requested. Even a decree enjoining further use of the current text would not be without precedent, given the West Clark (Indiana) biology book suit. But such an order would require a finding that the continued use of the approved text violates certain constitutional rights just as the use of *A Search for Order* denied religious liberty. The review of the history book would have to be much more elaborate than the analysis made by the Indiana judge in the biology case; not only would a court need to study in detail what was said about blacks and whites, it would also have to ascertain whether vital elements of black history had been omitted. That task would be more extensive and more demanding than the process of finding a biology text to be unconstitutionally creationist. The need for expert witnesses—both educators and historians—would be far greater. And the element of judicial discretion and perception would be much broader. Nonetheless, a court cannot avoid a case properly before it simply because the process of adjudication is sensitive, demanding, or time consuming, or because it requires the expertise of specialists. The claim that the Mississippi history text is unusable because it is racially discriminatory—and thus denies black students the equal protection of the law—seems at least properly before the federal court.

The complaint goes further, though, and asks the court to enjoin state officials from discriminating against textbooks "containing perspectives on history at odds with those traditionally acceptable in Mississippi." At this point two problems of a different sort arise: First, a court would by granting such an order place itself effectively in the position of reviewing *every* textbook decision—not only in history but in other fields as well—for possible violation of the injunction. Second, and even more troublesome, the court would be forced to formulate and apply a new standard that substantially exceeds the racial equality guarantee of the Fourteenth Amendment. It is one thing for the court to hold that one text has been rejected or disparaged for unlawful reasons, or that another has been adopted and is being required in violation of black students' rights. It is quite another thing for a court to make sure that books are not rejected because their views vary from those "traditionally acceptable in Mississippi." The former reflects proper limits of judicial intervention; the latter is simply asking for trouble.

Given these hazards, it is not surprising that the court resolved the case on relatively narrow grounds. The district judge held in favor of the plaintiffs, but on grounds which were more procedural than substantive. The court declined to rule, as the plaintiffs had urged, that state approval of the "traditional" text constituted racial discrimination. Instead, the judge addressed the propriety of the rejection of the competing text, and held that the procedures by which that action had been taken were constitutionally defective. Without an adequate opportunity for the authors of competing works to obtain review of textbook commission decisions, a form of censorship could result. To the extent that the commission had rejected one text because they found abhorrent its view on race relations (a conclusion which gained some support from the evidence), its action was constitutionally illegitimate and justified judicial intervention. Thus the court ruled that the competing work must now be approved, unless the commission found it unsuitable on grounds other than its treatment of race relations. The district judge declined to go further, and cautioned that the federal courts "should not undertake to dictate a plan of textbook approval."

Sex

The claim that teaching materials are sexist parallels in many respects the claim of race bias we have just considered. There has been much recent litigation about other issues of sex differentiation—for example, two federal court cases striking down sex-based grade differentials for entry into academic high schools, numerous cases upholding the right of girls to compete in athletic programs, and a case (in which the Supreme Court was equally divided) about the constitutionality of separate girls' and boys' high schools in Philadelphia. There have also been earlier disputes about the curriculum. Several cases in the late 1960s reached conflicting results about school rules making home economics a degree requirement only for girls, or excluding female students from industrial arts classes. Usually local policies contain enough flexibility to keep these issues out of the courts.

More recently, the concern about the treatment of women in texts and other materials has intensified. Sex stereotyping has in fact been a cognate concern of the Council for Interracial Books. The removal of several allegedly "sexist" books from the Montgomery County, Maryland, public library drew national attention, as did a protest by the Women Library Workers of Los Angeles against circulation of the film "How to Say No to a Rapist and Survive."

Such essentially local tensions were overshadowed by national attention to teaching materials when the federal nondiscrimination guidelines were framed. Title IX of the Higher Education Act of 1972 bans discrimination on the basis of sex in a broad range of federally aided educational programs. All public schools and most colleges and universities, along with other types of institutions, are covered. An early draft of the regulations implementing Title IX would have mandated equal treatment of men and women in all texts and other teaching materials, but the final version of the rules, long delayed and extensively revised from the early draft, contained no such provision. The modification was explained in a lengthy statement by then Secretary of Health, Education, and Welfare Caspar Weinberger:

> The Department recognizes that sex stereotyping in curricula and educational materials is a serious problem to which Title IX could well apply, but the Department has concluded that specific regulatory provisions in this area would raise grave constitutional problems concerning the right of free speech under the First Amendment to the Constitution, and for that reason the Secretary has not covered this subject matter in the proposed regulations. The Department assumes that recipients [of federal funds] will deal with this problem in the exercise of their general authority and control over curricula and course content. For its part, the Department will increase its efforts, through the Office of Education, to provide research assistance, and guidance to local education agencies in eliminating sex bias from curricula and educational materials.

Perhaps the most elaborate focus on the issue of sex bias has come in California. State law requires that all instructional materials portray the diversity of society, specifically "the contributions of both men and women in all types of roles, including professional, vocational, and executive roles," and precludes adoption of any materials which reflect adversely on any persons because of their sex. Under these provisions the State Board of Education has issued rather detailed guidelines. Among the desiderata are these: Descriptions demeaning or patronizing toward females must be avoided; references to men and women must be approximately equal in number, "except as limited by accuracy"; there must be approximately even division of "mentally and physically active, creative, problem solving roles and success or failure in these roles" between men and women; emotions "should occur randomly among characters regardless of gender"; "traditional activities engaged in by characters of one sex should be balanced by presentation of nontraditional activities for characters of that sex"—and so on through a long list of forbidden sex stereotypes.

The role of the courts in the area of sex-biased materials remains to be determined. No suits appear to have been filed, either challenging the fairness of current curricula or materials or protesting the nonadoption of more balanced materials. At least two legal commentators have, however, argued that a cause of action should be recognized to the extent that administrative remedies are not adequate to redress sexual stereotyping. Such a suit would have several premises: First, that the use of sex-biased materials denies equal opportunity (although the Supreme Court has been less rigorous in reviewing gender-based differentials than those based on race). The specific claim would be that "the inferior education provided for girls as compared with boys violates the equal protection clause. . . . The schools are operating on the basis of a presumption that all female children, simply because of their sex, are limited to the traditional female role; the curriculum has the effect of perpetuating that presumption." A second basis for such a suit would be the claimed denial of a more elusive interest in personal liberty, or possibly privacy: "To the extent that the public schools interfere with this right by controlling and limiting a child's autonomy in these areas, the schools are violating a fundamental right"—essentially by analogy to the role of courts in judging the validity of school rules on length of male students' hair. Such a claim would not necessarily be limited to girls:

> Sex stereotyping denies both boys and girls basic personal liberty to develop as individuals, not to be required to conform to standard personality types; the denial is more destructive to girls since boys are encouraged to have a positive self-image and an expansive view of their own potential while girls are taught that they are inferior, are given a negative self-image and a limited view of their own potential.

As in the matter of race, the fate of such claims may depend largely on how they reach the courts. One can imagine a parent so outraged by unequal treatment of the sexes in the curriculum that he or she would be willing to risk prosecution for truancy by taking a child out of school in protest. As with the Blackfoot Indian case, the courts should at least be willing to consider the merits of such a claim, and might excuse the truancy by finding sufficient provocation in a demeaning and destructive learning environment. Reversal of a single conviction would at most have a collateral effect on the curriculum, and would leave the broader issue open.

The other possibility, a civil suit to compel the elimination of "sexist" materials, should be analyzed very much as we analyzed the Mississippi history textbook case. The basic constitutional principles may be less clear, since the standard for gender-based classifications is less consistent and less rigorous than that which governs racial classification. Problems of proof would probably be more difficult, since the body of expertise is less well defined in the sex stereotype area. Among other differences, the absence of the long history of litigation over school segregation would remove from this field one obvious source of expertise available in the race area. The problems of reviewing even a single challenged work, and of determining a proper constitutional standard, would be at least as complex in regard to sex as in regard to race. Yet the guiding principle seems the same: Courts should not be totally insensitive to the claims of students or parents that instructional materials deprive them of rights and interests of constitutional stature. Any judicial entry into this sensitive area should serve the limited purpose of judging a specific claim rather than supervising the broad curriculum or the textbook adoption process.

The Holocaust

A quite different set of issues has been raised by the recent decisions of several school districts to require a unit about the Holocaust. Such a requirement has already been instituted in Philadelphia and has been seriously considered in New York City. The Philadelphia unit, incorporated in the ninth grade world history course, relies upon primary sources (for example, passages from Hitler's *Mein Kampf*) as well as secondary accounts of the mass extermination of Jews in pre–World War II Western Europe. The adoption of this unit drew sharp criticism from a Philadelphia German-American organization, which feared that "Nazi and German would be identical in the American mind" and that students would form an impression that "Nazis were the only ones who committed crimes against humanity and that Jews were the only ones who suffered to any great extent." When the New York City unit was under discussion, similar feelings emerged. The *New York Times* recognized editorially many of the risks in adopting such a unit, and suggested that account should also be taken of the economic recovery of postwar Germany, but argued in the end that "the annihilation of European Jewry should be a mandatory subject."

There appears to have been no litigation regarding the Holocaust units. It is not hard to imagine, however, several types of parents who might wish at least to have their children excused from such a unit, and perhaps to have it removed completely from the curriculum. We might begin with Jewish parents, themselves refugees of Nazi Germany, who wish nothing more than to forget the trauma of the Holocaust. There is, of course, no guarantee that the curriculum will avoid all possibly offensive or anti-Semitic references; recall, for example, the court's rejection of a Jewish parent's protest against the teaching of *The Merchant of Venice* and *Oliver Twist*. ("If evaluation of any literary work is permitted to be based on a requirement that each book be free from derogatory reference to any religion, race, country, nation or personality, endless litigation respecting many books would probably ensue, dependent upon sensibilities and views of the person suing.") Yet the Jewish parent's claim against the Holocaust unit would be stronger in several respects: First, the focus is not great literature that happens to include anti-Semitic figures, but rather a newly fashioned unit designed to remind others of a period of history which may reopen old wounds that have slowly and painfully healed. Second, the emphasis of the Holocaust unit is very narrow and specific—more analogous, perhaps, to the literary study of Henry Ford's *Protocols of Zion* or the writings of George Lincoln Rockwell. Third, the context is also different; in the *Oliver Twist / Merchant of Venice* case, teachers were required to tell students that characters in the novels or plays were not typical of any racial or religious group, nor "intended to be regarded as reflecting discredit on any race or national group." It would be very difficult by comparable disclaimer to remove the pain of having to relive the Holocaust for the Jewish family seeking a new life in a new world.

Consider a case at the other end of the spectrum—relatives of a Nazi war criminal, who are equally anxious to forget the Holocaust. They may fear that such a unit would renew hostility not only from Jewish students but from others who have a less personal aversion to the excesses of Nazism. Again, the starting proposition is clear enough: Nothing in the Constitution guarantees complete freedom from unpleasant experiences in school, or ensures that every reference to one's relatives will be reassuring. But these parents would assert an obvious difference between discussion of Nazi Germany in modern world history, and a unit which by its focus could be threatening as well as painful. For survivors of the Nuremberg courtroom as for the survivors of Auschwitz and Dachau, the desire to forget the Holocaust may be a compelling one.

Third, suppose an American Indian family feared that special emphasis to one form of genocide would divert attention from others. They could argue, notwithstanding the horror of the Holocaust and the general value of studying man's inhumanity to man, that better material exists closer to home in the savagery of the white man's relentless westward movement.

Finally, one could posit the objection of a parent who has no direct connection with the Holocaust or with other victims of acts of genocide, but simply feels that no single period of history should receive special attention in response to the wishes of a particular racial, national, or religious group.

In none of these cases does there seem any basis for enjoining the teaching of the unit; even the relatives of Nazi war criminals can at most claim that study of the Holocaust may arouse dormant hostility. But the possibility of excusing a particular child poses a different set of issues. The weakest claim for excusal is that of the noninvolved child whose parents simply object to what they consider a distortion of history; such a dispute belongs in the principal's office and not in the courts. The challenge of the Native American is more difficult, but goes really to the *exclusion* of a unit about mistreatment of Indians rather than to the *inclusion* of a unit recounting the persecution of the Jews.

The two remaining cases are somewhat harder. It would be tempting to dismiss both claims as simply inappropriate for the courts. Yet there may possibly be constitutional dimensions lurking in both cases, and for that reason the bare possibility of judicial intervention should remain open. The Jewish parent and child could conceivably assert a claim of religious discrimination—not in the intent of the unit (the purpose of which is, in fact, precisely the opposite), but rather in its effect. If, therefore, school officials refused to exempt the child whose parents wished to avoid the legacy of persecution which they feared a Holocaust unit might revive, and if they went to court, a court might grant a dispensation on essentially religious grounds.

The Nazi's relative might receive a different form of protection, alleging discrimination on the basis of national origin. Proof of such a claim would be difficult. One would have to demonstrate that the unit had a genuinely anti-German bias, rather than simply an intent to present the aberrations of Nazism. A few disclaimers—along with an account of the German economic recovery, as the *New York Times* editorial suggested—would go far to refute any suggestion of discrimination against a particular national group. Nothing less than proof of such discrimination should entitle the German-American child to dispensation and such evidence would be difficult to find with respect to a carefully fashioned Holocaust unit. In any case, the conclusion that the courts might be open to consider extreme cases offers little solace to most parents or students who might object to such a unit; only the clearest showing of a substantial constitutional violation would justify judicial intervention.

Privacy

Another area of parental concern well beyond the familiar bounds of constitutional litigation is the desire to move some subjects out of the classroom and keep them in the home. There are certain privacy claims which may succeed to the extent they invoke the guarantee of religious freedom—for example, the sex education cases and suits challenging on similar grounds mandatory physical education classes. Many privacy concerns are only peripherally religious in nature, however, and they fare less well in the courts. There have been strong objections in conservative rural areas toward attitude testing, role-playing exercises, sociodramas, and other activities which call upon the child to reveal personal and family beliefs and views. The extent of such concern emerges from an amendment to the Elementary and Secondary Education Act in 1978; the amendment provides: "no student shall be required, as part of any applicable program, to submit to psychiatric examination, testing or treatment or psychological examination, testing or treatment, without the prior consent of the parent." A basis for the amendment is reflected in a supportive statement by California Senator S. I. Hayakawa: "To inquire into the sexual attitudes and beliefs of 8-year olds, to probe their psychic and emotional problems, real or imagined, rather than into the level of their intellectual achievements— these are serious invasions of privacy." Some states also require parental consent for various forms of testing.

The remedy for such allegedly intrusive practices lies in the legislature and in educational administrative agencies, and not in the courts. The Constitution does protect personal privacy as such from governmental invasion. In one recent case, the Supreme Court struck down a New York ban on contraceptive advertising in part because the state law interfered with the right of parents to guide the development of their children. But when the dispute is between the parents and the schools, courts are properly reluctant to apply external standards to pedagogical procedures under the "privacy" rubric. If parents do not like to have their children asked certain kinds of questions or required to take part in discussions, dramas, or role-playing activities, the political and administrative process offers the sole avenue of relief.

Patriotism, Politics, and the Like

The role of political values and issues in the curriculum is surely not new. From early times, those who shape the curriculum and select teaching materials have seen the vast potential for inculcation (or avoidance) of certain ideologies in the classroom. The pressures have come from both sides—forces, on the one hand, seeking to ban certain materials or even subjects as "un-American" or "alien"; and concurrent pressure to prescribe certain subjects in order to enhance political values or principles.

The complex of curricular requirements is deep and pervasive. A recent survey conducted by the American Bar Association reveals the following pattern:

Thirty-eight states have statutes requiring the inculcation of specific values and attitudes. Of these 38 states, at least 12 charge teachers with responsibility for building the moral character of their students. Statutes dating back several generations tend to stress, in rather quaint language, such characteristics as piety, truth, benevolence, sobriety, frugality, and similar virtues. For example, a California statute calls on teachers to teach their students to avoid "idleness, profanity, and falsehood, and to instruct them in manners and morals. . . ." Similarly a Maine statute calls on educators to "impress on the minds" of their students: "the principles of morality and justice and social regard for truth; love of country, humanity and a universal benevolence; sobriety, industry and frugality; chastity, moderation and temperance."

Statutes in a number of states also endorse "civic virtues." The Maine statute quoted above goes on to link moral characteristics with their tendency "to preserve and perfect a republican constitution, secure the blessings of liberty and to promote students' future happiness." At least 12 states seek to instill "patriotism," "loyalty," "love of country" or "devotion to American institutions and ideals." Indiana, South Carolina, and Vermont statutes speak of "good" citizenship or behavior.

In addition to these general prescriptions, the statutes of many states contain more specific mandates. Seven states, for example, require teaching about Communism in terms which unmistakably reveal a pejorative view—stressing, for example, the "evils" of Communism, or its "destructive effects," or exposing its "threat to our system." Some such mandates even specify the teaching materials, while others prescribe the outcomes and the content of the unit without mandating a particular text.

Such requirements as these, although they may be objectionable to many teachers, parents, and students—and although they seem increasingly anachronistic as the memory of the McCarthy era fades—are unlikely subjects for judicial challenge. In fact, curricular policies of this type would seem legally vulnerable only to the extent that a teacher's freedom of thought and inquiry was directly impaired. The Supreme Court decision most closely in point may suggest the limited potential of the Constitution in this area. Two decades ago, the Washington legislature required that all teachers swear a standard disclaimer-type loyalty oath. But the law also forced teachers to promise that they "will by precept and example promote respect for the flag and the institutions of the United States of America and the State of Washington." The lower courts sustained this provision, and an appeal brought it to the Supreme Court in 1964. The Justices did not question the legitimacy of the state's objective, but did hold that language so broad and imprecise could not be used to place teachers in peril of losing their jobs. The operative terms of the law, said the Court, were "unduly vague, uncertain and broad" and conscientious teachers could really have little idea of the duties they assumed by entering the Washington public school classroom.

The Washington law differed from the curricular mandates at least in two respects. One, which may have been more psychological than legal, was the linking of the affirmative duty with the already abhorrent disloyalty disclaimer provision, thus suggesting that one could only be "loyal" by carrying out both parts of the vaguely worded law. The other difference, legally more significant, was the clear linking of the affirmative duty to the teacher's employment status; since the obligation was a condition for continued employment, the teacher who failed in some respect to meet the statutory duty risked losing his or her job. The typical curricular mandate does not have quite such a bite; teachers are merely urged or directed to promote certain values— or to avoid others—in the classroom, without a statement that the failure to do so will risk loss of employment. Even where the basis of such a mandate may be more dubious in its origins than those we have surveyed here—for example, the Florida law requiring teachers to "inculcate every Christian virtue"—courts may be reluctant to strike down such requirements unless an individual teacher has been placed in jeopardy for noncompliance. If, as the federal courts have held, Florida teachers may be told to "inculcate every Christian virtue" even when teaching non-Christian children, a wholesale invalidation of most "patriotic" or "American" value mandates seems highly unlikely.

If we move from the level of comprehensive statutory requirements to the district level, "patriotism" and politics may assume a slightly different role. To the aggrieved parents in Kanawha County, West Virginia, no issue was of greater concern than "Americanism"—the feeling that the more "modern" texts disparaged traditional values and virtues while subtly promoting alien or hostile principles. Many of the most critical comments of the local reviewers revealed such concerns, quite as much as religious issues which drew most of the national attention. Often heard in Charleston were comments about the undermining of parental authority, the lessening of respect for the American flag and tradition, and a lack of commitment to traditional principles. Kanawha County was, as many observers noted at the time and since, classically a value conflict which simply happened to focus on the curriculum in the public schools. Given the centrality of this issue in Charleston and elsewhere, it is reasonable to ask whether any judicial remedy does or should exist.

There is one relatively easy starting point. The public schools cannot become forums for proselytizing, and must remain neutral on partisan issues. An easy case is one upholding the nonrenewal of a teacher who exhorted his students on behalf of a candidate for a local political office shortly before election day; such conduct, the court concluded with little difficulty, fell outside the teacher's freedom of speech. Of course the answers are not always quite so easy. The New York teacher who showed his students how he felt about the Vietnam War by wearing a black armband to class was held entitled to reinstatement, but only after the court considered the sophistication of his students, the nature of his courses, and the absence of other forms of antiwar advocacy in his classroom.

There are obvious differences between such cases and the

situation in Charleston. For one, it is not clear that a parent or taxpayer suit could force the dismissal even of a proselytizer if the school administration or board chose to retain him. For another, the claim that a classroom has become a partisan forum goes well beyond saying that the social studies curriculum is not sufficiently "American." A court can readily perceive that a school board is trying to maintain partisan (or religious or ideological) neutrality in its classrooms and would probably uphold even rather drastic means addressed to that end. But the court could head into the wilderness with little guidance if it agreed to determine what measure of "traditional American values" or "patriotism" was proper in the public school curriculum.

Thus it seems quite clear that courts should not, and would not, intervene from either direction in value conflicts. The few cases warranting such intervention are the extreme ones we have noted—the outrageously vague Washington statute requiring teachers to "promote" respect for the flag and for national and state institutions on the one hand, or the blatantly proselytizing teacher on the other hand. Other disputes over the role of political values and ideologies in the curriculum should be left to the political process. The group which wishes more civil liberties or less anti-Communism taught in the schools must pursue its political remedies, along with those parents or taxpayers who desire more traditional patriotism or greater stress on the strengths of free enterprise. Many abuses and excesses may exist, and may persist because they fall beyond the reach of the law. Even substantial perversions of the school curriculum fall short of the kind of clear constitutional violation with which the courts are properly concerned.

9
PUBLIC REGULATION AND THE
PRIVATE SCHOOL CURRICULUM

JUST BEFORE THE start of the 1977 school year, the Attorney General of Kentucky ruled that children enrolled in private schools not approved by the State Board of Education would be declared truant. Parents of children attending nonapproved schools would be subject to prosecution and, upon conviction, could face one year in jail and a $500 fine. This ruling reflected a finding by the Kentucky Board of Elementary and Secondary Education that twenty church-related schools failed to meet the state's minimum standards for educational quality. Those criteria went well beyond such routine matters as health, safety, and the condition of physical facilities. Kentucky authorities were also concerned about the competency and qualification of teachers in the private schools, the subjects offered, and the contents of the school libraries.

At once a group of newly disapproved schools—most of them affiliated with fundamentalist religious groups—brought suit to challenge the authority of the state to remove their accreditation. They were joined in court by a group of pastors, parents, and students, all of whom claimed that the actions of the Commonwealth deprived them of religious freedoms. The state replied that Kentucky law conferred not only authority but responsibility to see that private as well as public schools met general standards of educational quality; such criteria were imposed alike on religious and secular independent schools. The issue was joined, and the matter went to trial. Some months later the judge ruled in favor of the private schools, the pastors, parents, and students.

The relationship between state regulation and the curricula of private (or independent) schools is complex. Several legal propositions may help to guide our discussion. They also suggest the difficulty of finding any simple solution to the dilemma posed by the Kentucky case.

First, it is clear that states must allow parents (who are able to pay) to choose private education. Even in the case of a wholly secular private school, the alternative to public education is one which the Constitution recognizes and protects.

Second, state regulation of the private schools and their curricula may, however, diminish the scope of that choice. Imposing upon the private sector all rules which apply to the public schools, for example, would give the alternative limited value and thus undermine the constitutional right of choice.

Third, the state has at least a practical need to impose some substantive standards on the independent schools—else the compulsory attendance laws would be ineffectual. Moreover, the state has a broader and more theoretical responsibility to ensure some consistency in the quality of education which all children receive, regardless of the affiliation of the school which provides it.

Fourth, at least in the case of church-related schools, excessive leniency toward the private sector might raise constitutional problems under the establishment clause. If the state, by an absence of effective regulation, made the private sector alternative *too* attractive, there might result covert sponsorship of religion to a degree which the First Amendment forbids.

Finally, excessive regulation might also raise an establishment clause problem. If the state through its education agencies became deeply involved in the day to day operations of church-related private schools, the constitutionally mandated wall of separation between church and state might be jeopardized.

It should now be clear that the problem posed by the Kentucky case is far from easy. Any court facing such challenge must take all five propositions into account in deciding to what extent state regulation is permissible, and in balancing the conflicting claims of private school parents and students and those of proponents of public regulation. This chapter offers some possible solutions, with particular attention to the curricula of the private schools.

A brief general background may be useful before turning to the current legal context. Clearly private education now offers a meaningful alternative to the public school system. Although fewer than 5 percent of all children in school presently attend a private institution, in some parts of the country the figure is much higher. It has been estimated, for example, that one-tenth of the white children in the southeastern states now attend private schools—some from a desire to avoid racial integration, and others by reason of religious preferences. There seems to have been a recent and dramatic growth in the number of "Christian" schools; perhaps as many as 5,000 such schools now exist, mostly products of the 1960s and '70s. Their origins are not altogether clear, for in addition to concerns about desegregation and secularization in the public schools, a lively evangelical movement has given an added impetus to separate schooling. In addition, there is the traditional Catholic parochial school system, which remains strong in major urban areas despite problems of finance and commitment in smaller communities. Other denominations also maintain parochial schools; there have long been conservative Lutheran schools, Jewish yeshivas, and loosely affiliated Episcopalian preparatory schools. Roughly one quarter of the private or independent schools in the country—the total number of which is put at roughly 19,000—are not affiliated with any church. This category includes country day schools which survive in many metropolitan areas, military academies, and specialized schools for students with academic, physical, or emotional problems.

Private schools are certainly not the exclusive province of the rich. Parochial schools, especially those in the inner city, attract many students from modest and even poor families. It has recently been estimated by the National Association of Independent Schools that the average family income of students attending all private schools in 1979 was about $16,000—a figure which surely includes many families far from wealthy. Some families—who pay private school tuition on top of the general tax costs of the public school system—are willing to make a substantial sacrifice to give their children an alternative education.

Until quite recently relations between the states and the private schools have been distant and harmonious. Most states impose few criteria for approval—health and safety rules, for example, pertaining both to the physical welfare of students and teachers and to the condition of buildings and facilities. Although the authority to regulate has always existed, Coons and Sugarman observe that "in reality . . . state regulation is usually so minimal as to accomplish little, at least in educational terms." They cite the California statute which demands only that teachers in private schools be "persons capable of teaching," and they add that "little effort is made to enforce even this or other petty constraints in the educational code." Despite the rather substantial number of students enrolled in California private schools—some 400,000 at last count—the state "is content to let the family decide whether the private education now provided is in the interest of the child."

Such has been the traditional pattern across the country. But the recent and rapid growth of private academies, especially in the southeast, had redefined the relationships in several ways. A 1978 survey in the *New York Times* reports: "So many church-sponsored grammar and high schools have been opened in the United States in the last decade that education officials in some states are now beginning to monitor their effectiveness, thereby precipitating serious church-state conflict." Such is clearly the origin of the Kentucky controversy; there have been similar confrontations in Ohio, North Carolina, and Indiana, among other states. These conflicts seem confined to the areas in which the private school movement has substantial momentum, but the dispute will undoubtedly widen as the Christian academy spreads beyond the traditional Bible Belt.

Proof that the problem is not confined to the southeast comes from a recent and poignant incident in upstate New York. A Baptist minister near Syracuse was brought before the family court in part because he spanked his fifteen-year-old daughter for wearing slacks in violation of the family's strict moral code. Once the court got into the case, it discovered that the daughter had been attending the Fremont Christian Academy, an unaccredited private church-related school. The judge ordered that the daughter be transferred to the public schools, a step which the father took under protest because he feared a "moral degeneration" in the public system. This part of the order, as well as the no-spanking decree, has been appealed. It is quite possible that New York will soon be called upon to moderate the tension between a strong family preference for an unaccredited private school and the state's policy of uniform approval of all educational programs. New York—and California, quite as surely—may not be so different from the Bible Belt after all.

The Legal Context

One would expect more guidance from the courts on the private school regulation issue than we will find. Ironically, the closest Supreme Court case to the issue of the Kentucky case is also the earliest. In 1923, the Court in *Meyer* v. *Nebraska* had little difficulty striking down a state law which forbade the use of foreign language before the ninth grade in the schools of the state. The case specifically involved the use of German to teach Bible stories in Lutheran and Reformed parochial schools. But the Court's ruling went well beyond the facts of the case. Moreover, the Court did observe that "the power of the state to compel attendance at some school and to make reasonable regulations for all schools . . . is not questioned." What was questioned, and held to exceed state power, was the banning of a mode of instruction. Today courts might reach the same conclusion on the basis of First Amendment interests—either freedom of religion or freedom of expression. But in the 1920s it was not yet settled that the Bill of Rights applied to the states. Thus the Court took the broader ground of due process, holding that states lacked in the most basic sense the authority to do what Nebraska had tried to do to the private schools. The subtler question of what regulations or controls might be appropriate obviously did not concern the Court.

The other early and relevant case was *Pierce* v. *Society of Sisters*, two years after *Meyer*. There the Court held invalid an Oregon law which required all children to attend public schools. The basis of judgment was also the general guarantee of the Fourteenth Amendment:

> The fundamental theory of liberty upon which all governments in the Union repose excludes any general power of the State to standardize its children by forcing them to accept instruction from public teachers only. The child is not the mere creature of the State; those who nurture him and direct his destiny have the right, coupled with the high duty, to recognize and prepare him for additional obligations.

Here, as in *Meyer*, the Court took pains to point out what was *not* being decided, lest anyone read into the opinion a threat to state authority over education:

> No question is raised concerning the power of the State reasonably to regulate all schools, to inspect, supervise, and examine them, their teachers and pupils; to require that all children of

proper age attend some school; that teachers be of good moral character and patriotic disposition; that certain studies plainly essential to good citizenship be taught; and that nothing be taught that is manifestly inimical to the public welfare.

The intervening years have eroded somewhat the qualifications of *Meyer* and *Pierce*. Many decisions have restricted the power of school districts to determine—through loyalty tests and the like—whether teachers are of "patriotic disposition." There would be serious doubt today about the validity of a law or school board rule banning certain subjects as "inimical to the public welfare," although narrower restrictions might (as we have seen in previous chapters) survive.

Today it is tempting to think of *Pierce* as a religious freedom case, since the named plaintiff was in fact a Roman Catholic order. Such an inference would be quite misleading; not only had the religious freedom guarantees of the First Amendment not yet been brought to bear on actions of the states, but the other plaintiff in the case was a secular miliary academy to whose constitutional plea the court was equally sensitive. *Pierce*, like *Meyer*, would presumably be decided the same way today on First Amendment grounds, but its general due process origins are important to keep in mind as we approach the contemporary complex of secular and sectarian independent schools.

Meyer and *Pierce* have received consistent reaffirmation from the Supreme Court. Perhaps the clearest recent reliance on these precedents came in *Yoder*, the case sustaining the exemption of the Wisconsin Amish. There the Court defined for the first and only time the permissible scope of compulsory attendance laws, and ruled that the Amish had indeed stated a compelling case for exemption from the public school system beyond the eighth grade. At least one portion of the Court's opinion has direct bearing on the scope of state power to regulate independent schools:

A State's interest in universal education, however highly we rank it, is not totally free from a balancing process when it impinges on other fundamental rights and interests, such as those specifically protected by the Free Exercise Clause of the First Amendment and the traditional interest of parents with respect to the religious upbringing of their children so long as they, in the words of *Pierce*, "prepare them for additional obligations." Only those interests of the highest order and those not otherwise served can overbalance legitimate claims to the free exercise of religion.

Yoder is understandably the cornerstone of arguments advanced by the Kentucky Christian academies and other beleaguered private schools. But the force of the analogy is limited. The actual scope of the dispensation offered by *Yoder* is quite narrow; one commentator finds it "doubtful that any [other] extant religious or social group could satisfy the strict standards of *Yoder*." The exemption may be for the Amish alone, and at that only beyond the eighth grade, with the implication that other sects would fare less well. Indeed, even the Amish might be unable to obtain a similar dispensation from attendance laws at the elementary or junior high school level. Second, the issue in *Yoder* was not one of alternatives to the public schools, but of complete exemption. While the case for a total dispensation might seem harder to make, the claim of *family* superintendence of the child's maturation is far more compelling from the Amish than would be a different religiously based plea for an alternative *school* setting. Third, the *Yoder* court did not declare open season on compulsory attendance laws or rules; as in *Meyer* and *Pierce*, the Justices recognized that compulsory education requirements reflected a "compelling state interest" to which great deference must be given. Finally, the Amish did not seek to have their children untaught beyond the eighth grade level, but offered in extenuation an admittedly informal system of vocational training which the Court found responsive to the somewhat insular needs of the Amish community. Thus it would be unwise to read *Yoder* as undermining the general authority of states either to compel attendance at *some* school or to impose qualitative standards on *all* schools. *Pierce* recognizes only that states must leave free the choice of school, while *Yoder* adds that a compelling claim of religious liberty may conceivably outweigh certain civic interests, of which uniform high school attendance is one. More should not be read into either case.

A quite different set of cases has also helped to determine constitutional boundaries between government and private (especially religious) education. There have been many different attempts to make state funds available in some form to church-related schools, mainly to offset the "double burden" which the parent pays to exercise the choice that *Pierce* guarantees. For three decades, hardly a term of the Supreme Court has passed without at least one case on the docket involving the constitutionality of such a measure to aid parochial education. Volumes can be (and have been) written about these decisions. Any summary here, necessary for a full appreciation of the legal context, must be brief and superficial.

It all began in 1947, when a sharply divided Court held that a New Jersey school district did not breach the wall of separation between church and state by providing transportation for parochial school students on the same terms as public school pupils. Although the plan offered reimbursement to parents for transportation costs privately incurred, the majority held that government had not gone beyond "neutrality" in its relation to religion—rather like assigning police officers to direct traffic on Sunday mornings after church. Moreover, the Court stressed that the benefit of the New Jersey program ran to the children rather than to the church—although surely the parochial schools derived indirect benefit from such an arrangement.

There matters rested for some twenty years. Intervening decisions dealt with the role of religion in the *public* schools—differentiating between in-school and out-of-school religious instruction programs, and banning devotional prayers and Bible readings at the start of the school day. It was not until 1968 that the Court again reviewed the status of aid to private church-related schools. This time again the decision went narrowly in favor of the challenged program, a New York law making secular textbooks available to students in parochial schools. With a few minor exceptions, however, these two decisions—the bussing reimbursement and textbook loan cases—mark the limits of permissible aid to church-related schools.

Other forms of assistance which go further or in different directions—reimbursement to parochial schools for buying texts and other materials; partial payment of teachers' salaries for teaching nonreligious subjects; payment to parents to offset the costs of private school tuition, or tax credits and exemptions to such parents; grants for facilities to parochial schools; funds for pupil field trips; and even the lending of general instructional materials—have all been held invalid in recent cases. About the only other programs that have survived the careful scrutiny of the Supreme Court have been aid in meeting the costs of state-required testing; subsidies for diagnostic testing by public employees on the private school's premises; and remedial or counseling services off the school premises. (Even where the activity is unquestionably secular, the Court has insisted—most recently in a 1980 New York case—that reimbursements be scrupulously audited so that no public money could possibly be diverted for sectarian purposes.)

The distinctions in this area have become very fine indeed. Secular textbooks, for example, may be loaned for the use of parochial school students, while audio-visual materials may not; the books are used primarily at home, while slides and films would be used only in a religion-dominated school setting and could thus serve more directly to advance the interests of religion. Bussing of children to and from school is permissible, while transportation for field trips is not; the former is a part of a general service provided for the safety of all pupils, while special buses for field trips would specially enhance the program of the religious school rather than simply help get the student to school and back.

Three factors underlie these sophisticated and elusive distinctions: In order to be valid, a state program which aids religious education "first . . . must have a secular legislative purpose; second, the principal or primary effect must be one that neither advances nor inhibits religion; finally, the statute must not foster an excessive entanglement with religion." The Court has been especially concerned with the third of the criteria, and has often held that even state programs with clearly secular goals are invalid because their administration would involve public officials in the affairs of religious schools—for example, would require them to differentiate between religious and secular activities—to a degree the establishment clause was meant to forbid. It may be feasible for the state to transport children to and from the school door and to administer certain kinds of tests without intruding excessively in the affairs of the private religious schools. But almost any other form of aid—even such closely related practices as bussing for field trips, and lending audio-visual materials—the Court has placed on the forbidden side of the line.

What do the parochial school aid cases have to do with regulation of the church school curriculum? There is at least a general connection: While *Pierce* says that the state must allow parents to choose private education if they wish, the parochial aid decisions prevent the state from making that choice too easy or too attractive. The touchstone has been one of neutrality. Government must neither help nor hinder the exercise of parental choice. Private schools must be allowed to exist and must be given breathing room, but they must not be helped in ways that get government too deeply into the business of aiding religion.

The injunction against public subvention of sectarian schools is made more acute by the fact that most of these schools are operated by a single church. In Ohio, whence comes a major

share of the Supreme Court's parochial aid docket, 96 percent
of the non-public-school students attend church-related schools
and 92 percent are in Catholic parochial schools. Yet the constitutional problem would be equally severe whatever the denomi-
nation. In the southern states, where the fundamentalist Protestant sects have generated most of the recent growth in sectarian
schools, the injunction against state support is equally clear. The
only alternative is one which in most states would be politically
unacceptable—a program of private school aid limited to *secular*
institutions. Apart from the political controversiality of any such
law, it would surely be vulnerable in the courts to a claim of
denial of equality by parochial schools excluded from its benefits
solely because of their religious affiliation. Thus the extent to
which government may aid any form of private education is in
fact quite limited.

Until recently this was about all the parochial school aid
cases contributed to our current dilemma. In the summer of
1979, the Supreme Court moved in a related context one step
closer to the Kentucky conflict. The National Labor Relations
Board had asserted jurisdiction over the faculty in several Chicago parochial schools. The Archdiocese argued that federal
supervision of an election among its teachers would violate the
First Amendment. In fact there were two quite distinct First
Amendment claims: one, that the free exercise of religion should
bar a federal agency from interfering in what might well be
doctrinal matters—for example, deciding whether a teacher had
been fired for reasons of theology or on some other ground. The
other claim derived directly from the parochial aid cases: that
the process of policing the unfair labor practice laws would risk
the very kind of "entanglement" between government and religion which had tainted many of the state school aid laws.

The Supreme Court ruled in favor of the church, but did
not reach these constitutional issues. The majority held simply
that Congress had not meant to authorize the Labor Board to

organize the faculties of parochial schools. (Four Justices found this rationale rather disingenuous, and insisted that the constitutional issue should be faced.) The majority drew heavily upon the parochial school aid cases to suggest the kinds of hazards it felt Congress wished the NLRB to avoid:

> Inevitably the Board's inquiry will implicate sensitive issues that open the door to conflicts between clergy-administrators and the Board, or conflicts with negotiators for unions. . . . The church-teacher relationship in a church-operated school differs from the employment relationship in a public or other non-religious school. We see no escape from conflicts from the Board's exercise of jurisdiction over teachers in church-operated schools and the consequent serious First Amendment questions that would follow.

Thus the Supreme Court majority, though purporting to avoid a tough constitutional issue, served notice how it would probably rule on that issue. For the National Labor Relations Board—or any other government agency—to get as deeply into the internal affairs of a religious school as the NLRB often does with private employers might well cross the forbidden line of constitutional separation. Thus, for the first time, the parochial aid cases seem to have some bearing on the scope of *regulation* as well as of *subvention*, and may move one step closer to unlocking the Kentucky Christian academy puzzle.

Another recent case reinforces the concerns cited by the Supreme Court in the Chicago parochial school case. The Minnesota Human Rights Department ruled in 1978 that a parochial school could not, under the state's civil rights law, refuse to hire an otherwise qualified teacher solely because he planned to remarry after a divorce. The teacher was a Catholic, and possessed all the requisite academic credentials, but school officials found his marital status abhorrent to their values and principles. The Human Rights Department had rejected the school's contention that adherence to Canon Law principles was a bona fide religious qualification for employment, and ruled that the school must rehire the teacher. The Minnesota Supreme Court reversed the agency, however, and found in favor of the school. The court relied on *Pierce*, finding that the exercise by parents of a meaningful choice among educational options allowed the parochial school to insist within its faculty on such standards as strict adherence to church principles. Even though the school employed some non-Catholics, it could still insist that a *Catholic* teacher not flout the values of the church in his private life. It was central that "the school's purpose is to establish an entire program geared toward the education of young people in the Catholic faith"—a goal which would be subverted by the ruling of the Human Rights Department. (It was not clear whether the constitutional rights recognized by the court were those of the school, or those of parents and students who had chosen such a school for religious reasons. *Pierce* itself was somewhat unclear on the relative priority of school and parental interests, and that ambiguity has persisted in later cases.)

If *Pierce* and *Yoder* suggest a free exercise clause ground for the exemption plea of the Kentucky Christian academies, then the Chicago parochial school case suggests a corresponding rationale under the establishment clause. The extent to which these precedents actually do stay the hand of state government from regulating the private school and its curriculum is an issue to which we shall turn very shortly. Before doing so, one other line of relevant cases deserves some attention.

Race and the Private School: The Admissions Issue

If the courts have been deferential to the independent school in some matters, they have been far less so with regard to racially discriminatory admissions policies. As early as 1964, the Supreme Court held that Virginia could not set up and support a system of "private schools" for whites only while closing the public schools. But the growth of "white academies" throughout the South continued apace during the late 1960s, and the issue was bound to return to the Court in a different form. In 1973 the Justices unanimously held that Mississippi could not constitutionally provide free textbooks for pupils at private non-sectarian schools and academies which had racially exclusive admission policies and were in fact totally segregated. The Court stressed the importance of textbooks to the education program of the segregated schools, and then declared:

> The Constitution does not permit the State to aid discrimination even where there is no precise causal relationship between state financial aid to a private school and the continued well being of that school. Given the purpose and the effect of the Mississippi law, against the background of efforts to desegregate the public schools, it could not survive scrutiny under the Equal Protection clause.

The same question arose several years later from a different perspective. Acts of Congress passed shortly after the Civil War give "all persons" the same right to make and enforce a contract "as is enjoyed by white citizens." Black parents brought suit against a white academy claiming that under this law they had a right to admission notwithstanding the formally private character of the school. In *Runyon* v. *McCrary*, the Supreme Court had first to decide whether the old law reached such conduct—which they unanimously held it did—and then whether the Constitution supported such an assertion of federal power. The answer on the second question was also affirmative; such a law, held to reach the admission policies of private academies, was well within the power of Congress to implement the Fourteenth Amendment's guarantees of racial equality. In the course of the opinion, Justice Stewart added a comment potentially relevant to the curricular issue:

> No challenge is made to the [private boards'] right to operate their private schools or the right of parents to send their children to a particular private school rather than a public school. Nor do

these cases involve a challenge to the subject matter which is taught at any private school. Thus, the [schools] remain presumptively free to inculcate whatever values and standards they deem desirable. *Meyer* and its progeny entitle them to no more. . . . It does not follow that because government is largely or even entirely precluded from regulating the childbearing decision, it is similarly restricted by the Constitution from regulating the implementation of parental decisions concerning a child's education.

Since the *Runyon* decision, there have been several pertinent developments in the lower courts. The federal court of appeals which covers the southeastern states has rejected a constitutional claim which *Runyon* did not reach—that a policy of excluding blacks from a church-related school may be defended on grounds of religious liberty. The contention is that while Congress may have the power to force a *secular* academy to admit blacks, that power may not extend to a *sectarian* school without abridging the free exercise of religion. The court of appeals, however, balanced the conflicting interests in favor of free access for the black applicant against the school's claim of religious liberty.

The case touched very closely the questions that are the focus of the Kentucky litigation. Black parents had sought the admission of their children to the Dade Christian School in Miami, but were informed that the school had a racially exclusive policy. They then brought suit in the federal district court, claiming that the post–Civil War law gave them a federally protected right of access. The trial court held in their favor, even before the Supreme Court had decided the *Runyon* case. When the issue reached the court of appeals, after *Runyon*, the district court judgment was affirmed. The school officials maintained that the exclusion of blacks was within their religious liberty, and that *Runyon* therefore had not decided the central issue. The appellate court made rather short shrift of this claim, finding "strong evidence that school segregation is not the exercise of religion" in the "absence of references to school segregation in written literature stating the church's beliefs, distributed to members of the church and administrators of the school. . . ." Moreover, much of the testimony of the school officials seemed to treat racial segregation as an operating policy rather than a divine command: "if belief in school segregation was religious in nature, neither the officers of the school nor the congregation of the church was aware of it." It was, instead, "nothing more than a recent policy developed in response to the growing issue of segregation and integration. . . ."

One member of the appellate court concurred in the judgment, but felt the constitutional issue was more complex. In his view, the claim of religious freedom advanced by the private school could not simply be dismissed by an essentially "factual" analysis of church publications. There was inescapably a legal question which lay buried in the particular case or would surely surface in the next such case to reach the court. The basic tension between the claims of the black parents to equal access and those of the white parents to religious liberty must be faced. The concurring judge would uphold the former interest over the latter—at least in the absence of a religious freedom claim far more compelling than any suggested by the Dade Christian School. He would leave open the possibility that some religious group might be able to show that the exclusion of blacks was vital to its worship or belief, but such a demonstration was unlikely and remote in the setting of the segregated southern white academy.

One other recent case deserves mention here, if only because it has been poignantly noted in the media. A white girl attending a private Christian school in northern Virginia was expelled because she had developed a romantic relationship with a black classmate. Such liaisons violated the racially segregationist policies of the school. Her parents brought suit in the federal court, claiming that expulsion for such a cause violated the girl's civil rights. The district judge rejected that claim, holding that the school was within its legal rights to enforce in this way its scripturally based racial tenets: "The religious belief involved in this case is the [school's] conviction that the Bible forbids interracial romancing, dating and/or marriage." Unlike the majority in the Dade Christian School case, the district court in Virginia felt no need to test the religious basis of the expulsion, but simply accepted the school's allegations at face value and summarily validated its disciplinary rules.

Cases involving racially discriminatory admission and exclusion policies of private schools offer limited guidance to our basic inquiry. On one hand, they do suggest that courts may—where a very strong countervailing constitutional interest appears—be willing to intervene in the governance of a church-related school. On the other hand, the admission cases present no issue of curriculum or even of teacher selection. One can imagine a suit brought by the parent of a black child, once admitted to a formerly segregated academy, claiming the curriculum was so manifestly "racist" as to deny equal opportunity. The same court which had been willing to set aside the color bar would now be most unlikely to carry its concern into the classroom, laboratory, or study hall of the private school. Indeed, the Supreme Court in *Runyon* stressed that no such issues were involved in the admission question. Thus the racial admission cases, significant though they are in defining the relationship between government and private education, stop short of the precise question we are now seeking to answer.

The Kentucky Case Revisited: The Privacy of the Private School Curriculum

With the benefit of this legal background, we now return to the Kentucky Christian academy case. Clearly the Supreme Court has not spoken on the precise question of constitutional limits on state power to control the curricula of private schools.

The case closest to the mark is *Meyer* v. *Nebraska,* and the issue which is of concern to us figured minimally in the Court's broad discussion of state power and individual liberty. Nor do the comments in *Pierce, Yoder,* and *Chicago Archdiocese* resolve the present dispute. All the Court has done in these later cases is to set broad outer limits to the inquiry—recognizing the role of general state regulatory interests in dealing with private schools, while leaving open the degree to which those interests may reach the content of the curriculum. The Kentucky case does not arise on a totally blank slate, though it clearly charts new ground.

Several factors would be important in resolving the conflicting claims posed by such a case: the extent of state regulation; the purpose of the state regulation; the precise impact of the regulation on the curriculum; the nature of the constitutional claim presented by the school, the parents, and the students; and the alternatives available to the state (if any) for accomplishing the same result. Each of these elements deserves at least brief attention.

First, the *extent* of state regulation seems highly relevant. As we noted earlier, the tradition in most states has been one of *laissez-faire,* with approval or accreditation of private schools contingent only upon proof of satisfactory physical facilities and a faculty of a certain size, and meeting an occasional curricular requirement such as offering American history to all juniors or seniors. Only in a few states, and rather recently, have the requirements become sufficiently detailed to cause concern.

Ohio has long had on of the most extensive state regulatory schemes. A stated percentage of teachers in all private schools must be certificd by the state; others must be provisionally certified. The number of school days is mandated by state law. School officials are required to "cooperate with the community" in various ways. The length of the school day is implicitly prescribed by the statute, and even the subjects to be taught within the day are enumerated in the law. Thus it was hardly surprising that the one private school challenge to reach a state supreme court arose in Ohio. In a prosecution for truancy, parents of children attending the Tabernacle Christian School claimed that the pervasive state regulation impaired the free exercise of their religion and that of the school community. The Ohio Supreme Court, in *State* v. *Whisner*, agreed with the parents and held much of the state law invalid, at least as applied to religious schools.

Of special concern to the court was the scope and extent of the state regulatory system. The parents and the school had argued that if the school day were prescribed in such detail, and so many secular subjects required, insufficient time would remain for religious instruction, Bible study, and other sectarian subjects which made the private school unique and different from the public schools. The exercise of the constitutional choice guaranteed by *Meyer* and *Pierce* would be severely limited if state law so nearly preempted the school day for secular study. The court observed of the crucial requirements and their effect: "we think that [the regulations] unduly burden the free exercise of religion and 'interfere with the rights of conscience' by requiring a set amount of time to be devoted to subjects which, by their very nature, may not easily lend themselves to the teaching of religious principles (e.g., mathematics)." Toward the end of the opinion, the court summarized its concern:

> In our view, these standards are so pervasive and all-encompassing that total compliance with each and every standard by a non-public school would effectively eradicate the distinction between public and non-public education, and thereby deprive [the parents] of their traditional interest as parents to direct the upbringing and education of their children.

Moreover, the court felt that such interests of the state as were validly served by the challenged regulations could be met by less restrictive means, such as those on which most other states relied to govern their private schools.

Such regulations might conceivably have been justified by

a compelling state interest; even in *Yoder*, the powerful religious freedom claim of the Amish might have yielded if Wisconsin could have shown a dispositive reason for keeping children in public school beyond the eighth grade. Suppose, for example, the state required (as many do) that all children in school receive certain immunization or have regular chest x-rays. The schools may in fact provide the only effective control point for enforcement of such laws. Should a particular school refuse on grounds of religious conviction to enforce these general health and safety laws, the courts would surely resolve the conflict the other way, and find the state's interest superior to a strong religious liberty claim on the part of school and parents. But the situation in the *Whisner* case was not of that sort. The state's asserted interest in uniformity of curricula, and its wish to see that all children received a well-rounded education, did not (the Ohio court felt) outweigh the powerful religious freedom claim of the parents and the school. Of course that latter interest was presented in the most compelling way, since the issue arose through a criminal prosecution for truancy. But even a civil suit—seeking state approval or accreditation, or eligibility for public funding, for instance—would not have come out differently. The resolution of the three central factors—the extent of state regulation, the impact of regulation on the religious element of the curriculum, and the strength of the state's regulatory interests—would undoubtedly have been similar regardless of the posture of the case.

If the minimal regulation of states like California represents one extreme, the Ohio structure marked the other. Kentucky is somewhere in between. In addition to the usual health and safety standards, Kentucky law requires that students attend school for a minimum number of days each year, that teachers be certified by the state, that the library contain a certain number of titles, and that textbooks used in the schools be chosen from the state's approved list. In no sense is religious study foreclosed by state structuring of the school day, as in Ohio. Yet the nonaccredited Kentucky academies vigorously challenged the teacher certification standards and the textbook approval requirement.

The Kentucky trial judge struck down all but the health and safety requirements. After finding as a "fact" that "compliance with the various regulations for approval and/or accreditation mandated by the state would violate the religious convictions of [the parents]," he ruled specifically against the teacher and textbook criteria. The court made rather light of the state's interest in regulating even the competency of teachers, apparently persuaded by some evidence that graduates of fundamentalist schools did as well on standardized tests of secular material as did graduates of the public school system.

The Louisville *Courier Journal,* in an editorial the next day, found the trial court decision "far beyond the precedents." The editorial contrasted the pervasive regulation which the Ohio Supreme Court had struck down with the operative policies of the Kentucky Board of Education: "The State accepted as a matter of course the right of such schools to teach whatever religious tenets they saw fit. . . . Under succeeding administrations in the Department of Education, the state leaned over backwards in allowing religious schools to handle as they pleased such religiously sensitive subjects as biology." Even though certain portions of the law might be legally vulnerable, the editorial argued that the trial judge had ruled too broadly.

The two requirements that are most troublesome are indeed those dealing with teacher certification and textbooks. It should not be too hard to support the requirement that some (or even all) of the teachers in private schools should be licensed by the state. Only in this way does the state really have any control over the qualifications, preparation, and experience of persons to whom a vital public function is entrusted. If, for example, the state may rigidly control the qualifications of persons permitted to instruct their children at home, it would be perverse to deny the state comparable control over the credentials of persons performing the same function in private schools. Moreover, it seems unlikely that a teacher certification requirement would raise substantial constitutional problems. The state surely has no monopoly on teacher training. Persons who attend approved programs at Spalding, Bellarmine, Georgetown, or Central may be licensed to teach as readily as those who graduated from the University of Kentucky or the University of Louisville. Unless the teacher certification process somehow disadvantages persons of particular religious convictions, or requires some experience or study which is abhorrent to religious belief, the challenge to this part of the Kentucky law seems ill founded.

The textbook regulation is, however, quite another matter. Its effect is to prevent religious schools from using books that have not been approved for the public schools. The range of approved texts will be limited at least by practical considerations, including the primarily secular interests of public school teachers, administrators, and parents. Thus it is unlikely that all books attractive to private schools would find their way onto the state approved list in the first place. But there is a more serious and substantial limitation to the state approval process. Recall the West Clark, Indiana, decision—removing from the state approved list *Biology: A Search for Order* because its treatment of the origins of human life "established" a particular religious view. Presumably the Kentucky courts would reach the same conclusion. Thus the state could not allow the use in its public schools of a creationist biology text. Under the Kentucky law, such a decision would also deny to students in Christian academies the right to use *Search for Order*, and for reasons quite unrelated to its soundness in treating the secular aspects of biology. Here the free exercise clause and the establishment clause collide with each other: What is guaranteed by one provision of the First Amendment may appear to be forbidden by another clause. In the end, one component of religious liberty must yield to the other.

At the very least, private schools should be free to use certain otherwise adequate texts which would not appear on the state approved list for establishment clause reasons. Constitutionally, the state may not *approve* a book like *Search for Order* for public school use. Yet the state should not *deny* its use in private academies where a study of creationism may be the major *raison d'être*. Faced with this conflict, a court might simply strike down the textbook approval requirement entirely, and leave the state free to devise a less restrictive alternative—conscious that the government does have an interest in the accuracy and soundness of teaching materials as well as in the qualifications of teachers in the private schools. Or the court might take a more limited approach—for example, to validate the textbook approval procedure, save in subjects like biology where a direct conflict of values could be shown, and there recognize a specific exemption. Such a judgment might involve the court in the process of reviewing disputed adoptions, a role in which judges are usually not comfortable, but such a result might be preferable to striking down an entire program which is elsewhere valid and workable.

The objection of the Kentucky private school parents goes further, however, and should be more fully stated. They are immediately concerned about being denied the use of congenial texts in subjects like biology. But they also bridle at being forced—even in wholly secular fields like English and history—to adopt books which they may find offensive even to the point of sacrilege. As one of the witnesses said during the trial, "Some of those texts [on the approved list] are anti-Christian, they use excessive profanity and are highly descriptive of sexual acts and so forth. We feel it's a violation of our constitutional rights to force us to use those books." This claim may well be the most difficult of all. We have seen that parents of public school students—in Kanawha County, West Virginia, for example—could not force the removal of texts and other materials on such grounds. Whether they claimed an abridgment of free exercise or an establishment of "irreligion" or "nonreligion," the claim foundered in federal court both in Charleston and in Houston.

Now the argument comes full circle. The West Virginia federal judge could in good conscience send a parent away without recourse against the public schools because the alternative of private education was always open. Whether or not the family could afford the tuition at the Christian academies in the Charleston area, their right to elect an alternative educational setting was legally available. So long as that option existed, the public schools remained free to use materials that might offend even the religious sensibilities of some parents. But if state law now limits the private schools to materials that have been approved for use in the public schools, the constitutionally essential alternative may in fact cease to exist. If a parent is now told that the Christian academies must use the same D.C. Heath language arts series he found so offensive in the public school, the whole issue becomes far more complex. The federal judge can no longer with such confidence decline to review the public school materials if those are also, *de facto*, the private school materials. The choice of an alternative school site may continue to exist, but if the child finds the same curriculum and the same textbooks when he gets there as he left behind in the public school, the difference becomes more one of form than of substance.

The dilemma is therefore acute. It may be most intense in the case of religious values, but should not be so limited. Two factors suggest a broader focus. One, of course, is the *Pierce* case itself, which grounded the right of choice on due process rather than on free exercise of religion, and whose benefits flowed as much to the Hill Military Academy as to the Society of Sisters. To the extent that *Pierce* ensures a substantively meaningful choice, and not simply a right to attend school in a facility under nonpublic control, it requires that nonreligious concerns be taken into account. There is another dimension of more recent origin. In chapter six we considered the scope of academic freedom in the public schools, and recognized substantial limitations reflecting the state's power to decide what shall be taught in schools which it finances, superintends, and certifies. Surely the scope of academic freedom can be no narrower in the private schools, and in fact it should be substantially broader. Thus a state law which limits private schools to the use of materials that have been chosen for public schools may extend governmental authority well beyond its origin and rationale. The source of the power to choose texts for the public schools applies with greatly attenuated force in the private sector. If, therefore, a claim of academic freedom challenges that power—admittedly with far less force in elementary and secondary education than at the college or university level—the balance may well be tipped in favor of the private schools' freedom of choice. Even where the subject matter is not religiously sensitive, or the parental objection is not religiously based, there is grave doubt whether the state can limit all schools to using materials which have been approved for the public school system.

Two final comments round out this discussion. We are understandably uneasy about striking down all state power to approve materials for the private schools. While it is unlikely that most such schools would use inadequate or inaccurate texts if left to their own devices, a case for some state oversight remains. There may be several practical and legally valid solutions. One would be the appointment of a commission drawn from the independent sector to approve a much broader list of texts, including some (like *Biology: A Search for Order*) which could not lawfully be adopted for the public schools. Another approach would rely upon the accreditation process of the regional associations, which do examine teaching materials and course content during initial approval and reinspection visits. The third and least appealing alternative would be to leave intact the basic structure, subject to judicial review of special conflicts. The prospect of having the courts police the textbook selection process is not an attractive one, but might at least resolve the immediate dilemma.

Our second conclusion is essentially a plea for diversity in education. There is not, and by nature cannot be, much choice in the public school system of the nation. As consolidation into ever larger districts diminishes those pockets of variety and uniqueness which once existed in a more localized system, the potential of the private sector for differentiation assumes growing importance. State concern for the basic quality of private education cannot be seriously doubted. But within the broad limits which states feel bound to impose in fulfillment of their responsibility to children, there is much to be said for permitting, and even encouraging, experimentation in the private sector. Whatever can be done, therefore, to allow the private academies of Kentucky to choose their own texts—even at the risk that they will make choices which would restrict rather than enlarge the intellectual horizons of their students—should be allowed by a tolerant and diverse system of education.

10

THE CURRICULUM AND
THE COMMUNITY

DISPUTES OVER CURRICULUM are ultimately broader than bilateral debates between parents and principals. The larger community also has a substantial interest in the public schools and what they teach. If we limit our attention to parents, teachers, librarians, and administrators, we miss much of the larger significance of what is happening today and is likely to continue to affect the public school curriculum. In fact, the portion of the taxpaying community who at any given time actually have children enrolled in the public schools will continue to diminish as the birth rate declines and the number of childless couples and small families continues to grow. Thus the relationship between the larger community and the public school curriculum becomes a critical element for understanding.

The community has various interests in the schools, what they teach, and how well they do it. Persons who employ graduates of the local high schools have an obvious stake in the curricula, well beyond the vocational or technical programs. Others may regard the school system as a source of regional or local pride; quite apart from the value of public education as an inducement for new business and industry, communities often compete with one another in the quality of schools along with other dimensions. Thus the nonparent taxpayer has reasons for

212

being willing to help support a school system from which members of his immediate family will never receive an education.

There is, however, a broader and more elusive community interest in public education. It is, quite basically, the function of the public schools to inculcate values in children during their formative years. The primary source of indoctrination has been and remains the home and the family. But as soon as the child begins to attend school, the larger part of the weekday is spent outside the home and the major initiative passes to persons other than immediate family members. If children are to learn about the values and principles of a democratic society, the social studies classroom may be a more effective medium than the family dinner table. And if children fail to acquire such values, beliefs, and commitments, it is increasingly the school system that receives the blame.

The inculcation of values and principles must come chiefly through the formal curriculum. Some subjects may be relatively exempt from this role—mathematics, for example, and the vocational and technical courses. But the potential contribution of the curriculum to the inculcation of values is broader than might at first appear. Not only most of social studies, but all of English beyond the level of technical competence in written and spoken communication, are value-sensitive. The relevance of biology is apparent from the textbook controversies we have examined. Other sciences may be less value-implicated, although there are aspects of physics and chemistry that are not wholly neutral. Thus in fact a broad range of subjects are potential vehicles for the transmittal of the values and principles of the community.

The curriculum becomes a focus of controversy because not all parts of the community agree on the values that should be taught. Indeed, there are disagreements on the extent to which particular subjects do in fact play such a role. The biology course which simply traces the origins of human life in evolutionary terms may seem to many parents value-free or neutral; but to the deeply religious fundamentalist, such an approach is selective or judgmental and may be alien even to the point of sacrilege. A contrasting approach, which made no mention of either theory of the origin of life, may satisfy the fundamentalist but would seem seriously deficient to the evolutionist. In a different context, the English literature course which includes the writings of certain contemporary authors may seem to many parents simply an accurate mirror of current society. But to the deeply devout or traditional parent, inclusion of such materials condones an abhorrent societal trend and thus reflects a major value judgment. Much the same can be said in other areas; the curriculum which seems neutral or value-free to some persons may to others imply clear and substantial judgments.

The special relationship between community and school has long been respected by the courts. The Supreme Court has often declined to become a "super school board" and has stressed the primacy of local and professional judgment about curricular and other matters. "By and large," the court has said, "public education in our Nation is committed to the control of state and local authorities. Courts do not and cannot intervene in the resolution of conflicts which arise in the daily operation of school systems and which do not directly and sharply implicate basic constitutional values." The Court has stressed "the State's undoubted right to prescribe the curriculum for its public schools. . . ." Although the Court has not always accepted the judgment of local or state officials, the degree of deference marks as exceptional the occasions of intervention.

A 1979 Supreme Court case illustrates the nature of this balance. New York enacted a law which barred any noncitizen from a public school teaching position. Aliens were ineligible for such positions regardless of the country of origin, the subject to be taught (for example, foreign languages), or other evidences of the applicant's loyalty to the United States. Previously the

Court had held that citizenship requirements would be sustained only if the state could demonstrate some rational relationship between the requirement and the particular position. The Court now sustained the citizenship requirement. A major premise of the decision was the function which teachers play in the inculcation of values and principles—not only teachers who taught social studies, but all teachers throughout the public school system.

This case serves to reaffirm the Supreme Court's traditional deference to local and state community judgments about the role of values in the public school and its curriculum. If the New York legislature believes that only United States citizens can be trusted to impart the state's values, traditions, and beliefs, that judgment will be respected—even though aliens may not be excluded from certain other public service positions. The key seems to be the importance which the relevant community attaches to the value-inculcating function of its school teachers.

The role of "community" emerges elsewhere in the school context. Earlier we discussed the *Yoder* case, in which a majority of the Supreme Court created for the children of the Old Order Amish an exception to the Wisconsin mandatory attendance law. A central premise was the Court's recognition of the self-contained religious community within which education of the Amish youth would continue after they left the public school system. Had there not been such clear evidence of community concern for education and its larger values, the result would probably have been different—as it has been on almost every other occasion the compulsory attendance laws have been challenged. The majority in *Yoder* was obviously impressed by the ways in which the Amish alternative education served the special needs of a largely insular community: "The independence and successful social functioning of the Amish community for a period approaching almost three centuries . . . is strong evidence that there is at best a speculative gain, in terms of meeting the duties of citizenship, from an additional one or two years of compulsory formal education." Thus the *Yoder* case stands apart from all other challenges to compulsory education because the nexus between the alternative educational system and a community was both cohesive and insular.

The nature of the community interest, then, is substantial, and the courts have paid it substantial deference. But the courts have also recognized that the Constitution limits the ways in which the community governs its schools. As a starting point, we might consider the very definition of the relevant "community"—who may make decisions about the public schools. New York some years ago enacted a law which allowed only parents of school children and owners of real property to vote in school board elections. The premise was that only such persons were "primarily interested" in school matters, and only they should vote. A young man who lived with his parents after graduating from college, and was very much interested in the schools, tried to vote but was barred by this law. He brought suit challenging this restriction, claiming that school board elections were at least as important to him as to many people whom the law enfranchised. The Supreme Court majority agreed, finding it irrational to bar such a person from voting while giving the vote to, for example, "an uninterested, unemployed young man who rents an apartment in the district." School elections, in short, were too important to exclude interested citizens on wholly arbitrary grounds. If New York had proved that some strong governmental interest justified its voting classification, that might have been another matter. But without a much stronger claim than the state had in fact made, access to the governance of the public schools could not be so severely limited.

The Constitution sets even greater limits on community control of the *substance* of education. Suppose, for example, the white citizens who constitute the majority of a community decide to relegate black children to separate schools. This was essentially the issue which reached the Supreme Court in 1954 as

Brown v. *Board of Education.* The Court held that education was too vital a civic function to permit the majority of the community to disadvantage the minority even to the extent of racial separation among superficially equal facilities. The importance of education required that no part of the community be denied access on grounds (for example, race) which are constitutionally invalid. It is well to recall the Court's conviction about the value of education as a premise to this judgment:

> Today, government is perhaps the most important function of state and local governments. Compulsory school attendance laws and the great expenditures for education both demonstrate our recognition of the importance of education to our democratic society. It is required in the performance of our most basic public responsibilities, even service in the armed forces. It is the very foundation of good citizenship. Today it is a principal instrument in awakening the child to cultural values, in preparing him for later professional training, and in helping him to adjust normally to his environment.

Racial segregation is not, of course, the only area in which the Supreme Court has overridden the judgment of a community about public education. Intervention goes back at least to the *Pierce* case, holding that communities may not require all their children to attend the public schools. Later cases have reaffirmed this principle on more clearly religious liberty grounds. In the 1950s, for example, the San Francisco suburb of Piedmont enacted a zoning law which forbade the building of parochial schools within the town limits. Usually the courts give great deference to zoning laws, recognizing that the ability of a community to shape its development depends upon the use of its zoning powers. But when zoning impairs religious freedom, as it did in Piedmont, then the wishes of the majority must yield to the constitutional liberties of the minority. Those liberties may, as in this case, include educational opportunities—apparently important enough to Piedmont's rather small Catholic population to warrant taking their case to the state's highest court. Thus the powers of the community to standardize education are in this crucial respect subject to limitations of the Bill of Rights.

Religious liberty has compelled another form of judicial intervention in the governance of the schools. The importance of education, and the amount of time which students spend in school, made inevitable frequent community attempts to extend religion into the classroom. Such extension has taken many forms —religious instruction, Bible readings, and devotional prayers. The courts have sought to distinguish permissible and impermissible recognition of religion in the public school classroom. While religious instructors may not come into and use school classrooms, students may be excused early to attend off-campus religious classes. Prayers and passages from Scripture may not be used for devotional purposes, but the Bible may be studied in literature and history classes. In these and other ways the courts have accommodated the very strong pressures for recognition of religion—especially strong in deeply religious communities—with the religious neutrality which the First Amendment commands. Clearly the Constitution deprives the local community of a desired opportunity to infuse faith into the fabric of civic life. Thus emerges another critical limitation upon the degree to which the will of the community may shape the public schools.

When we leave the relatively familiar limitations of racial equality and religious neutrality, the analysis becomes more difficult. If, for example, the community decides that certain forms of student protest should be forbidden, rights of free expression are implicated. When the conflict is clear, as in the *Tinker* case, courts will not hesitate to hold that the community has overstepped its constitutional authority. But the degree of deference to the judgment of the school board or the administration is apparent in such a case; recall, for example, the potential importance in *Tinker* of evidence that the wearing of black armbands disrupted regular school activities. While the principal could not simply have alleged such disruption without proof, the *Tinker* court would have deferred to a judgment based plausibly on the need to maintain order. In other recent cases involving controversial student insignia, underground newspapers, and the like, courts have in fact reached a different result. Throughout these cases runs a recognition not only that school authorities represent (and presumably reflect) the will of the community to which they are accountable, but also that their continuing support depends upon their not departing too far from the expectations and wishes of that community. Schools are fragile and dependent institutions, and even judges appreciate that fact.

In quite a different sense, decisions like these do not reject community judgment, but may be seen as looking to a different and larger community. The Bill of Rights and the Fourteenth Amendment have, after all, quasi-popular and democratic origins. At one time a national consensus determined that government should avoid supporting or favoring religion, even when it would be easy and tempting to do so. Thus when a court strikes down a prayer or religious exercise in the public schools which the local majority strongly support, it is asserting the primacy of one community (the national community from which our basic liberties derive) over the transient views of the local community. In the long run, the courts have said, we best meet the expectations of that historic national community if we avoid prayers and Bible readings, allow students to wear black armbands, and do not separate children of different races on ethnic grounds.

A similar analysis extends to the curriculum of the public schools. In most respects the courts permit the community to determine what shall—and shall not—be taught in the schools. In theory at least, each community may decide for itself what subjects to include in or exclude from the curriculum. When the Supreme Court declared that Arkansas could not forbid the teaching of evolution in its public schools, the majority went out of its way to reaffirm the scope of state and local initiative in curricular matters. One Justice suggested that if Arkansas wished to avoid the whole controversy, it could eliminate all biology courses, since nothing in the Constitution requires that any particular subject be taught. But so long as biology was included in the curriculum, the state could not shape the content of that course to reflect a particular theology. Nor, presumably, could even the choice of secular subjects reflect a sectarian preference —if, for example, home economics were dropped solely because of opposition of a religious group. But a decision to eliminate (or not to offer) biology as a way of avoiding controversy altogether would seem to fall within the permissible zone of community judgment. Graduates of such a truncated program would suffer in the competition for college and in other ways; but nothing in the Constitution ensures that they will receive a complete or rounded education. If biology could be eliminated, or not offered, then almost any other course could be included or excluded, as a federal constitutional matter, by the consensus of the local community. Only where curricular actions either reflect a constitutionally impermissible motive, such as forbidding the teaching of evolution, or clearly infringe individual rights and liberties, as in the discharge of an outspoken teacher, are the courts likely to reverse the community's judgment.

The application of this reasoning is not always easy. Perhaps the most difficult case in terms of conflict between community consensus and constitutional principle is that of the West Clark, Indiana, biology textbook. Clearly the community wanted its children to learn about creation in the biology course, and therefore chose a particular textbook, against the recommendation of a parent-teacher committee. The court concluded that the text reflected a sectarian viewpoint so extensively that its adoption would represent an establishment of religion. There is no question that such a decision deprives the community of an important element of curricular choice—probably cutting far deeper than the Supreme Court's decisions banning devotional prayers and Bible reading.

It is not so clear, however, that the Court has wholly disabled the West Clark schools from deferring to community preference even in this sensitive area. Surely the retention of the forbidden text in the school library would not violate the Constitution. Should teachers suggest that students wishing to learn more about creation might consult the text in the library, such a reference would surely be allowed, at least so long as the teachers were not actually proselytizing. Lectures in each of the biology classes about the contrasting theories on the origins of human life would surely be permissible. Even offering an alternative biology course for students whose parents objected to the regular course might be allowed, although the use of public funds to develop such a unit might pose a different establishment clause problem. In any event, there remain open to the devoutly religious community several possibly satisfactory alternatives short of requiring all students to use a creationist textbook.

If West Clark requires a delicate balance between community and Constitution, the *Cary* (Colorado) case is even more complex. As we saw in chapter six, the school board approved some 1,275 works for use in the English literature courses, but refused to approve ten other titles. A group of teachers took the issue to court, and the federal district judge ruled in their favor on the substantive issue. His premise was that if the schools created such a course in the first place—an elective for mature high school seniors—it could not later pick and choose among the materials to be studied. The whole purpose of such an elective was to enable seniors to explore the full range of modern literature; that goal would be thwarted by the board's intervention. Such a judgment is consistent with other cases in which courts have said, in effect, to governmental bodies: "You may not have a legal duty to create such a program, but if you do, you may not then censor its content." There would have been no First Amendment violation if the Colorado board had simply decided not to offer senior English literature; but once having included that course in the curriculum, there was an implied commitment not to censor the books that could be assigned.

When the case reached the court of appeals some months later, the constitutional claim took a different turn. The appellate court stressed that it was up to the states whether public education would be offered at all, and that the Supreme Court in *Rodriguez* had ruled that "There is no constitutional right to an education." Two critical sentences followed:

> [T]hese local decision-makers may determine what subjects are taught, even selecting ones which promote a particular viewpoint. . . . It is legitimate for the curriculum of the school district to reflect the value system and educational emphasis which are the collective will of those whose children are being educated and who are paying the costs.

If the Adams-Arapahoe school board wanted to limit the English literature course to 1,275 of the proposed 1,285 titles, that was their option, notwithstanding the constitutional claims of the teachers. (There were, of course, no parents of students in the Colorado suit. The content-selection issue arose between the board and the teachers. The presence of others among the plaintiffs would have complicated the analysis. Here the court could defer to the wishes of the community, apparently conveyed by the elected board; there was no opposing voice other than that of the interested teachers.)

This result would have pleased Stephen Goldstein, whose views we noted earlier. Goldstein has argued forcefully for the primacy of community judgments in curricular matters:

> Although teachers' professional training and experience may give them special competency in matters of pedagogical methodology, often curricular decisions involve important value judgments con-

cerning the proper allocation of societal resources of the aims sought to be accomplished by public education. These are ultimately political questions, which the expertise of teachers does not provide any special competency in answering.

Earlier in the same article Goldstein suggested that "if the purpose of teaching is to instill values, there would seem to be little reason for the teacher, rather than the elected school board or other governmental body ultimately responsible to the public, to be the one who chooses the values to be instilled." Thus the conflict between teacher and community would be resolved in the community's favor, even though the teacher's freedom of curricular choice and expression suffers.

Yet there is a critical difference between cases like *Cary* and those in which the school board simply decides not to offer a course or even to discontinue a course that has become controversial. Decisions of the latter sort are among those that the community should be free to make—as long as constitutional liberties are not directly infringed in the process. But the decision to regulate the content of a course already in the curriculum seems a quite different matter. It is one thing for the board to decide on adoptions of textbooks—and in the process to reject certain titles because the content is too spicy or potentially offensive. It is quite another for the board to tell teachers charged with exploring the frontiers of contemporary literature that certain border zones are off limits. The latter is what the Adams-Arapahoe board did; thus the constitutional judgment of the district court in the teachers' favor seems quite sound.

A contrasting situation is suggested by recent events in the small community of Warsaw, Indiana. At least one teacher was discharged, books were burned, materials banned, and other measures of reprisal were taken or threatened. One element of the Warsaw saga bears directly on the current topic. After a year of community turmoil over the school curriculum, the school board decided to eliminate several courses which had fueled the fire. Black literature, folklore and legend, science fiction, detective and mystery fiction, and several other elective options were eliminated by board action at the end of the year. Clearly some of these curricular changes were prompted by the board's dislike of materials assigned in the courses. The pattern was complicated, however, by the substitution of what might be termed "basics"—greater emphasis on English composition, grammar, and other communication skills. Required courses replaced some of the previous electives, and the whole language curriculum became substantially more traditional.

Here the tension between community authority and curriculum becomes acute. On one hand, the reason for eliminating such courses hardly comports with principles of intellectual freedom. Students in the system will have far less opportunity for enrichment and excitement. The challenge for teachers will surely diminish. In the broadest sense, freedom of expression will be stifled as a result of such massive curricular changes. Yet these actions of the Warsaw board may well lie beyond the reach of the courts, for several reasons. For one, the motives of the board are not unmistakably clear; the substitution of "basic skill" courses at a time of great national concern with student literacy is surely a valid, and perhaps even laudable, action. The board could, of course, have left the controversial electives in place and still strengthened the basic skill program—but that is a political judgment the board should be free to make. Moreover, not all the courses which are changed in any given year are the target of controversy; in large school districts the process of evolution and change is constant, and the reason for abolishing some courses and initiating others may often be obscure. Third, and most important, elected school boards and appointed administrators should be free within very broad limits to make such changes without fear of judicial intervention. If every course change had to be justified on a content-neutral ground, the whole process of educational change would be stifled. The values and concerns of the community must be to some extent expressed through the curriculum, as the Supreme Court has consistently recognized.

Several different values argue for limiting judicial intervention to clear violations of constitutional liberties. Deference to the democratic political process is surely one such value; school boards are elected as part of the process of self-governance, and should have commensurate powers. For the very reason the Supreme Court has said that New York may not restrict voting in school elections to parents and property-owners, latitude should be given to the results of a governance system that represents the whole community. Second, the schools depend substantially and increasingly on the community for financial support. In times of scarce public resources—threatened further by tax-reduction measures like California's Proposition 13—it is important that courts not jeopardize unduly the precarious relations between the schools and those to whom they must look for support. Broad judicial restriction of community curricular choice could seriously impair the vital bond or affinity between the schools and their constituents. And as the percentage of the population (especially in the upper socioeconomic brackets) who are parents continues to decline, the importance of nonparent community support will be even greater.

Third, there are important limitations inherent in the nature and functions of courts. Policing the content of public education is surely not a task for which most judges are equipped or in which they would be comfortable. To insist that a desegregation decree be carried out in good faith and with reasonable dispatch is one thing—and for that reason courts will often retain jurisdiction in racial suits. But to review the content of texts or courses on a regular basis is quite another matter, for all the reasons we suggested in discussing the suit over the Mississippi history textbook adoption. The injunction that courts not become "super school boards" is a serious one, for reasons that extend to judicial competence as much as to comity among branches of government.

Finally, there is a strong positive value in educational diversity. Communities have varied and distinctive values and goals, and that variety should be reflected in the curricula of their schools. To the extent that courts impose national values and precepts, the natural diversification process would suffer. Conversely, reasonable steps that will encourage the survival of diverse local values and initiatives—within broad constitutional limits—should be encouraged. A reasonably tolerant attitude by courts faced with curricular challenges will surely help.

BIBLIOGRAPHIC NOTES

Important references to court decisions, documents, and other materials cited in the text have been grouped here under appropriate chapter headings. No attempt has been made, however, either to furnish a complete bibliography on the subject with which this book is concerned, or to provide the reference for each individual item of information. A law review article would, of course, contain such precise references, as would a legal treatise. But it was felt that such detail would impair the readability of this book and would misrepresent its purpose. Accordingly, only essential documentation has been provided.

A few introductory notes about citation of legal materials may facilitate the use of this section. Many court decisions have been summarized or referred to in the text, and are identified in these notes. All but a handful of these cases were decided by appellate courts, reviewing the decision of a trial court or of a lower appeal court. Many are decisions of the United States Supreme Court, recognizable by the citation to a volume of the *United States Reports*. (Such a citation is in the form "100 U.S. 200," which indicates that the case cited, or the opinion of the Court in that case, is in Volume 100 of the *United States Reports*, beginning at page 200. Dating from the first year of the Supreme Court, the series is now approaching its four hundred fiftieth volume. The same system of page and volume references is used below in references to articles in journals and reviews.)

There are also decisions of the lower federal courts. These appear in two series of reports, both issued by the West Publishing Company rather than by the courts or the government. Decisions of federal courts of appeals appear in the *Federal Reporter*, Second Series, which is nearing its six hundredth volume. (The form would be "100 F.2d 200" and would typically include the circuit in which the case was decided.

There are ten federal circuits, numbered roughly from east to west across the country, and one in the District of Columbia.) Decisions of the federal district (trial) courts appear in the *Federal Supplement*, which has run to almost five hundred volumes. (They are cited in the form "100 F. Supp. 200," usually followed by a reference to the judicial district—about one hundred throughout the United States—in which the case was decided.) Although nearly all decisions of federal courts of appeals are published in the *Federal Second*, only those district court decisions appear in the *Federal Supplement* that have been submitted by the judge as having special merit or novelty.

Finally, there are references to a smaller number of state court decisions. Only in New York are state trial court opinions reported regularly. For all other states, the decisions of the highest court appear in regional reporter series—Northeast, Northwest, Pacific, Southern, etc.—all in the second series. Opinions of intermediate appellate courts appear for some states but not all. Until recently every state also published an "official" report of its high court decisions. That practice has been declining, however, with increasing reliance on the "unofficial" (but often the only) report that appears in the West Company regional reporters. (A typical citation would be "100 N.E.2d 200 (Mass. 1965)" for a case decided by the Supreme Judicial Court of Massachusetts in 1965 and reported in the hundredth volume of the *Northeast Reporter*, Second Series, page 200.)

Some of the cases cited here have not yet been reported in either official or unofficial volumes, and others (for example, trial court decisions in states other than New York) never will be. Information about such cases is gleaned from various sources. Usually cases of importance involving educational issues will at least be noted in the *New York Times* the following day. Within two or three weeks, an abstract of the opinion may well appear in the *United States Law Week*, published in Washington weekly by the Bureau of National Affairs. This loose-leaf service distributes promptly the full text of U.S. Supreme Court decisions and of selected congressional enactments; it also culls the state and lower federal court advance sheets (preliminary reports) for cases of special importance. These are abstracted or summarized and distributed in the weekly supplement.

One general work deserves special mention at the outset. The *Newsletter on Intellectual Freedom*, published six times each year by the Office of Intellectual Freedom of the American Library Association, is a priceless resource. Its issues contain innumerable case summaries, brief articles, surveys, and other current data pertaining to the topics of this book. One could hardly approach the subject without frequent recourse to the *Newsletter*. References will appear throughout this essay to the *Newsletter*, simply cited as *NIF*, and the citation should be clear.

Chapter I: The Courts and the School Curriculum

The sources of material on the case studies in chapter one vary widely. In large part, these abbreviated accounts derive from fuller reports in daily newspapers, national magazines, and the like, although in several instances there has also been litigation. No attempt can be made here to offer a complete summary; only the briefest of references are offered for additional study.

Much of the material about the West Clark, Indiana, biology textbook controversy comes from reports in the Louisville *Courier-Journal* during the period June 1976 through September 1977. The court decision which held unconstitutional the optional use of *Biology: A Search for Order in Complexity* was never officially reported, and never appealed above the state trial court. The citation is Hendren v. Campbell, 45 U.S. Law Week 2530 (Marion Co. Superior Ct., April 14, 1977); the opinion is set forth in full in National Association of Biology Teachers, *A Compendium of Information on the Theory of Evolution and the Evolution-Creationism Controversy* (1978), pp. 31–42.

The Kanawha County, West Virginia, controversy was also the subject of extensive newspaper and media coverage, in the national as well as the regional press, especially during the summer and fall of 1974. A detailed treatment is found in J. Hefly, *Textbooks on Trial* (1976), and in the inquiry report of a panel of the National Education Association, entitled *Kanawha County West Virginia: A Textbook Study in Cultural Conflict* (1975). Also helpful is a long essay in the *New Yorker* for September 30, 1974, pages 119–127, under the title "U.S. Journal: Kanawha County, West Virginia." The one reported court decision that came out of the controversy, and which held that the use of allegedly irrelegious teaching materials violated no provision of the Constitution, was Williams v. Board of Education of Kanawha County, 388 F. Supp. 93 (S.D.W.Va.), affirmed 530 F.2d 972 (4th Cir. 1975).

Much of the material about the Fogarty case and St. Anthony, Idaho, comes from a long article in the *Los Angeles Times*, March 12, 1978, part IV, pages 1, 16–19. The editorial in the *Idaho State Journal* appeared on April 12, 1978, section A, page 4. The case, which has not yet been decided, is Fogarty v. Atchley, a civil action in the United States District Court for the District of Idaho.

The Chelsea, Massachusetts, case is Right to Read Defense Committee v. School Committee of the City of Chelsea, 454 F. Supp. 703 (D. Mass. 1978). Additional material comes from various newspaper stories both in Boston and occasionally in the national press.

The two cases on the Michigan sex education question come from different courts. The case challenging the restrictions upon sex education instruction in the Michigan schools is Mercer v. Michigan State

Board of Education, 379 F. Supp. 580 (E.D. Mich. 1974). The case which approached the issue from the opposite side and challenged the law requiring some sex education (though accompanied by an excusal provision), was Holboth v. Greenway, 218 N.W.2d 98 (Mich. App. 1974). The subject of sex education is discussed more fully in chapter eight.

The tribulations of Siba Baum, the Blackfoot Indian girl, are chronicled in several stories in the New York Times, Oct. 18, 1977, p. 39; Oct. 30, 1977, § I, p. 24; and Jan. 24, 1978, p. 59. An account of the litigation against Man: A Course of Study is found in NIF, Jan. 1977, p. 15. The civil damage suit against the Princeton, Ohio, school board alleging injury as the result of assigned material is found in Cincinnati Enquirer, Mar. 21, 1973, p. 1.

Chapter II: The Roots of Controversy

Two cases begin the chapter, and both reflect earlier litigation over the issues which have recently entered the courts in much larger volume. The case brought by the Jewish parents challenging the use of Oliver Twist and Merchant of Venice is Rosenberg v. Board of Education of the City of New York, 196 Misc. 542, 92 N.Y. Supp. 2d 344 (1949). The Baltimore teacher's unsuccessful quest for vindication after his dismissal for assigning Brave New World is reported in Parker v. Board of Education, 237 F. Supp. 222 (D. Md.), affirmed 348 F.2d 464 (4th Cir. 1965), cert. denied, 382 U.S. 1030 (1966).

General materials on the changing curriculum can be found in, e.g., L. Cremin, The Transformation of the School (1962); A. Applebee, Tradition and Reform in the Teaching of English: A History (1974); and S. Lynch and B. Evans, High School English Textbooks: A Critical Examination (1963). Prof. Donelson's comments appear in "Censorship Comes to Adolescent Literature," in Jenkinson, ed., Organized Censors Rarely Rest—A Special Issue of Indiana English, Fall, 1977, pp. 10–14. The Barber column appears in New York Times, March 23, 1975, § IV, p. 16. The Anderson comments are quoted in New York Times, July 10, 1977, § IV, p. 9. Prof. Burress's comments are found in Davis, ed., Dealing with Censorship (1979), pp. 14–47 (a report of the 1977 censorship survey of the National Council of Teachers of English). The litigation over Man: A Course of Study is summarized in NIF, January, 1977, p. 15.

On the development of parental protest or "Parents' Lib" movements, see especially two major stories, in New York Times, November 13, 1977, § IV, page 4; and "School Protest: It's Tough When One Mother Tackles the System," in National Observer, Dec. 5, 1975, p. 9. Fred Hechinger's comments on the textbook controversies are found in *New York Times*, Jan. 8, 1980, § IV, page 4, and April 8, 1980, § IV, p. 4.

The two challenges by black parents to allegedly racist materials are both reported in the *Newsletter on Intellectual Freedom*. The action of the New Trier (Illinois) School Board in removing *Huckleberry Finn* from the required reading list is reported in *NIF*, September 1976, p. 116. The controversy within the Oakland (California) schools over *Daddy Was a Numbers Runner* is found in *NIF*, May 1977, p. 71.

The lengthy excerpt from the work of Professors Coons and Sugarman is from J. Coons and S. Sugarman, *Education by Choice: The Case for Family Control* (1978), pp. 42–43.

Judith Krug's comments about the rise of censorship in the late 1970s are reported in *New York Times*, Jan. 2, 1979, § IV, p. 12. The *Phi Delta Kappan* article is found in the May 1980 issue, pp. 608–12. The Kilpatrick column, suggesting the interesting analogy between community control in New York City and in West Virginia, appeared in *Cincinnati Enquirer*, Oct. 22, 1974, p. 5. Prof. Jenkinson's observations are found in Davis, ed., *Dealing with Censorship* (1979), p. 5.

The intriguing suit filed by the Irwin family—and apparently never brought to trial, or at least never decided—is reported in *Cincinnati Post*, Mar. 27, 1979, p. 1.

Chapter III: A Right to Be Educated?

On the general legal issues raised in this and succeeding chapters, a most valuable survey is found in "Education and the Law: State Interests and Individual Rights," 74 *Michigan Law Review* 1373–1502 (1976). Two very recent and more specialized legal studies are also quite helpful. They are "Note, Schoolbooks, School Boards, and the Constitution," 80 Columbia Law Review 1092 (1980); "Note, Challenging Ideological Exclusion of Curriculum Material: Rights of Students and Parents," 14 Harvard Civil Rights–Civil Liberties Law Review 485 (1979).

The New York malpractice case is Donohue v. Copiague Union Free School District, 64 App. Div. 2d 29, 407 N.Y.S.2d 874 (1978), aff'd, 408 N.Y.S.2d 584 (1979). Comments on the decision are found in 43 *Albany Law Review* 339 (1979); 7 *Fordham Urban Law Review* 117 (1979); and a more general comment on the issue in Elson, "A Common Law Remedy for the Educational Harms Caused by Incompetent or Careless Teaching," 73 *Northwestern U.L. Rev.* 641 (1979). The earlier California case is Peter W. v. San Francisco Unified School District, 60 Cal. App. 3d 814, 131 Cal. Rptr. 854 (1976).

The *New York Times* editorialized twice on the Donohue case—on the intermediate appellate decision, on March 9, 1977, p. 28; and on the Court of Appeals decision (that of the state's highest court), on June 23, 1979, p. 20.

The earliest desegregation cases, in which the Supreme Court declined to find any constitutional violation in the historic racially separate school systems, were Cumming v. Board of Education, 175 U.S. 528 (1899) and Gong Lum v. Rice, 275 U.S. 78 (1927). During the 1930s and '40s the Court several times insisted that higher education facilities that were racially separate be equal, or held unconstitutional facilities which were demonstrably or inherently unequal, e.g., Sweatt v. Painter, 339 U.S. 629 (1950). Brown v. Board of Education, 349 U.S. 294 (1954), eventually found racially segregated elementary and secondary schools violative of the equal protection clause of the Fourteenth Amendment.

The decision striking down the Virginia "school closing" plan was Griffin v. County School Board, 377 U.S. 218 (1964). The school finance decision, upholding the Texas educational support system despite its inequities, was San Antonio School District v. Rodriguez, 411 U.S. 1 (1973). The case defining the rights of non-English-speaking children in the public schools is Lau v. Nichols, 414 U.S. 563 (1974). The claims of handicapped students have been extensively considered by the lower federal courts, and on November 3, 1980, the United States Supreme Court agreed to review the question whether federal statutes grant such students a private right to insist upon such special services as interpreters for the deaf. University of Texas v. Camenisch, 616 F.2d 127 (5th Cir. 1980), cert. granted, 49 U.S.L. Week 3322 (U.S. Supreme Court 1980). The "Black English" case is Martin Luther King Junior Elementary School Children v. Ann Arbor School District Board, 48 U.S.L. Week 2058 (E.D. Mich. 1979).

On the general issue of "unconstitutional conditions" and the legal differences between "rights" and "privileges," see R. O'Neil, *The Price of Dependency* (1970); Van Alstyne, "The Demise of the Right-Privilege Distinction in Constitutional Law," 81 *Harvard Law Review* 1439 (1968).

The flag-salute case is West Virginia State Bd. of Education v. Barnette, 319 U.S. 624 (1943). The later case in which the Supreme Court struck down school rules barring the peaceful wearing of black armbands is Tinker v. Des Moines School District, 393 U.S. 503 (1969). Several years later, in Goss v. Lopez, 419 U.S. 565 (1975), the Court held that students are entitled to some measure of due process before being suspended or expelled. The analysis of the Goss decision quoted in the text is from "Project: Education and the Law," 74 *Michigan Law Review* 1373, at 1480 (1976). For other comments, see Kirp, "Proceduralism and Bureaucracy: Due Process in the School Setting," 28 *Stanford Law Review* 841 (1976); and Letwin, "After Goss v. Lopez: Student

Status as a Suspect Classification," 29 *Stanford Law Review* 627 (1977). The later Supreme Court case, declining to set constitutional limits on corporal punishment in the schools, is Ingraham v. Wright, 430 U.S. 651 (1977). For a perceptive analysis, see Rosenberg, "Ingraham v. Wright: The Supreme Court's Whipping Boy," 78 *Columbia Law Review* 75 (1978).

Chapter IV: The Right *Not* to Be Educated

General studies of the topic of this chapter may be found in several recent books and articles: D. Schimmel and L. Fischer, *The Rights of Parents in the Education of Their Children* (1977); Association for Supervision and Curriculum Development, *Partners: Parents and Schools* (1979); Hirschoff, "Parents and the Public School Curriculum: Is There a Right to Have One's Child Excused from Objectionable Instruction?" 50 *Southern California Law Review* 871 (1977); Bereday, "Values, Education and the Law," 48 *Mississippi Law Journal* 585 (1977); Moskowitz, "Parental Rights and State Education," 50 *Washington Law Review* 623 (1975): and two student notes, "Parental Rights: Educational Alternatives and Curriculum Control," 36 *Washington and Lee Law Review* 277 (1979); and "Parental Control of School Curriculum," 21 *Catholic Lawyer* 197 (1975). Much of the general analysis with which the chapter opens relies upon discussion in these works.

The case granting a limited exemption for the Wisconsin Amish beyond the eighth grade is Wisconsin v. Yoder, 406 U.S. 205 (1972). The earliest of the Nebraska cases was Sheibley v. School District No. 1, 31 Neb. 522, 48 N.W. 393 (1891); the later case was Kelly v. Ferguson, 95 Neb. 63, 144 N.W. 1039 (1914). The California case involving a parental objection to dancing classes is Hardwick v. Board of School Trustees, 54 Cal. App. 696, 205 Pac. 49 (1921). The Colorado Supreme Court decision recognizing broad parental discretion to determine the curriculum is People ex rel. Vollmar v. Stanley, 255 Pac. 610 (Colo. 1927). These cases are discussed in Hirschoff, *supra*, 50 *Southern California Law Review* 871, 886–90.

On the general subject of home instruction as an alternative to compulsory school attendance, see Moskowitz, *supra*, 50 *Washington Law Review* 623, 630–36. The 1980 Michigan case was widely noted in the media, e.g., *Milwaukee Journal*, May 4, 1980, part 6, p. 17.

The U.S. Supreme Court struck down the West Virginia flag-salute requirement in West Virginia Board of Education v. Barnette, 319 U.S. 624 (1943). Several years earlier, the Court had reached the opposite conclusion in Minersville School District v. Gobitis, 310 U.S. 586 (1940), which was overruled in *Barnette*. The very recent case upholding the

New York requirement of citizenship as a condition of teaching is Ambach v. Norwick, 441 U.S. 68 (1979); the Court had earlier ruled both ways with respect to citizenship tests for other types of public employment. The federal court of appeals case involving the Chicago teacher's objection to certain indicia of "patriotism" in the classroom is Palmer v. Chicago Board of Education, 603 F.2d 1271 (7th Cir. 1979). The juvenile mental commitment procedure case is Secretary of Public Welfare of Pennsylvania v. Institutionalized Juveniles, 442 U.S. 640 (1979). On the Supreme Court's view of the parental interest in the dissemination of contraceptives and birth control information, see Carey v. Population Services International, 431 U.S. 678 (1977). On deprogramming, one representative suit is Orlando v. Wizel, 443 F. Supp. 744 (W.D. Ark. 1978).

The legality of sex education programs has been extensively tested. For representative decisions upholding such programs, see Citizens for Parental Rights v. San Mateo County Board of Education, 51 Cal. App. 3rd 1, 124 Cal. Rptr. 68 (1975); Hopkins v. Hamden Board of Education, 29 Conn. Supp. 397, 289 A.2d 914 (1971). And see, for general discussions of the cases and issues, Bolmeier, *Sex Litigation and the Public Schools* (1975); "Sex Education: The Constitutional Limits of State Compulsion," 43 *Southern California Law Review* 548 (1970).

Chapter V: Religion and the Schools

On the complex set of relations between religion and the public schools there are innumerable books, articles, notes, and comments. Most address a particular facet—the legality of governmental aid for church-related schools, for example, on which see Choper, "The Establishment Clause and Aid to Parochial Schools," 56 *California Law Review* 260 (1968); or the legality of prayer, Bible reading, and other religious activities in the public schools, on which one might consult Fordham, "The Implications of the Supreme Court Decisions Dealing with Religious Practices in the Public Schools," 6 *Journal of Church and State* 44 (1964). On the special set of issues with which we are here concerned, there is an earlier "Note, Humanistic Values in the Public School Curriculum: Problems in Defining an Appropriate Wall of Separation," 61 *Northwestern University Law Review* 795 (1966); and an excellent recent analysis, "Note, Freedom of Religion and Science Instruction in Public Schools," 87 *Yale Law Journal* 515 (1978), to which reference is made at several points in this chapter.

The two Kentucky cases have now both reached decision in the state's highest court. The private school or Christian Academy accreditation case is The Kentucky State Board for Elementary and Secondary Education v. Rudasill, 589 S.W.2d 877 (1979); the Ten Commandments case is Stone v. Graham, 599 S.W.2d 157, reversed, 49 U.S. Law Week 3369-70 (U.S. Supreme Court, 1980).

The early Supreme Court decision allowing use of public funds to transport students to religious schools is Everson v. Board of Education, 330 U.S. 1. (1947). The later case upholding the New York program of lending secular texts to church-related schools is Board of Education v. Allen, 392 U.S. 236 (1968). Later cases, taking a rather restrictive view of the scope of permissible aids, are Lemon v. Kurtzman, 403 U.S. 602 (1971); Meek v. Pittenger, 421 U.S. 349 (1975); Wolman v. Walter, 433 U.S. 299 (1977); and most recently, Committee for Public Education v. Regan, 100 S.Ct. 840 (1980). The Regan case did allow reimbursement of church-related schools for the performance of certain state-required testing and record-keeping functions.

In Zorach v. Clauson, 343 U.S. 306 (1952), the Supreme Court permitted a "shared time" program for after-school religious instruction. But in Engel v. Vitale, 370 U.S. 421 (1962), and in School District v. Schempp, 374 U.S. 203 (1963) the Court struck down the saying of prayers and the devotional reading of passages from the Bible in the public schools as violations of the establishment clause of the First Amendment.

The Washington State Supreme Court decision on the validity of a university Bible study course in Calvary Bible Presbyterian Church v. Board of Regents, 436 P.2d 189 (Wash. 1968).

The two recent cases on the Bible study credit issue are both from federal district courts. The Tennessee case is Wiley v. Franklin, 468 F. Supp. 133 (E.D. Tenn. 1979); modified 474 F. Supp. 525 (E.D. Tenn. 1979). For a later and contrasting view of the same court, see 497 F. Supp. 390 (E.D. Tenn. 1980). The Utah case is Lanner v. Wimmer, 463 F. Supp. 867 (D. Utah 1978). The Michigan *Slaughterhouse Five* case is Todd v. Rochester Community Schools, 41 Mich. App. 320, 200 N.W.2d 90 (1972). The transcendental meditation case is Malnak v. Yogi, 440 F. Supp. 1284 (D.N.J. 1978), affirmed, 592 F.2d 197 (3rd Cir. 1979). A casenote and comment appears in 16 *San Diego Law Review* 325 (1979).

The Florida Bible distribution and "Christian virtue" case, on rehearing in the court of appeals, is Meltzer v. Orange County Board of Public Instruction, 577 F.2d 311 (5th Cir. 1978). The case involving the dismissal of Mrs. Joan LaRocca for allegedly religious proselytizing is noted in *New York Times*, June 27, 1978, p. 28.

The religious music controversy has come to the courts in several forms. The Sioux Falls, South Dakota, case is Florey v. Sioux Falls School District, 464 F. Supp. 911 (D.S.D. 1978), affirmed, 619 F.2d 1311 (8th Cir. 1980). The California religious music controversy never reached the courts; the materials consist of various memoranda and reports provided by Mr. Roger D. Wolfertz, assistant chief counsel of the California State Department of Education, through a letter to the author, dated April 17, 1978.

There are now two separate cases challenging the Ten Commandments procedure. The Kentucky case is Stone v. Graham, 599 S.W.2d 157, reversed, 49 U.S. Law Week 3369–70 (U.S. Supreme Court, 1980). The North Dakota case, Ring v. Grand Forks Public School District No. 1, 483 F. Supp. 272 (D.N.D. 1980), reached a contrasting result on slightly different facts.

The "monkey trial" resulted in a decision of the Tennessee Supreme Court in Scopes v. State, 154 Tenn. 105, 289 S.W. 363 (1927), which was recalled in LeClerq, "The Monkey Laws and the Public Schools: A Second Consumption," 27 *Vanderbilt Law Review* 209 (1974). The later Supreme Court case striking down the Arkansas law on the teaching of evolution is Epperson v. Arkansas, 393 U.S. 97 (1968). The Tennessee statute was finally held invalid in Daniel v. Waters, 515 F.2d 485 (6th Cir. 1975). The *New York Times* survey showing a revival of interest in teaching of creationism appears in *New York Times*, April 7, 1980, p. A1.

A good account of the California creationism-evolution controversy appears in "Note," 87 *Yale Law Journal* 515–17 (1978); many of the papers presented to the California Board of Education by persons opposing creationism are found in National Association of Teachers of Biology, *A Compendium of Information on the Theory of Evolution and the Evolution-Creationism Controversy* (1979), pp. 49–66.

The decision vindicating the Gastonia, North Carolina, school teacher who gave her students a Darwinian answer in class is Moore v. Gaston County Board of Education, 357 F. Supp. 1037 (W.D.N.C. 1973). The Mississippi case involving the ingenious challenge to a creationist mandate on grounds of educational quality is Smith v. State, 242 So.2d 692 (Miss. 1970).

The two cases involving challenges to an allegedly "secular" curriculum on establishment grounds both produced substantial district court decisions but summary affirmances by the respective courts of appeals. The West Virginia case is Williams v. Board of Education, 388 F. Supp. 93 (S.D.W.Va. 1975), affirmed, 530 F.2d 972 (4th Cir. 1975); the Texas case is Wright v. Houston Independent School District, 366 F. Supp. 1208 (S.D. Tex. 1972), affirmed, 486 F.2d 137 (5th Cir. 1973), cert. denied, 417 U.S. 969 (1974). Both cases, and the issues they raise (and which are explored in this text), are discussed at some length in "Note, Freedom of Religion and Science Instruction in Public Schools," 87 *Yale Law Journal* 515 (1978). One might also see "Commentary: 'Secular Humanism' as An Established Religion?—A Response to Whitehead and Conlan," 11 *Texas Tech Law Review* 51 (1979).

Peripherally relevant Supreme Court decisions are those holding that a state may not deny a notary public commission to an atheist, Torcaso v. Watkins, 367 U.S. 488 (1961); and broadening the definition of "religion" for purposes of conscientious exemption from the draft laws, Gillette v. United States, 401 U.S. 437 (1971).

The Iowa accommodation appears in National Association of Biology Teachers, *NABT News and Views*, April 1978, p. 5 ("Position of the Iowa Department of Public Instruction Regarding Creation, Evolution and Public Education").

Chapter VI: Dirty Words and Suspect Books in the Classroom

Among the many publications dealing with freedom of expression for the teacher in the secondary classroom, four might especially be mentioned at the start of this section of the essay: Goldstein, "The Asserted Constitutional Right of Teachers To Determine What They Teach," 124 *Univ. of Pennsylvania Law Review* 1293 (1976); Kalven, "A Commemorative Case Note; Scopes v. State," 27 *Univ. of Chicago Law Review* 505 (1960); Nahmod, "Controversy in the Classroom; The High School Teacher and Freedom of Expression," 39 *George Washington Law Review* 1032 (1971); Schauer, "School Books, Lesson Plans and the Constitution," 78 *West Virginia Law Review*, 287 (1976).

Material on the Fogarty case comes, as we noted in chapter one, largely from the article in the *Los Angeles Times*, March 12, 1978, part IV, pp. 1, 16–19. The complaint filed with the United States District Court for the District of Idaho adds further allegations.

The Supreme Court decision recognizing the validity of lower or different standards in defining obscenity for minors is Ginsberg v. New York, 390 U.S. 629 (1968).

For a general discussion of the constitutional rights and liberties of public employees including teachers, see R. O'Neil, *The Rights of Government Employees* (1978). The Supreme Court decision defining the rights of the outspoken teacher is Pickering v. Board of Education, 391 U.S. 563 (1968). The two federal appellate cases involving teachers engaged in antiwar protest are James v. Board of Education, 461 F.2d 566 (2d Cir. 1972) (black armband), and Russo v. Central School District No. 1, 469 F.2d 623 (2d Cir. 1972) (refusal to lead the flag salute). The teacher who departed from his assigned responsibility by lecturing on American policy in the Far East was dismissed in Goldwasser v. Brown, 417 F.2d 1169 (D.C.Cir. 1969).

The excerpt from Prof. Nahmod's article is at page 1050. The Oregon classroom speaker ban case is Wilson v. Chancellor, 418 F. Supp. 1358 (D.Ore. 1976).

The major Supreme Court loyalty oath case is Keyishian v. Board of Regents, 385 U.S. 589 (1967). The earlier Supreme Court cases are Meyer v. Nebraska, 262 U.S. 390 (1923), and Pierce v. Society of Sisters, 268 U.S. 510 (1925). The other relevant Supreme Court cases discussed in this section are Epperson v. Arkansas, 393 U.S. 97 (1968), and Tinker v. Des Moines School District, 393 U.S. 503 (1969).

The statement by Professor Emerson comes from T. Emerson, *The System of Freedom of Expression* (1970), pp. 609–10. The two New York federal teacher cases cited earlier are James v. Board of Education (black armband), and Russo v. Central School District No. 1 (pledge). The *Brave New World* case is Parker v. Board of Education, 237 F. Supp. 222 (D. Md.), affirmed, 348 F.2d 464 (4th Cir. 1965).

The two cases involving teachers in New England are Keefe v. Geanakos, 418 F.2d 359 (1st Cir. 1969), and Mailloux v. Kiley, 323 F. Supp. 1387 (D. Mass. 1971), affirmed, 488 F.2d 1242 (1st Cir. 1971). The federal appellate case involving the Illinois teachers is Brubaker v. Board of Education, 502 F.2d 973 (7th Cir. 1974). The case involving the demotion of the North Carolina fifth grade teacher for circulating the "vulgar" note to her class is Frison v. Franklin County Board of Education, 596 F.2d 1192 (4th Cir. 1979). The Alabama case involving the assignment of *Welcome to the Monkey House* is Parducci v. Rutland, 316 F. Supp. 352 (M.D. Ala. 1970). The most recent and relevant of the federal cases is one which ordered the reinstatement of a Texas teacher who had been discharged for his slightly unorthodox classroom treatment of the Civil War: Kingsville Independent School District v. Cooper, 611 F.2d 1109 (5th Cir. 1980).

The Colorado case involving the deletion of ten titles from the approved list is Cary v. Board of Education of Adams-Arapahoe School District, 427 F. Supp. 945 (D. Colo. 1978), affirmed, 598 F.2d 535 (10th Cir. 1979). The *Spoon River Anthology* case is Kramer v. Scioto-Darby City School District, Civil Action 72-406, Southern District of Ohio, March 8, 1974 (not officially reported).

Chapter VII: Libraries, Librarians, and Censorship

There are relatively few general works on the theme of this chapter—the removal of library materials. An excellent collection of pertinent essays is D. Berninghausen, *The Flight from Reason: Essays on Intellectual Freedom in the Academy, the Press and the Library* (1975). On the legal issues, one might refer to O'Neil, "Libraries, Liberties and the First Amendment," 42 *Univ. of Cincinnati Law Review* 209 (1973); O'Neil, "Libraries, Librarians and the First Amendment," 4 *Human Rights* 295 (1975); and "Comment, Constitutional Aspects of Removing Books from School Libraries," 66 *Kentucky Law Journal* 127

(1978). The *New York Times* editorial remarking on the nature of the library profession appears in *New York Times*, July 29, 1973, p. 30. The earliest of the cases dealing directly with library materials was Presidents Council, District 25 v. Community School Board No. 25, 457 F.2d 289 (2d Cir. 1972). The Supreme Court decision regarding the location of the exercise of First Amendment freedoms, specifically in the context of the rock musical *Hair*, is Southeastern Promotions, Ltd. v. Conrad, 420 U.S. 546 (1975). Prof. Becker's article appears in *NIF*, July 1978, pp. 83–84, 105–08, under the title "The First Amendment and Public Libraries."

The Strongsville, Ohio, case was decided by the court of appeals as Minarcini v. Strongsville City School District, 541 F.2d 577 (6th Cir. 1976). The Chelsea case is Right to Read Defense Committee v. School Committee of the City of Chelsea, 454 F. Supp. 703 (D. Mass. 1978). The Island Trees case is Pico v. Board of Education, Island Trees Union Free School District, 474 F. Supp. 387 (E.D.N.Y. 1979), reversed, 49 U.S. Law Week 2274 (2d Cir. 1980). The Vermont case is Bicknell v. Vergennes Union High School Board of Directors, 475 F. Supp. 615 (D.Vt. 1979), affirmed, 49 U.S. Law Week 2274 (2d Cir. 1980).

The case in which the Supreme Court recognized the propriety of relief for groups for whom the political process offered inadequate recourse is Baker v. Carr, 369 U.S. 186 (1962), involving legislative reapportionment. Such disputes had previously been held to be "political questions" beyond the competence of the courts.

Chapter VIII: Beyond the First Amendment

The Supreme Court's cautions about the risks of venturing too deeply into the management of the school systems of the country appear in Epperson v. Arkansas, 393 U.S. 97 (1968), the case striking down the ban on teaching of evolution, to which we gave attention in chapter six.

On the validity of sex education requirements, which have been almost uniformly sustained, see "Annotation, Validity of Sex Education Programs in Public Schools," 82 *A.L.R. 3rd* 579 (1978): "Note, Sex Education: The Constitutional Limits of State Compulsion," 43 *Southern California Law Review* 584 (1970).

The Mississippi history textbook case is Loewen v. Turnipseed, 488 F. Supp. 1138 (N.D. Miss. 1980). The controversy surrounding the work of the Council on Interracial Books for Children was spurred by the publication in 1976 of *Human—and Antihuman—Values in Children's Books—A Content Rating Instrument for Educators and Concerned Parents*. For an indication of the depth of concern which the publication evoked within the library community, see "Editorial: Would-Be Censors of the Left," *School Library Journal*, November 1976, p. 7.

On the question of sex bias in textbooks and other materials, see National Project on Women in Education, *Taking Sexism Out of Education* (1977); Hodgson, "Sex, Texts and the First Amendment," 5 *Journal of Law and Education* 173 (1976); "Comment, Sex Discrimination: The Textbook Case," 62 *California Law Review* 1312 (1974). The Supreme Court case reviewing (but failing to decide) the legality of sex-segregated public schools in Vorchheimer v. Philadelphia School Board, 532 F.2d 880 (3d Cir. 1976), affirmed by an equally divided court, 430 U.S. 703 (1977).

There is no litigation with regard to the Holocaust issue. It might be well to recall the 1949 case, Rosenberg v. Board of Education, 196 Misc. 542, 92 N.Y.S.2d 344 (1949), which refused to enjoin the careful classroom use of *Oliver Twist* and *Merchant of Venice* despite complaints by Jewish parents. Some material may be available from the Simon Wiesenthal Center for Holocaust Studies in Los Angeles, a national organization devoted to the continuing appreciation of the horrors of the Holocaust. Expressions of concern from the Philadelphia German community about the curricular unit are found in *New York Times*, Sept. 18, 1977, p. 23; the editorial about the possibility of a similar unit in the New York City schools is in *New York Times*, Nov. 9, 1977, p. 36.

There are many cases implicating privacy concerns of religiously conservative parents. They are seldom successful. See, e.g., Davis v. Page, 385 F. Supp. 395 (D.N.H. 1974), seeking excusal not only from music and health education classes but also from all classes in which audio-visual equipment was used. For a similar approach, see Smith v. Dallas County Board of Education, 480 F. Supp. 1324 (S.D. Ala. 1979), upholding placement testing programs despite objections based on privacy. On the other hand, see Moody v. Cronin, 484 F. Supp. 270 (C.D. Ill. 1979), striking down a state law requiring participation in physical education classes—to which religiously conservative parents had objected because "indecent apparel" must be worn. Such cases are quite rare, and courts seek to avoid collision between such school policies and religiously based privacy claims.

On the general subject of curricular mandates, see Shelton, "Legislative Control over Public School Curriculum," 15 *Willamette Law Review* 473 (1979). The survey of curricular requirements cited in the text was done for the Youth Education for Citizenship program of the American Bar Association in 1974–75 and covered the statutes of all states at that time.

The Supreme Court decision striking down the Washington loyalty oath is Baggett v. Bullitt, 377 U.S. 360 (1964). The case dealing with the Florida "inculcate every Christian virtue" law is Meltzer v. Board of Public Instruction of Orange County, 577 F.2d 311 (5th Cir. 1978).

Chapter IX: Public Regulation and the Private School Curriculum

There has recently been substantial writing on the topic of this chapter. See, for example, "Comment, Regulation of Fundamentalist Christian Schools: Free Exercise of Religion vs. The State's Interest in Quality Education," 67 *Kentucky Law Journal* 415 (1979); "Note, Separation of Church and State: Education and Religion in Kentucky," 6 *Northern Kentucky Law Review* 125 (1978); and "Note, Secular Control of Non-Public Schools," 82 *West Virginia Law Review* 111 (1979).

The case involving the accreditation of the Kentucky Christian academies is The Kentucky State Board for Elementary and Secondary Education v. Rudasill, 589 S.W.2d 877 (1979).

On the general growth of private schools and the basis of the legal conflict, see *New York Times*, April 28, 1978, p. 1; *New York Times*, Jan. 26, 1979, p. A8. For the estimate of parental income, see John C. Esty, Jr., President, National Association of Independent Schools, letter to the *New York Times*, June 17, 1979, § IV, p. 18.

The assessment of the degree of current control of private schools is from J. Coons and S. Sugarman, *Education by Choice: The Case for Family Control* (1978), p. 41.

The early Supreme Court cases are Meyer v. Nebraska, 262 U.S. 390 (1923), and Pierce v. Society of Sisters, 268 U.S. 510 (1925). The later cases dealing with permissibility of governmental aid to church-related schools include Everson v. Board of Education, 330 U.S. 1 (1947) (bussing to and from school); Board of Education v. Allen, 392 U.S. 236 (1968) (lending of secular textbooks); and other cases cited in chapter five, the most recent of which is Committee for Public Education v. Regan, 100 S.Ct. 840 (1980).

The recent case in which the Supreme Court construed the National Labor Relations Act not to extend to the faculty of parochial schools, and thus avoided the lurking constitutional issue, is National Labor Relations Board v. Catholic Bishop of Chicago, 440 U.S. 490 (1979). Valuable background analysis is found in Warner, "NLRB Jurisdiction Over Parochial Schools," 73 *Northwestern University Law Review* 463 (1978).

The case involving the Minnesota Human Rights Department order regarding the remarried teacher at a religious school is Steeber v. Benhilde-St. Margaret's High School, 47 U.S. Law Week 2308 (Minn. Dist. Ct. 1978).

The Supreme Court case enjoining the closing of certain portions of the state school system to forestall desegregation is Griffin v. County School Board, 377 U.S. 218 (1964). The later case holding that states may not lend textbooks to students in private schools with racially discriminatory policies in Norwood v. Harrison, 413 U.S. 455 (1973). Runyon v. McCrary, 427 U.S. 160 (1976) later reached the issue of racially discriminatory admissions policies, and recognized a right of nondiscriminatory access under federal civil rights statutes.

The case involving the racially segregated policies of a Christian academy is Brown v. Dade Christian Schools, Inc., 556 F.2d 310 (5th Cir. 1977). The later case in which the district court declined to order the reinstatement of the white student expelled for romantic relations with a black classmate is Fiedler v. Marumsco Baptist Church, 486 F. Supp. 960 (E.D. Va. 1980). The court of appeals later reversed, and ordered the students readmitted, 631 F.2d 1144 (4th Cir. 1980). See generally on these cases, "Note, A Sectarian School Asserts Its Religious Beliefs," 32 *University of Miami Law Review* 709 (1978).

The Ohio Christian school regulation case is State v. Whisner, 351 N.E. 2d 750 (Ohio 1976). For the possible application of *Whisner* to the Kentucky situation, see "Comment, Regulation of Fundamentalist Christian Schools," 67 *Kentucky Law Journal* 415 (1979).

Chapter X: The Curriculum and the Community

There are few separate discussions of the legal role which community values play in the governance and shaping of school systems. One essay may be helpful in sorting out the issues—Bereday, "Values, Education and the Law," 48 *Mississippi Law Journal* 585 (1977). The caution about the role of the Supreme Court in the superintendence of the schools is contained in Epperson v. Arkansas, 393 U.S. 97 (1968). The Supreme Court decision upholding New York's requirement that teachers be United States citizens is Ambach v. Norwick, 441 U.S. 68 (1979).

In Kramer v. Union School District, 395 U.S. 621 (1969), the Supreme Court recognized the interest of the unmarried non-property-owner in shaping the decisions of the community about its schools, and thus broadened the franchise for these purposes.

The West Clark, Indiana, biology textbook case is Hendren v. Campbell, 45 U.S. Law Week 2530 (Marion County, Indiana, Superior Court, 1977). The Colorado textbook selection case is Cary v. Board of Education of Adams-Arapahoe School District, 427 F. Supp. 945 (D. Colo. 1978), affirmed on different grounds, 598 F.2d 535 (10th Cir. 1979). The Warsaw, Indiana, case is Zykan v. Warsaw Community School Corp., 631 F.2d 1300 (7th Cir. 1980).

344.73
On 58

113 654